SAN JOSE

SILICON VALLEY

PRIMED FOR THE 21ST CENTURY

Sponsored by the San Jose Metropolitan Chamber of Commerce.
Above, right, and cover photos by Pat Kirk.

SAN JOSE
& SILICON VALLEY

PRIMED FOR THE 21ST CENTURY

Written by Chris Di Salvo
Corporate profiles by Judith Harkham Semas
Featuring the photography of Pat Kirk

Photo by Pat Kirk.

San Jose & Silicon Valley: Primed For The 21st Century

Produced in cooperation with the San Jose Metropolitan Chamber of Commerce.
180 South Market Street • San Jose, CA 95113 • (408)291-5250

By Chris Di Salvo
Corporate Profiles by Judith Harkham Semas
Featuring the Photography of Pat Kirk
Contributing Photographer: Dana L. Grover

Community Communications, Inc.
Publishers: Ronald P. Beers and James E. Turner

Staff for *San Jose & Silicon Valley: Primed For The 21st Century*

Publisher's Sales Associates	Paula Haider and Robbie Wills
Executive Editor	James E. Turner
Managing Editor	Candy Strickland
Design Director	Camille Leonard
Designer	Scott Phillips
Photo Editors	Scott Phillips and Candy Strickland
Production Managers	Corinne Cau and Cindy Lovett
Editorial Assistants	Katrina Williams and Kari Collin
Sales Assistant	Annette Lozier
Proofreader	Connie Sessions
Accounting Services	Sara Ann Turner
Printing Production	Frank Rosenberg/GSAmerica

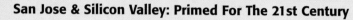

Community Communications, Inc.
Montgomery, Alabama

James E. Turner, Chairman of the Board
Ronald P. Beers, President
Daniel S. Chambliss, Vice President

©1997 Community Communications
Photography ©1997 Pat Kirk Photography
All Rights Reserved
Published 1997
Printed in Canada
First Edition
Library of Congress Catalog Number: 97-16064
ISBN Number: 1-885352-56-5

Part One

From California's First City to Capitol of Silicon Valley page 14

While the United States was struggling for its independence in 1777, 66 Spaniards founded the first civil settlement in California. The site was along the east bank of the Guadalupe River in the fertile valley at the south end of San Francisco Bay. The settlement called the Pueblo de San Jose de Guadalupe, named in honor of St. Joseph, was established to raise crops and cattle.

Downtown San Jose: Refreshed, Revitalized & Thriving page 30

Out of the depths of darkness, San Jose's revitalized downtown is thriving. As little as 15 years ago, if you walked downtown you would have found it somewhat deserted. Today, downtown flaunts high rises, fine restaurants, major hotels, theaters, and many corporate headquarters.

San Jose & the Surrounding Cities of Silicon Valley page 50

The entrepreneurial spirit is alive and well in Silicon Valley. Today, San Jose is the most important high-technology center in the country.

Building a Transportation System page 64

San Jose International Airport, three miles from downtown, is served by 13 major airlines and opened a state-of-the-art terminal in 1991. A 21-mile Light Rail Transit System connects downtown with residential San Jose to the south and Santa Clara to the north. Four major freeways, Interstate Highways 280, 680, 880, and U.S. 101 converge on San Jose along with the newest freeway addition, Highway 85.

San Jose & Silicon Valley: Leading Center for Medical Treatment page 76

The area's health care resources are a source of great pride to the local community. Hospitals, specialized care facilities, and growing maintenance organizations are explored in this chapter.

San Jose & Silicon Valley Offer Educational Choices page 92

San Jose and Silicon Valley provide a selection of school districts that offer a variety of educational choices in learning. Besides a strong public school system, many private schools in San Jose and Silicon Valley are rated the best in the nation.

Photo by Pat Kirk.

San Jose & Silicon Valley: Region of Diversity page 108

You may be sitting on the lawn at the Children's Discovery Museum listening to the San Jose Symphony on July 4th and surrounding you is an adventure of culture. The city is alive with a blend of Latino, Asian, Black, Filipino, and Indo-American communities, all working, living, and playing together.

Neighborhoods Create A Sense of Community in San Jose & Silicon Valley page 126

The neighborhoods that comprise San Jose and Silicon Valley insert charm into this sprawling area giving this large metropolitan city a feeling of neighborliness and a sense of community.

Arts & Cultural Affairs page 148

If you have a desire to see national art exhibitions, check out the San Jose Museum of Art. If technology is your interest, the Tech Museum of Innovation is your answer. San Jose boasts 30 galleries and museums and is also home to world-class performing art companies.

Lifestyle-Sports & Recreation page 166

When it comes to lifestyle, San Jose and Silicon Valley have it all. Rated as the nation's number one discretionary income spenders by *American Demographics Magazine*, San Joseans not only work hard, but like to play hard as well. The San Jose Arena, which opened in September, 1993, is home to National Hockey League's San Jose Sharks, and also hosts other events such as concerts, ice shows, and circuses. For the outdoor enthusiast, there are over 3,000 acres of park land where residents can swim, throw a football, or catch a baseball.

Part Two

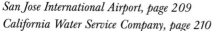

Film processing for Pat Kirk by Vision Color Lab.

Foreword

*T*he San Jose Metropolitan Chamber of Commerce is proud to represent one of the most dynamic business communities in the world. The products and ideas that flow from San Jose and Silicon Valley play a key role in maintaining our nation's global economic leadership.

Yet, Silicon Valley's legendary high-technology base is well-complemented by its top ranked quality of life. *Fortune* magazine says "San Jose/Silicon Valley is one of the nation's economic powerhouses…and still far and way the single most important high-technology center in the U.S." At the same time, San Jose and Silicon Valley consistently rank high in quality of life studies by national magazines and universities.

This melding of economic strength with delightful touches—great weather, outstanding culture and arts, distinct and diverse neighborhoods, and a growing sense of community—is what this book is all about.

Its intended audience includes people from around the world who may recognize Silicon Valley from superficial media reports, but who do not know the multi-level depth of our community. Its audience also includes people who already live here, but want to learn more about their home city and living environment.

The San Jose Metropolitan Chamber of Commerce is pleased to present this book to showcase San Jose and the Silicon Valley. This is a community that is indeed primed for the 21st century. It will continue to be a leading community in which to live, and the leader in technological advancement for the progress of humankind throughout the world.

Steve Tedesco
President & CEO
San Jose Metropolitan Chamber of Commerce

◆

SANTA TERESA

807

Preface

*H*aving lived in San Jose and Silicon Valley my entire life, I remember the days of there being absolutely nothing to do here in regards to entertainment. I also remember when downtown San Jose was a thriving mecca and when retail and business deserted it for nearby Valley Fair Shopping Center. I can still visualize the many orchards in the valley where teenage summer jobs consisted of cutting apricots.

As a teenager in the 1960s, we spent most of our leisure time listening to music at a friend's house. If we wanted to attend concerts or sporting events, San Jose and Silicon Valley residents made the long trip up to San Francisco, known to many as "the city."

As we approach the 21st century, San Jose has an identity all its own. For many, there is something to do just about every day and night of the week. In fact, most of us can't fit all of it into our busy Silicon Valley schedules. For example, today residents and visitors alike are fortunate to have the availability of the San Jose Arena, a $140 million, 450,000-square-foot, state-of-the-art building that holds 20,000 seats for concertgoers and 18,000 for hockey fans. When Barbara Streisand held her first concert tour in years, she chose the San Jose Arena as her Bay Area concert venue and I was in the audience.

The trend in retail throughout the country exhibits itself through suburban malls, and San Jose has experienced a rebirth. High-technology business, which San Jose is known for, has located here. And downtown San Jose is so well planned that there are many fine restaurants, parks, and fountains for workers to stroll through during their off hours.

Recently, San Jose State University completed Paseo de San Carlos, a $3.2 million project that connects San Jose State University to downtown San Jose. Traffic is closed through the campus, and a pedestrian walkway with grass, fountains, and benches exists on the former San Carlos Street. Now, university faculty, students, downtown residents, and business people can stroll onto the campus or downtown, pause to eat their lunch on a park bench and enjoy a college landscape that is a part of downtown San Jose.

Downtown San Jose is truly the hub of Silicon Valley. Almost every day of the business work week, one can find members of Silicon Valley corporations conducting conferences and meeting at the many venues in downtown San Jose. As downtown San Jose evolves, it is giving Silicon Valley a geographic, cultural, and business focus. The superior image of downtown San Jose held by Silicon Valley business and industry is a sign of growing maturity.

Local photographer Pat Kirk has captured the essence of San Jose and Silicon Valley in his outstanding photographs of the area. Also, Judy Semas has done an excellent job in profiling the many corporations and business entities of the area. Jim Tucker, director of communications for the San Jose Metropolitan Chamber of Commerce, pointed me in the right direction for research and is an outstanding editor.

When I first received the assignment of writing this book, even though a San Jose native, I was dismayed at how I would write 30,000 words about San Jose and Silicon Valley. In retrospect, the area is so full of life, congeniality and prosperity, it wouldn't be hard to write an additional 30,000 words.

I commend my husband Joseph Di Salvo for applauding my efforts, and when I was overwhelmed with information he encouraged me every step of the way. Writing this book is a project that I am sure will stand out in my mind for many years to come. San Jose and Silicon Valley is my home and it is where I live, work, and play. I was born here, attended school, and am raising my family here. While I miss the agricultural environment, I am proud of what the area has become: a vibrant, alive, and fine community.

My hope for this book is that visitors realize the importance of San Jose and Silicon Valley, appreciate its history and richness, and that residents value what they already have by living and working here, and continue to contribute in making this one of the best places to live in the country.

Chris Di Salvo
Author

◆

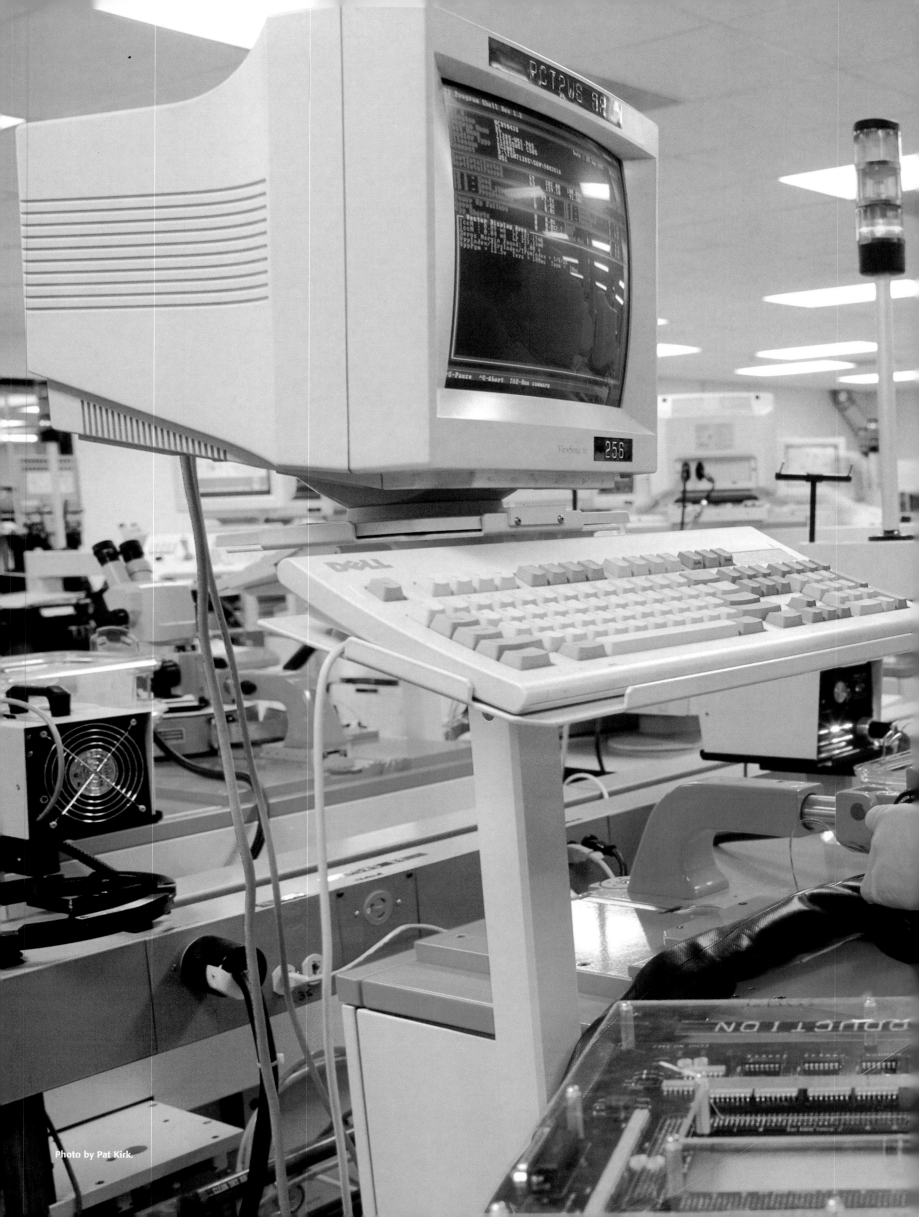

Photo by Pat Kirk.

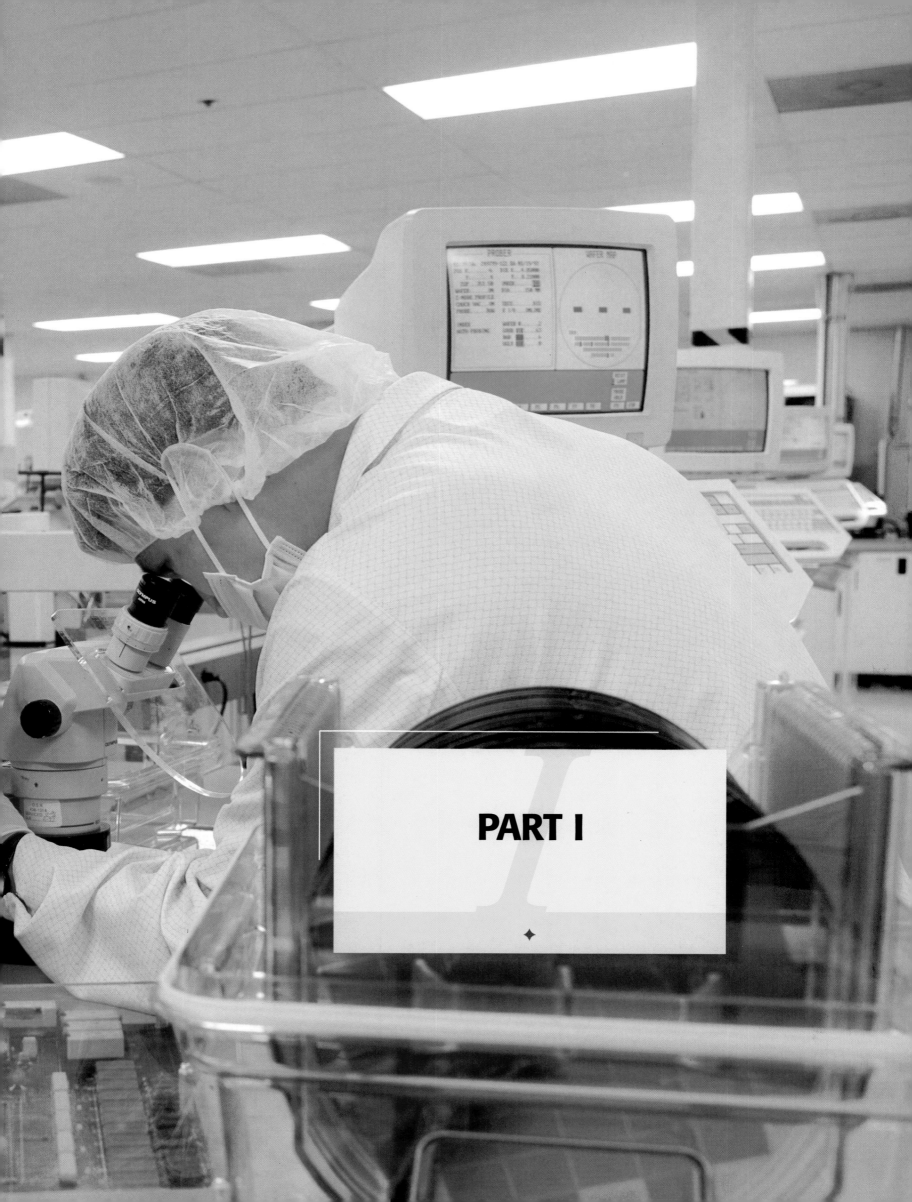

PART I

Photo by Pat Kirk.

Chapter One

From California's First City to Capital of Silicon Valley

◆

Pueblo de San Jose de Guadalupe Founded in 1777

More than 200 years ago, led by Comandante Don Jose Moraga, from the Presidio of San Francisco, nine soldiers, five civilians, one servant, and their families from the San Francisco and Monterey presidios founded Pueblo de San Jose de Guadalupe on November 29, 1777. Most of the party had experience in agriculture.

The exact site of Pueblo de San Jose de Guadalupe was bordered by the east bank of the Guadalupe River and the present West Hedding, North First, and Hobson Streets. Pueblo de San Jose de Guadalupe was the first civil settlement of California and was named after St. Joseph.

This group of settlers must have been awestruck when they saw this beautiful valley of the California Coast Range, part of a complex series of mountains paralleling the coastline of California. The San Jose plain is the largest of the valleys separating the radiating files of this mountain system.

Soon, however, the Spanish settlers of Pueblo de San Jose de Guadalupe must have wondered why they left Mexico. They were nearly driven away by floods from the shallow, choked Guadalupe River. Dams broke, crops washed away, and adobe houses melted into the soil.

Conflict with Mission Santa Clara

Adding to their problems, the new residents of Pueblo de San Jose de Guadalupe were not welcomed to the area with open arms. Close by, the Fathers at Mission Santa Clara resented having a civil settlement so close to the mission. Besides questioning its right to be there, they feared

The Mission Santa Clara was a source of conflict between the Fathers at the mission and the new settlers of Pueblo de San Jose de Guadalupe. Due to the frequent flooding of the Guadalupe River, the pueblo was moved to higher ground, and thus, Pueblo Nuevo (New Town) was born.

its soldiery and other worldly features would have an ill effect on the morals of the Indians who resided at the mission.

At that time, the pueblo's right of location proved to be the most gnawing bone of contention. The Fathers felt that the land on both sides of the Guadalupe belonged to the mission and that San Jose was encroaching on mission pasturage. They angrily complained to the Comandante and Governor. They even appealed directly to the Viceroy. However, in the end the Viceroy expressed sympathy but sided with the Pueblo because his men had established it and had no intentions of moving it elsewhere. Therefore, on September 1, 1800, the Viceroy decreed the Guadalupe River the legal boundary between the pueblo and mission. This gave San Jose part of the mountains which lie toward the coast so that the settlers could provide themselves with timber and wood.

At about the same time, the flooding of the Guadalupe River often left the pueblo a bog until May or June. Commissioner Ygnacio Vallejo, the Governor's representative, concluded in 1785 that the pueblo could never prosper under such conditions. He notified Moraga, and a solution was reached to move the pueblo to a safer location.

By the end of 1797, an undisclosed number of San Jose's citizens had already moved to higher ground. Thus, Pueblo Nuevo (New Town) was born. It extended southward from just north of the present St. John Street to about midway between San Carlos Street and Auzerais Avenue, and from the easterly line of Market Street to the westerly line of San Pedro Street.

Mexico Becomes Independent of Spain

In 1821, Mexico declared its independence from Spain. On April 11, 1822, California took the oath of allegiance to Mexico when Governor Pablo Vicente de Sola and his troops replaced the Spanish flag with that of Mexico at the Presidio of Monterey.

During the transition from Spanish to Mexican rule, San Jose faced an uncertain future. There were hostile Indians to the east, foreign ships in

The first group of settlers to discover the beautiful valley were awestruck when they saw it with its complex series of mountains paralleling the coastline of California.

the Pacific, and an emperor of uncertain tenure in Mexico City. On the other hand, the San Jose residents showed no disposition to resist a change in administration.

Dependent upon supplies and goods brought by Spain to the commissary stores, Mexico would not be able to maintain the aid or replace the supplies Spain had provided. Californians had to find other solutions for their problems. This weakened their sense of dependence on Mexico. Mexican authority proved indecisive and some of the measures the government took were unfortunate and unpopular, such as sending convict colonists and troops to California. As a result, Californians became conscious of their own identity both as a people and an area.

United States Obtains California through the Mexican American War

The United States declared war on Mexico in 1846. On June 14, 1846, a party of American settlers hoisted the Bear Flag of the California Republic at Sonoma. In San Jose, an unidentified person raised the flag on July 11, only to have it cut down immediately by angry natives.

It wasn't until Thomas Fallon of the American Volunteers hung it on a flagstaff that it stayed fluttering in the air. In his dispatch to his commander, Fallon wrote, "I am happy to inform you that we have hoisted the star spangled banner on the 14th instant, and we hope it may wave and dispense its blessings throughout this country."

Fallon, a young Irishman, was a 25-year-old emigre from Ireland. He recruited fellow Irishmen and struck out for the West Coast. In 1844, he linked up with one of John C. Fremont's early exploring expeditions to California. Fallon spent much of the summer of 1846, marching from place to place with about 20 volunteers trying to catch up to and reinforce Fremont. After the Mexican American War, Fallon settled in Santa Cruz. He moved to Texas for two years but returned to San Jose to open up a saddle shop in the center of town.

Fallon was elected mayor in 1859. Through his real estate dealings, he became one of the wealthier residents. His fine residence was located at San Pedro and St. John Street. Today, the refurbished Fallon House is

a San Jose landmark that showcases 15 fully furnished rooms, open for the viewing public.

Transition to American rule was relatively peaceful. For a time, the Americans kept the existing form of government, although some variations were incorporated. That served to minimize any social dislocation, especially since Californios—as those of Spanish and Mexican descent were called—were often included in the governing bodies.

Captain Thomas Fallon, of the American Volunteers, was elected mayor of San Jose in 1859. Through his real estate dealings, he became one of the wealthier residents.

California Gold Rush-1848

Gold was discovered in Coloma in 1848. The men of San Jose, as in most California settlements of that time, took off for the Sierra foothills to discover gold. However, most San Joseans were wise enough to recognize that their true fortune came from their productive farms and ranches. They provided food for the miners and realized that this service was more lucrative than splashing through Sierra streams with pan and gun in hand.

By the end of 1848, little was left of the old pueblo. New faces, a new language, and new customs rapidly were replacing the old. Tents cluttered the still-open spaces, and wooden buildings rose to replace older adobes. San Jose was changing and facing a new destiny.

The raising of the American flag at the Pueblo de San Jose, California, by Captain Thomas Fallon.

Copyright Applied For
By Edwin A. Sherman.

San Jose, the First Capital of California

The governance of the pueblo was taken over by the Americans shortly after the Treaty of Guadalupe Hidalgo. Many of these Americans were speculators who came to California to seek their fortunes in the gold fields.

By 1850, San Jose had about 4,000 residents living in disorganized clusters of adobe, wood, and canvas buildings grouped roughly around the edges of the original Spanish plaza near Market Street. Livestock roamed the streets, and the chief source of water was a sometimes putrid ditch that meandered through the town.

About that time, a prime mover in the community was James Frazier Reed. Reed was a wagonmaster, miner, farmer, and land speculator. He was a particularly good lobbyist. It was Reed along with Charles White, another real estate investor, who put the wheels in motion

that would make San Jose the seat of the first capital of California.

After the end of the United States' war with Mexico, California was admitted as a state. U.S. Army General Bennett Riley, the military governor, called for a constitutional convention in Monterey, September 1, 1849, in order to establish a state capital.

The convention soon became a free-for-all to secure not only the honor of becoming the first capital of California but to try to derive economic benefits from this status. San Jose's convention delegation hoped that capital status would further inflate real estate values for resident Americans. To persuade conventioneers to name San Jose, Charles White and James Reed promised that impressive legislative chambers and fine accommodations would be provided.

White and Reed triumphantly returned to town to announce the selection of San Jose as the first capital of California. They were quickly disappointed to find that local government could not furnish a suitable meeting place for the legislature nor did it have the funds to make good the promises that both men had made in Monterey.

To live up to their promises, Reed and his friends formed a private fund to house the legislature. They raised $34,000 to purchase a two-story adobe structure that faced Market Street on the east side of the Plaza. Reed's associates loaned the funds to the town and in return took as security mortgages on public lands originally granted to the pueblo at the time of its founding.

The first session for the legislature occurred on December 17, 1849. From the beginning, the lawmakers were unhappy. The legislature hall was originally built as a hotel and contained few luxuries. If one were visiting the legislature in San Jose at that time, he would find a speaker perched in a species of a pulpit, and a floor covered with a number of small carpets that looked like each member contributed a patch.

The conduct of the lawmakers was abhorrent. The officials were bored because San Jose was a long way from home for most of them. The speaker had a habit of adjourning each session with "Let's go have a drink boys, let's go have a thousand of them." The legislature quickly earned the reputation of "Legislature of 1,000 drinks."

It was also common to see the lawmakers smoking and chewing tobacco during those sessions. Soon, bills were circulated to move the legislature to a more hospitable place. Finally, in 1851, an Act of Removal was passed and the capital was moved to Vallejo.

The legislators were not sorry to leave San Jose. One man wrote, "Very glad, hope to have some place to sleep now except on the floor, under cot, and bad living all for $35 a week."

The refurbished Fallon House is a San Jose historical landmark that showcases 15 fully furnished rooms open for the viewing public. (inset) The Peralto Adobe House, built in 1797, is one of the last remaining structures of the El Pueblo de San Jose de Guadalupe. Photos by Pat Kirk.

When gold was discovered in Coloma in 1848 the men of San Jose, as in most California settlements of that time, took off for the Sierra foothills to discover gold.

Basic San Jose Boundaries Established

Once the lawmakers left town, the U.S. Congress took action to validate the ownership of private lands in the state. In 1847, the San Jose Town Council partitioned the town and gave away lots of more than 6,000 feet square to the head of each household. They established three public squares and set aside land for a school site. The new border of the town was Julian Street on the north, Eighth Street on the east, Reed Street on the south and Market Street on the west.

San Jose City Hall Built in 1854

Shortly after the elections of 1854, a publicly owned city hall became a topic of conversation. Since 1850, the council and official staff had occupied rented quarters. After much discussion and an investigation, the council chose D. Emmanuelli's lot at 35 North Market Street as the site of the new edifice.

Construction began in November, with Levi Goodrich as the architect. The construction progressed on a crenelated brick structure that resembled a medieval castle and was operable by April 16, 1855 when the council held its first meeting.

San Jose Continues to Grow

As the seat of government for Santa Clara County, the city continued to grow slowly but steadily. Agriculture was the main industry because of room to expand, the mild climate, and rich soil. The area, contrary to the first legislature's experience, was indeed a pleasant place to live. Because of its agricultural bonanza, San Jose was known as the "Garden City," nestled in the "Valley of Heart's Delight."

After the end of the United States' war with Mexico, California was admitted as a state and San Jose was selected as the first capital of California. Peter Burnett was elected as its first governor.

$34,000 was raised to purchase a two-story adobe structure for the State House that faced Market Street on the east side of the Plaza. The first session for the legislature occurred on December 17, 1849.

The council chose D. Emmanuelli's lot at 35 North Market Street as the site of a new City Hall. Construction progressed on the crenelated brick structure that resembled a medieval castle and was operable by April 16, 1855 when the council held its first meeting.

As the seat of government for Santa Clara County, San Jose continued to grow slowly but steadily. Agriculture was the main industry because of the room in which to expand, the mild climate, and the rich soil. The area was indeed a pleasant place to live.

The packing and canning plants provided the manufacturing base of the Santa Clara Valley's economy throughout the first half of the 20th century.

Throughout the first half of the 20th century, the fruit and vegetable packing and agriculture industry continued to grow. Together with factories producing agriculture machinery, these packing and canning plants provided the manufacturing base of the area.

1930s Innovation Revolution

Stanford University, north of Palo Alto, is where the seeds of the innovation revolution were planted. During the 1930s, electronic wonders were stimulated through creative energies of teachers like Dr. Frederick Terman. He inspired students such as David Packard, William Hewlett, and the Varian brothers. The university encouraged its graduates to stay in the valley and start their own companies. Hewlett-Packard Company and Varian Corporation pioneered many technological advances during World War II.

World War II also brought new people to the area for military service or to work to support the war effort. Many stayed when the war ended. The next four decades saw booming subdivisions that expanded the boundaries of San Jose and surrounding cities. The material "silicon" was being used to manufacture semiconductors. As the high-technology based businesses grew, the area quickly became known as "Silicon Valley" throughout the world.

As the high-technology industries gained in importance, agricultural-related industries lost their dominance. During this period, San Jose was cited as the fastest growing city in America. San Jose's population jumped from 95,000 in 1950 to 849,400 in 1996. San Jose is now the third largest city in California and the 11th largest in the United States. Santa Clara County, the core of Silicon Valley, hosts a population of over 1.6 million. Today, valley residents enjoy economic opportunity, jobs, and a high standard of living. And, in the past few years, San Jose has been voted near the top of quality-of-life studies sponsored by various universities and national media.

San Jose is a 200-year-old city that refuses to act its age. As it looks toward the dawning of the 21st century, the city continues to offer opportunity for not only businesses but residents as well. San Jose and its surrounding cities together form an economic powerhouse that is recognized worldwide. ◆

Because of its agricultural bonanza, San Jose was known as the "Garden City," nestled in the "Valley of Heart's Delight."

Photo by Pat Kirk.

San Jose has been cited as the fastest growing city in America, and is now the third largest city in California and the 11th largest in the United States. **Photo by Pat Kirk.**

EL MESTIZAJE VA AL NORTE

PRIMERO LAS PALIZADAS

EL LLANO DE LOS ROBLES

Photo by Pat Kirk.

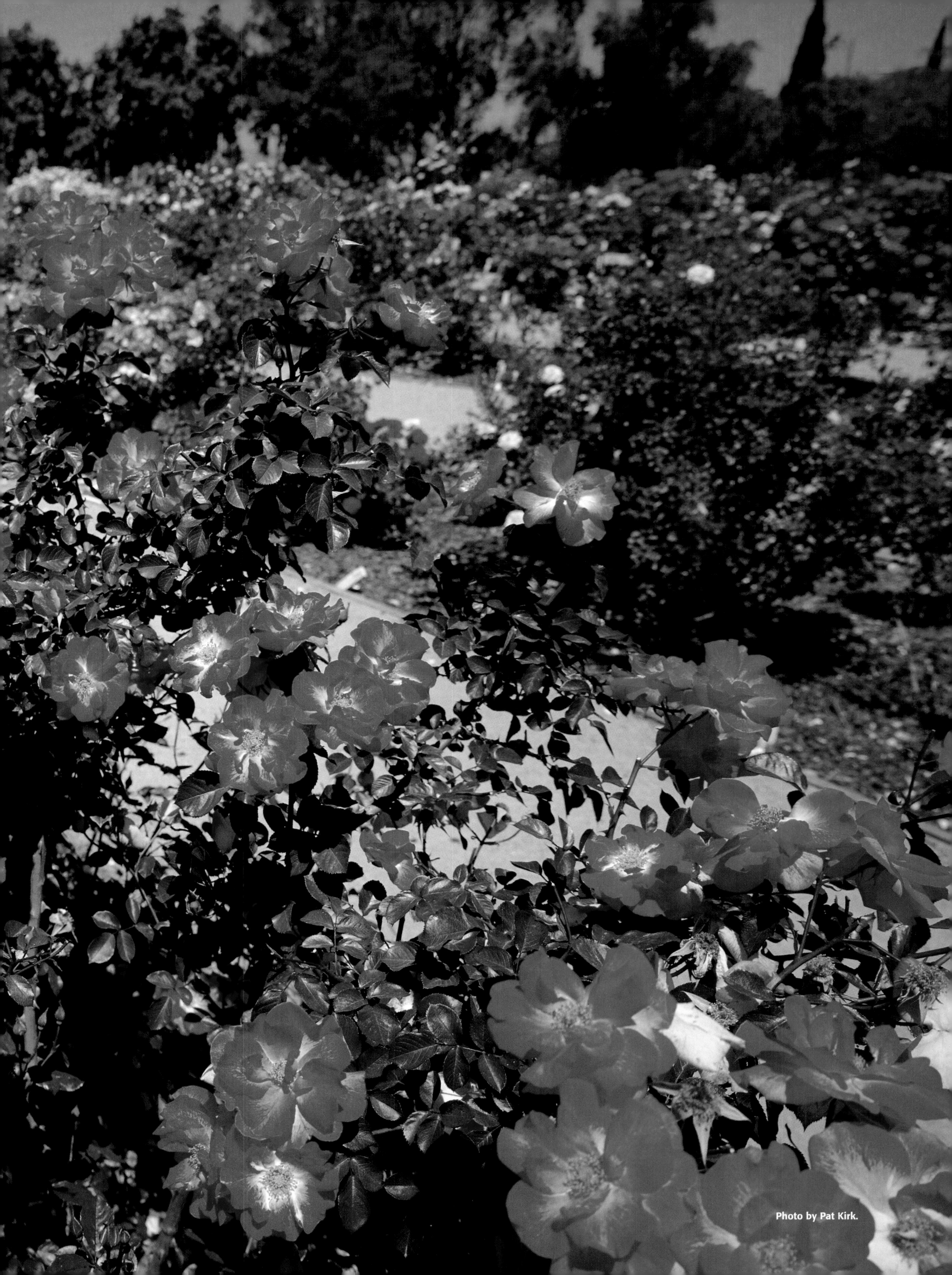

Photo by Pat Kirk.

Chapter Two

Downtown San Jose: Refreshed, Revitalized, & Thriving

Standing in the Redevelopment Agency of the City of San Jose lobby, on the 15th floor of the Fairmont Tower building, the view of downtown San Jose is not only breathtaking but awe inspiring. It is hard to believe that beginning in the 1960s retail, financial, and commercial institutions started to move out of downtown to outlying areas. Twenty-five years ago, downtown San Jose resembled a ghost town. The businesses and merchants moved out of the area, greatly reducing the hustle and bustle enjoyed during the 1950s. The abandonment of the downtown core lasted for approximately 25 years.

Today, an observer views business professionals working downtown in the many newly built and refurbished buildings, conventioneers rushing to attend sessions at the San Jose McEnery Convention Center, children playing in the water fountains at Plaza de Cesar Chavez, and diners enjoying lunch and dinner at the many outside eating areas of the cafes and restaurants.

San Jose was not alone in the trend of businesses and merchants abandoning their downtown area. The pattern for American cities at that time was to grow and expand into the suburbs. Thus, San Jose was doing just that, growing. Housing developments sprouted on empty land; Valley Fair Shopping Center was built to take over the retail needs; while downtown San Jose, the core of the city, lay dormant in a winter of discontent, waiting to bloom.

Identifying a need for a stable city center with the hopes of bringing back old business as well as new, the Downtown Working Review Committee (DWRC) was appointed by then Mayor Tom McEnery in 1978. The DWRC was a broad committee composed of community leaders and representatives of business, politics and residents. Former Mayor McEnery writes in his book, *The New City-State: Change and Renewal In America's Cities,* "Our redevelopment process placed a priority on community participation as we looked for successful strategies to

---

(left) *Downtown San Jose is designed so that city dwellers can live, work, and play in one area.* **Photo by Pat Kirk.**

Diners enjoy lunch and dinner at the many outside eating areas of the cafes and restaurants in downtown San Jose. **Photo by Pat Kirk.**

involve our citizens in this revitalization. I looked forward to a new downtown that fostered and protected urban traditions, like festivals celebrating diverse communities. We were interested in identifying all the elements that could nourish a town and bind it together."

And bind it together they did. Bordered by Highway 280 on the south, Highway 87 on the west, Julian Street on the north and Fourth Street on the east, downtown San Jose is an activity-filled center. "Downtown San Jose is designed so that city dwellers can live, work, and play in one area," says Dennis Korabiak, special projects coordinator of The Redevelopment Agency.

In the middle 1970s, San Jose was in the middle of a high-technology revolution. Many high-technology firms began in Santa Clara Valley and their success fueled the redevelopment process. As the Rincon industrial area developed in North San Jose, tax dollars became available to use for downtown improvement. The redevelopment process was made possible by California state law, which provides for the allocation of certain local tax revenues to eliminate conditions of blight.

Over the past decade, downtown San Jose has undergone a dramatic physical renaissance. New office and retail buildings, public facilities, transportation improvements, a luxury hotel, convention center, parks, and outdoor art have created a cosmopolitan environment. Downtown San Jose has also undergone an economic resurgence that includes an expanding market for business, retail, and visitors.

The original Downtown Working Review Committee accomplished 75 percent of their goals set forth in a Master Plan that began under the direction of Mayor McEnery in 1988. Eight years later, the Downtown Working Review Committee adopted the Downtown Strategy Plan to continue to guide development, growth, and preservation activities that assure the future development of downtown San Jose into the 21st century. Thus, the 2010 Downtown Strategy Plan was developed by RTKL Associates, Inc., and Economics Research Associates.

Utilizing the many needs and wants of residents and community leaders, they envisioned an active center city that functions 24 hours a day with a healthy mix of people and activities. Planning efforts were directed to create new development sensitive to historic places, creating a new downtown urban environment filled with places for people to work, walk, shop, and enjoy cultural and recreational activities. The program included office development, hotels, retail space, civic functions, new housing, and parking.

Today, navigating downtown San Jose is relatively easy. To combat commute traffic, light rail transit was developed in the 1980s. Light rail allows visitors the convenience of leaving their car at home and riding from South San Jose to downtown and north to Great America Parkway in Santa Clara. If you do need a car, parking is not a problem because there are nearly 20,000 parking places downtown. Once you are downtown, major landmarks are within easy walking distance.

Pedestrian and bicycle paths run along the west side of the city center at the Guadalupe River Park. **Photo by Pat Kirk.**

San Jose has seven sister cities throughout the world. Each city is commemorated with a special seating area along the Guadalupe River Walk. Above is the Dublin sister City Garden Area. **Photo by Dana L. Grover.**

Plaza de Cesar Chavez is a brilliant design success that has emerged as the heart of the city. **Photo by Dana L. Grover.**

Original Joe's is a San Jose landmark located at San Carlos Street and First Street. Photo by Pat Kirk.

A Pedestrian Visits Downtown San Jose

Stepping out into the California sunshine from the Fairmont Tower, you enter the Corona of Palms. Corona, which means circle in Spanish, is the area between the Fairmont Hotel and the San Jose Museum of Art, and faces Market Street. The palm trees give residents a little Hawaii in San Jose. A large bronze plaque is located in the sidewalk which exhibits the California Seal. The plaque celebrates San Jose as the first capital of California. Surrounding the circumference of the plaque are inscribed relevant quotes such as "Let's go have a drink, let's drink a 1,000 drinks." This inscription depicts the checkered early history of San Jose where the first legislature gained the name "Legislature of 1,000 Drinks" because they seemed to be going out for drinks more than conducting business. One of the many lovely pedestrian walkways incorporated within downtown, the Corona of Palms has easy access into a side entrance of the Fairmont Hotel. If one looks west, you will see Plaza de Cesar Chavez and to the east, The Pavilion, a dining-entertainment center.

In the 1980s, many major landmarks were built in downtown San Jose. The San Jose McEnery Convention Center was built on San Carlos Street between Market and Almaden Streets as an anchor of the city core. Hotels such as the Fairmont and Hilton were built to host conventioneers. The DeAnza Hotel on Santa Clara Street and the Hyatt Sainte Claire at Market and San Carlos Streets, historic San Jose buildings, were completely renovated and are truly charming.

As you walk west through Plaza de Cesar Chavez, the Park Center Plaza office complex faces you. Park Center Plaza was actually the first office complex built in the new downtown in the 1970s.

Turning left at Park Center Plaza and proceeding down Market Street, visitors come upon the San Jose Civic Auditorium and the Montgomery Theater. Next door, there is the construction site of the new technology museum, known as the Tech Museum of Innovation. Turning right onto San Carlos Street, one finds the present Technology Museum to the right and the spacious San Jose McEnery Convention Center across the street. The unique design of the convention center actually connects to the

Hilton Hotel on Almaden, with the Dr. Martin Luther King, Jr. Main Library in between both of these landmarks.

Along the west side of the city center is part of the Guadalupe River Park. There are pedestrian and bicycle paths along the river that eventually will connect downtown to the San Francisco Bay. Overlooking Guadalupe River Park is the Center for the Performing Arts, and River Park Towers, a multi-story office building. Across the street you will notice a distinctive purple edifice—the unique and creative Children's Discovery Museum. An expansive lawn area with its many trees and benches fronts the museum and on its east side lies the Guadalupe River.

Upon reaching Almaden Boulevard, you may want to stroll north to Santa Clara Street and visit the newly refurbished DeAnza Hotel or turn around and head back towards the Hyatt Sainte Claire. It may be time for a cup of cappuccino at Il Fornaio's Cafe or a tasty lunch or dinner at their formal restaurant.

Heading east along San Carlos Street at First Street you come upon Original Joe's, a San Jose landmark. Most of the time, the wait for a table is long but if you are game you may sit at the counter and be entertained by the many specialty chefs. Original Joe's borders the South First Street area, known as the SoFA. The SoFA contains cafes and many fine restaurants, the Camera One Theater which features first-run art films, an upscale pool hall establishment and the Institute for Contemporary Art. The SoFA area has its own summer festival each year, featuring arts and entertainment.

Continuing east on San Carlos Street, notice the federal and state buildings at First and Second Streets. When you reach Fourth Street, you come directly into the San Jose State University campus. Recently, San Carlos Street through the campus was closed to through traffic. A picturesque mall now stands and not only enhances the campus but provides a vital link to downtown San Jose.

Turn left onto Fourth Street and you will be allured into making a quick left on Paseo de San Antonio where you will find outdoor cafes and specialty shops. Overlooking the Paseo are new condominium and rental apartment developments that have a variety of downtown views. Housing developments like these are enticing suburban dwellers to trade their large sprawling homes for the convenience of living in the city center.

Continuing through the Paseo and across Second Street, you happen upon the United Artists Theaters. The outside of this building is an art piece in itself. There are eight projection screens showing not only scenes from movies but views of patrons as well. Ahead and on your right you will find The Pavilion which is becoming a dining and entertainment establishment in its own right. Cross First Street and you will happen upon one of the most enchanting views of downtown. Here you gaze at the Fairmont Hotel on your right but straight ahead are the fountains of Plaza de Cesar Chavez.

Plaza de Cesar Chavez is a brilliant design success that has emerged as the heart of the city because its fountains have been embraced by children and

The Civic Auditorium Complex features a 3,060-seat Civic Auditorium and a 30,000-square-foot Exhibit Hall. Photo by Pat Kirk.

The historic DeAnza Hotel on Santa Clara Street has been completely renovated and is truly charming. Photo by Pat Kirk.

The 20,000-seat San Jose Arena on Santa Clara Street, home to the San Jose Sharks, plays host to concerts, sporting events, and family entertainment. Photo by Dana L. Grover.

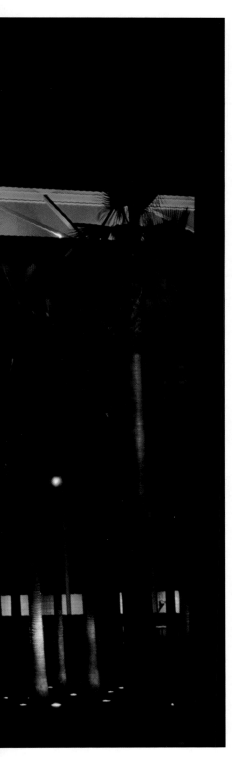

families. It is the home for numerous community events and festivals. On many weekends, you can find entertainment or other events occurring at Plaza de Cesar Chavez.

As you walk towards the Plaza, to the right, on the corner of San Fernando and Market Streets is the San Jose Museum of Art. The museum is located in the original San Jose Post Office building plus a recently expanded wing that houses more gallery space. Across San Fernando Street, St. Joseph's Cathedral-Basilica, another landmark structure, has been completely renovated.

Do not limit yourself to the described walking tour of downtown. If you feel up to it, you many want to walk down Santa Clara Street and tour the 20,000-seat San Jose Arena, home to the San Jose Sharks. The arena plays host to concerts, sporting events, and family entertainment. Barbara Streisand and Luciano Pavorotti gave sold-out performances there.

There are many old buildings being renovated and more restaurants and cafes to visit—one just needs to experiment. As you walk through downtown San Jose, listen to the children's laughter, glance at lovers strolling hand in hand while high-technology transactions occur on laptops and cell phones. Downtown San Jose radiates cleanliness, congeniality, and comfort. Whether you are a visitor or resident, downtown San Jose has become everyone's community.

The Mediterranean climate of San Jose has made it ideal to build archways over walkways that protect pedestrians from the rain in the winter months and the heat in the spring and summer months. **Photo by Dana L. Grover.**

Redevelopment Agency encourages retail businesses and restaurants to design an appealing facade by offering $10,000 grants for this purpose.

San Jose's investment in downtown has come close to $1 billion and is paying off. Many corporations are choosing to locate downtown. In 1996, Adobe moved its corporate headquarters and occupied a building with 1,000 workers. Adobe's second tower is under construction. Netcom, the rapidly growing Internet access company, moved 800 employees into the Horizon Center at Two North Second. An agreement to bring Software Publishing to downtown is in the works.

Future plans for the redevelopment of downtown are projected through the year 2030. A permanent home for the San Jose Repertory Theater will open late in 1997, and The Tech Museum of Innovation will open late in 1998. Of course, more office development is on the rise along with more housing. "The skyline is a chess board," says Carol Beddo of The Redevelopment Agency, "where buildings stand tall and the spaces between are as important as the buildings themselves." There continues to be a particular attention to detail and the use of the highest quality materials. This attention has created a downtown San Jose that is a pleasant place to live, work, and play. ◆

Downtown San Jose—An Investment for the Future

Downtown San Jose was designed by principal design consultants, Thomas Aidala and Frank Taylor. Aidala received the highest honor in American architecture in 1996. Largely because of Aidala, San Jose enjoys such niceties as the city seal stamped on manhole covers and the enticing, interactive fountain at Plaza de Cesar Chavez. Both Aidala and Taylor, executive director of The Redevelopment Agency, are as concerned about the subtle details of the downtown environment as with the grand high-rise buildings.

Restaurant owners are encouraged to offer sidewalk seating, and the Mediterranean climate of San Jose has made it ideal to build archways over walkways that protect pedestrians from the rain in the winter months and the heat in the spring and summer months. The

From auto shows...

...to high-tech trade shows, the convention center is a popular down-town destination. **Photos by Pat Kirk.**

(previous page) *The St. Joseph's Cathedral-Basilica, another land-mark structure, has been completely renovated.* **Photo by Pat Kirk.**

The San Jose McEnery Convention Center, considered the cornerstone of downtown, brings thousands of convention attendees from all over the world to San Jose each year. **Photo by Pat Kirk.**

San Jose State University, located in downtown San Jose, is the largest university in Santa Clara County and the oldest public college in the state. **Photo by Dana L. Grover.**

New fountains welcome visitors to the San Jose State University Campus. **Photo by Dana L. Grover.**

The unique and creative Children's Discovery Museum, distinctive in its purple walls, offer interactive exhibits that invite creativity and stimulate learning for children as well as adults. Photo by Dana L. Grover.

A large bronze plaque, located in the sidewalk, exhibits the California Seal that celebrates San Jose as the first capital of California. Photo by Pat Kirk.

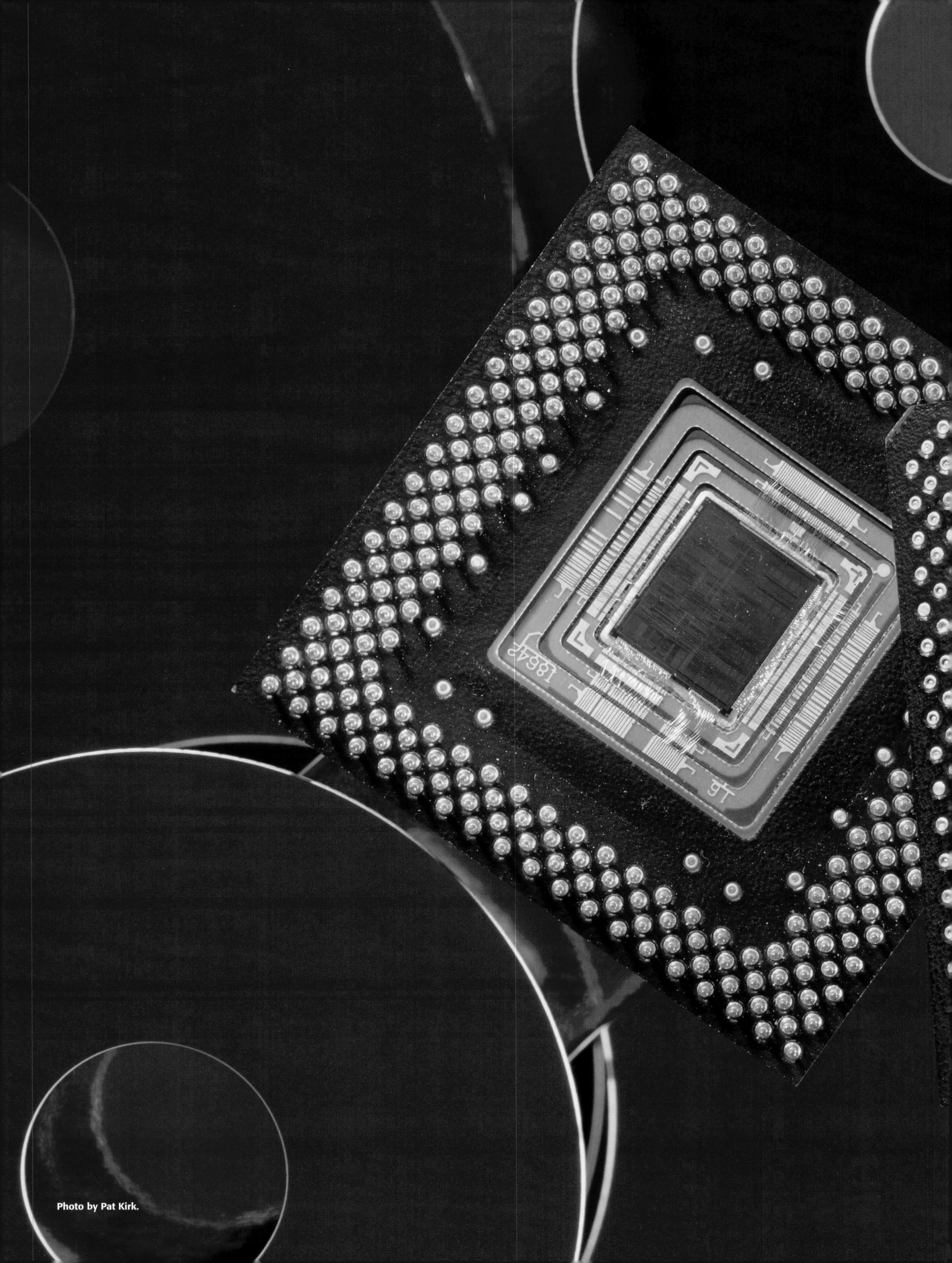

Photo by Pat Kirk.

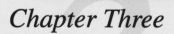

Chapter Three

San Jose & the Surrounding Cities of Silicon Valley

The Entrepreneurial Spirit

From the beginning, San Jose and the surrounding cities of Silicon Valley were positioned to succeed. First, the valley became an agricultural powerhouse; then, a technology powerhouse. Today, Silicon Valley is a wellspring of technology throughout the nation, a home to dreamers and doers encouraged by an entrepreneurial spirit that generates a powerful business climate.

Silicon Valley technology can claim its beginnings at Stanford University in Palo Alto during the 1930s. There, Frederick Terman, a teacher at Stanford, placed two graduate students together, William Hewlett and David Packard. These two engineers invented and developed devices to measure and control radio and sound frequencies. A buyer from Walt Disney Studios saw Hewlett's audio oscillator display at a meeting of the Institute of Radio Engineers in 1939 and ordered nine of them to assist in recording the sound-track for the award-winning movie "Fantasia." Flipping a coin to see whose name would come first on the company letterhead, Hewlett and Packard went on to establish one of the largest and most successful companies in the electronics industry.

Through the years, many technology companies were formed and more were born from others. As agriculture diminished and farmland was redesigned into technology parks, technologies such as the integrated circuit, microprocessor, personal computer, hard disk, laptop, mouse, and virtual reality were created. The list of products is endless with new technology emerging daily.

It is clearly known that Silicon Valley has an entrepreneurial spirit that surpasses other technology meccas in the country. Some claim the key to this valley is the available technology talent. Without great minds, you can not produce new and innovative technology like that produced by Hewlett-Packard and Apple Computer. Much of this talent comes directly from graduating classes of San Jose State University, Santa Clara University, Stanford University, and University of California at Berkeley and Santa Cruz. In addition, the valley boasts a highly ranked community college system which adds to San Jose's ranking as one of the top 10 cities in educated workforce. Out of 1.5 million adults who work in Silicon Valley, two-thirds are college educated.

Besides being a highly educated workforce, Silicon Valley employees have a strong work ethic. They make up a diverse community with many ethnic backgrounds who believe in working hard and doing their best.

Another major reason for the success of Silicon Valley is the availability of venture capital to support innovative startups. "Many redevelopment areas, such as Boston, depend on government funding. In Silicon Valley, there is an abundance of venture capital available that spurs economic growth," says John Weis, director, Neighborhood and Industrial Development Division, The Redevelopment Agency of the City of San Jose.

Hyundai America is located in Rincon de Los Esteros, part of the famed Golden Triangle that contains more than half the jobs that make up the Silicon Valley economy. Photo by Pat Kirk.

The Rincon de Los Esteros area is one of the largest industrial redevelopment projects and is home to many high-technology firms such as Atmel Corporation, a specialty computer company. **Photo by Pat Kirk.**

More than half of the venture capital firms in the world are located in Silicon Valley.

Many feel an important cause for the economic success of Silicon Valley is the fearless risk-taking attitude of so many of its residents. This entrepreneurial attitude along with brainpower and capital has made Silicon Valley the technological leader of the nation if not the world.

The following is a brief survey of activity in some key Silicon Valley cities:

San Jose

San Jose, Capital of Silicon Valley, is the corporate, financial, government and cultural center of the world's pre-eminent concentration of high technology businesses.

Actively seeking business investment, San Jose targets high-technology corporate headquarters, start-ups, research and development, sales offices, business services, industrial suppliers, distributors, environmentally-related businesses and retailers.

The city has made a concerted effort to recruit technology firms. In January 1990, the Redevelopment Agency adopted an aggressive program to promote the two largest industrial redevelopment project areas: Rincon de Los Esteros and Edenvale.

Rincon de Los Esteros is located between Route 237 and Interstate 880. Companies located there today are Cisco Systems, with nearly 1 million square feet and plans to expand into adjacent land; Atmel, 300,000 square feet; KLA 150,000 square feet; Hyundai America, 180,000 square feet; Conner Peripherals (now owned by Seagate), 150,000 square feet and more.

Since its inception in 1974, Rincon has developed into one of the most successful redevelopment industrial zones in the nation. As part of

High-volume production of anti-static delivery packaging for wafer components, circuit boards, and high-tech memory devices. Photo by Gene Antisdel, G2 Group.

Hewlett-Packard Company co-founders, Bill Hewlett and David Packard, visiting with children at The Tech Museum of Innovation. Photo by Pat Kirk.

Hewlett-Packard Company co-founder, Bill Hewlett, tests one of the company's early products, an audio signal generator. Photo courtesy of Hewlett-Packard Company.

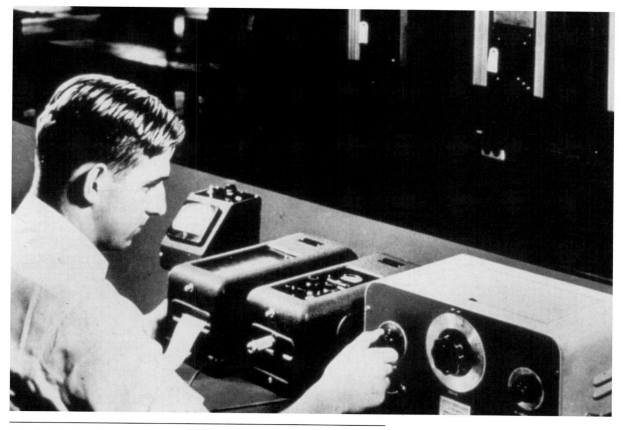

Hewlett-Packard Company co-founder, David Packard, calibrates HP's first major product, an audio oscillator, designed for testing and sound equipment. Photo courtesy of Hewlett-Packard Company.

As agriculture diminished and farmland was redesigned into technology parks, technologies such as the integrated circuit, microprocessor, personal computer, hard disk, laptop, mouse, and virtual reality were created. The list of products is endless with new technology emerging daily. **Photo by Pat Kirk.**

the competitive benefits of remaining in the valley, created some 7,000 new jobs.

Several of these and other earlier expansions were by specialty computer companies such as Atmel Corp., Altera Corp., and Cypress Semiconductor Corp. These companies focus their business on designing specialized devices that add value to products such as machine tools, cameras, automobiles, and microwaves. Other companies have developed products for the computer and wider electronics industry including peripheral equipment, networking systems, testing equipment, and integrated circuits.

Since 1990, the Redevelopment Agency has invested more than $100 million in infrastructure improvements in these two areas. Expenditures allocated were $42 million for Route 87, $20.2 million invested to accelerate the construction of Route 85, $18.7 million for the Guadalupe-Charcot overpass, $12 million for the Brokaw Road underpass, $900,000 for the Tasman Bridge, and $5 million for the construction of the Fontanoso Bridge. Other investments include median landscaping, gateway enhancement designs, signal lights and landscape master plans for both Rincon and Edenvale.

Two other areas included in the Redevelopment Agency Industrial Work Plan are the Monterey Corridor and the Julian-Stockton area. The Monterey Corridor, to the south of downtown, was organized as a redevelopment area in 1994. The City of San Jose is encouraging existing firms to expand within that area.

Cisco Systems, Inc., located in the Rincon de Los Esteros area, is the worldwide leader in networking for the Internet. **Photo by Pat Kirk.**

the famed Golden Triangle of Silicon Valley, more than 2,000 firms have located there to capitalize on the proximity to San Jose International Airport and the freeway system. Clearly the heart of the region, the Golden Triangle contains more than half the jobs that make up the Silicon Valley economy.

The recent increase in Rincon's corporate locations has utilized 112 acres over the last two years. There are still 483 prime acres to develop. It is projected that when the Rincon area is fully developed, there could be an additional 7,000,000 square feet of buildings and an additional 25,000 employees.

Another desirable San Jose industrial area is Edenvale. Edenvale is bordered by Cottle Road, Santa Teresa Boulevard, and Bernal Avenue in the southern part of San Jose. Edenvale was created to attract spinoffs and suppliers of its prime tenant IBM. At its peak in the 1970s, IBM's data storage manufacturing operations employed 15,000 people at its Cottle Road facility. Since the redevelopment area was created, approximately 200 firms employing 16,200 persons have located in the Edenvale area.

Since January 1994, corporate expansions in Rincon and Edenvale have totaled 1,351,000 square feet of new research and development, office, and manufacturing space. Much of this growth occurred from San Jose firms looking to expand at or near their locations, or from firms relocating from other areas of Silicon Valley as they seek room to grow. In the last three years, these expansions, by companies that recognize

The Julian-Stockton area, to the west of downtown, was created in 1984 to attract industries and offices in support of downtown development. Julian-Stockton's recent projects include the Arena, Guadalupe River Park, and the Villa Torino housing development.

When firms are interested in locating in San Jose, or expanding, the City of San Jose's Redevelopment Agency and San Jose Office of Economic Development (OED) staff work closely with city departments assisting companies through the development process. Real estate tours are held for corporate executives, real estate brokers, developers, and site selection consultants.

San Jose officials realize the time constraints facing businesses when relocating or expanding high-investment plants. The life cycles of technology products are brief, and new facilities must be up and running quickly in order to remain competitive. Every effort is made by San Jose staff to speed processing permits and construction.

There are a variety of business development programs to assist entrepreneurs available through the Office of Economic Development. For example, firms in an 18-square-mile central San Jose area called the Enterprise Zone are eligible for special tax incentives.

Firms locating in redevelopment areas—industrial or commercial—may be eligible for tax incentives as well.

The OED also offers a variety of financial assistance programs. The city participates in an industrial development bond program. Another program, Development Enhancement Fund, provides loan guarantees, subordinated direct loans and gap financing. A Revolving Loan Fund aids small firms. A special loan program helps firms in the Enterprise Zone. Yet another special program helps provide financing for firms using recycled feedstock. Finally, the city offers financial incentives to existing firms undertaking wastewater reduction modifications to help them meet environmental compliance.

The Export Resource Center (ERC), also a program through OED, is Northern California's most comprehensive source of international trade information. ERC is available to Silicon Valley businesses interested in conducting international trade. The center provides worldwide sales leads, export guides, an extensive periodical and computer library, and a database containing 80,000 U.S. and foreign firms. Participants are also encouraged to attend weekly export orientation seminars. The center is co-located in downtown San Jose with the U.S. Export Assistance Center, sponsored by the U.S. Department of Commerce. This cooperative effort between local and federal agencies is providing a full range of services for local exporters.

If you have a software idea and are financially strapped to test it, the Center for Software Development (CSD) is a public/private venture that enables software entrepreneurs to inexpensively test and debug software on virtually any platform combination. The CSD also offers technical/nontechnical resources that add to product quality and expedite time-to-market.

The OED also provides environmental and software business clusters. These successful incubators enable software and environmental startups to increase chances for success by working in a cooperative environment with firms in a similar industry. Shared benefits include below-market rental space, cooperative sharing of receptionist, copier/fax, meeting space, venture capital firm access, seminars, resources, and technical assistance.

The Cupertino area, located northwest of San Jose, is home to Apple Computer. **Photo by Pat Kirk.**

Besides being a domestic leader in technology, San Jose also ranks as an international trade leader. San Jose is grouped among North America's top 10 locations for international business, according to *World Trade Magazine.* In addition, *International Business Magazine*'s annual ranking of the nation's 100 fastest growing midsized international corporations finds one-fifth of them in Silicon Valley. North America's largest concentration of Pacific Rim Technology companies are also found here.

In recognizing San Jose and Silicon Valley's globalization, Mayor Susan Hammer was appointed chairperson of the President's Advisory Committee on Trade Policy and Negotiation. Mayor Hammer is responsible for a 40-member panel that advises the president on trade relationship and barrier issues.

Cupertino

Cupertino, located northwest of San Jose, is home to Apple Computer, Tandem Computers, a Hewlett-Packard campus, and about 50 other high-technology firms.

Because Cupertino benefited from the beginning of the high-technology boom, 85 percent of the city is built out and the vacancy rate for office space and research and development is very low. Currently, Cupertino's development activities include proposals for business expansion, hotel attractions, and apartment complexes.

In the near future, Symantec plans to build its 141,000 square foot headquarters at Cupertino's city center that will create over 500 jobs. Additionally, the Crossroads Center shopping center is expanding to 30,000 square feet and 100 more jobs.

Fremont

Northeast of San Jose, Fremont is surrounded by open space, hills toward the east, and the San Francisco Bay on the west. Fremont, located in the southern portion of Alameda County, is the fourth largest city in the San Francisco Bay Area with a population of 187,000. Its job profile and education level parallels that of other cities in Silicon Valley.

There are over 25,000 industrial and industrial services jobs in Fremont in a variety of sectors. These include 27 percent in computers/communication, 17 percent in automotive, 17 percent in miscellaneous manufacturing, 12 percent in innovative related services, 10 percent in semiconductors/equipment, 10 percent in business services, 3 percent in software and bioscience and 1 percent in environmental technologies.

The largest industrial companies in Fremont are in computers and the communications industry, and provide over 8,000 jobs. The semiconductor sector experienced a 71 percent job increase during a recent 12-month period. High-technology companies that are reinvesting and expanding in Fremont include: Cirrus Logic, Telco Systems, Cellotape, Grand Junction Networks, Elite Group, Therma, Wave, and West Coast Quartz.

Fremont is also home to New United Motors Manufacturing, Inc. (NUMMI), an automobile manufacturing plant which is a joint effort between General Motors and Toyota. Over 4,000 jobs are provided by NUMMI, the largest automobile manufacturing plant in California.

Recently, 2 million square feet of industrial space was approved for a group of biomedical device companies in Fremont. Fremont continues to maintain under a 4-percent vacancy rate for industrial space. According to Ann Draper, Fremont's Economic Development Director, Fremont is poised for a huge explosion of growth because there are 1,800 acres of land available for construction of new campuses. "Next to San Jose, we have the most land available for business growth."

The Fremont area is home to New United Motors Manufacturing, Inc. (NUMMI), the largest automobile manufacturing plant in California. Photo courtesy of New United Motors Manufacturing, Inc.

Los Altos

Situated between Northern California's employment centers–San Francisco and San Jose–Los Altos is an oasis of rolling hills and lush vegetation amidst the hustle and bustle of Silicon Valley.

Encompassing seven square miles, this scenic, semi-rural community has managed its growth with diligence and careful consideration for a high quality of life. Despite the urban expanse that surrounds it, Los Altos has retained charm and sense of community. Development has been carefully focused on residential, office, retail uses, and business services.

Menlo Park

Tucked between San Jose and San Francisco, in the southern part of San Mateo County, Menlo Park has a healthy economic climate. Economic activities range from highly desired office space on the renowned Sand Hill Road where many Silicon Valley venture capital firms are located, to a thriving downtown retail business district and an industrial area sporting Sun Microsystems, Raychem, FedEx, Boise Cascade and United Parcel Service. Menlo Park is also a popular site for startup software and biotechnology firms.

Being part of the Silicon Valley high-tech community and the San Francisco Bay Area business community, Menlo Park is a favorable location for business. That's why vacancy rates are near zero.

Recent economic expansion in Menlo Park includes the Sun Microsystems campus, located on the eastern edge near the Bay and Dumbarton Bridges. The campus contains one million square feet and created 2,500 jobs. Jefferson Place, a business park and industrial area, will be constructed in 1997 and will contain 210,000 square feet. The Center City Design Project is being built downtown near the El Camino Real corridor. The target of this project is to build on current retail, restaurant, and service uses, enhancing pedestrian traffic.

The Sun Microsystems campus, in the Menlo Park area, has created 2,500 jobs. Photo by Pat Kirk.

Milpitas

Once home to the Ford Auto Plant, Milpitas switched gears in the 1980s when the plant became the Great Mall of the Bay Area, one of the largest shopping outlets in California. Recently, the planning commission approved Phase II of McCarthy Ranch Marketplace, an additional retail outlet, totaling 108,000 square feet of retail space.

Besides retail business, Milpitas is thriving in Silicon Valley because of its many high-tech campuses. It is a progressive city with a strong pulse for quality living. Although Milpitas is a small city, with a population of 59,517, it is home to more Fortune 500 companies than any other city in the Bay Area. The largest manufacturing firms in the community are:

- LSI Logic
- Solectron
- Quantum
- Sun Microsystems
- Lifescan, Inc.
- Komag
- Read-Rite
- Octel Communications Group
- Adaptec, Inc.
- Linear Technology
- Xicor
- North American Transformer
- Adac Laboratories

Milpitas continues to thrive, and many people seeking a high quality of life choose the city for their home. Its close proximity to San Jose and other surrounding Silicon Valley cities gives it rich cultural and educational opportunities.

Mountain View

By night, Mountain View's population is 67,500; by day it swells to 100,000 as Bay Area residents commute to city businesses engaged in technology, scientific research, and service enterprises. Mountain View is experiencing a phenomenal period for its local economy. Real estate activity is high with a .56-percent vacancy rate (22,000 square feet) for R & D/office space in the Shoreline area and a 2.05-percent vacancy (124,000 square feet) in the rest of the city.

Silicon Graphics, Inc., continues to be the largest employer in Mountain View, with 4,400 employees and contractors in Mountain View and over 7,000 internationally. The firm occupies 29 buildings totaling almost 2 million square feet of office, research, and manufacturing space.

Netscape Communications, Inc., employs approximately 2,000 people, most in Mountain View. Netscape now occupies over 500,000 square feet of office space. The company continues to look for space to grow in the area and may double the size of their campus in the next two years.

LSI Logic in Milpitas. Photo by Pat Kirk.

Hewlett-Packard, a long-term corporate presence, is now the second largest employer in Mountain View, employing approximately 2,400. H-P occupies 842,000 square feet of office space in three locations. Recently, the finance and marketing functions moved to Middlefield Road, adding 525 employees.

Synopsis maintains its headquarters at 700 East Middlefield Road with 1,000 employees and continues to grow, hiring 50 people a month. They recently announced plans to expand to a new 210,000-square-foot complex in Sunnyvale.

Downtown Mountain View is also becoming a preferred location for new businesses involved in software and related high-technology fields. Recently, a $60 million revitalization of the downtown area was completed.

Businesses report that the availability of flexible space to accommodate expansion, proximity to major high-tech firms in Mountain View, and the option of late-night dining and coffee house ambiance make downtown Mountain View attractive to start-ups.

Palo Alto

Considered the birthplace of Silicon Valley, Palo Alto has successfully integrated elements of a flourishing business environment with quiet residential living. Located 14 miles north of San Jose, Palo Alto is a community of 58,000.

More than 80 percent of Palo Alto youth go on to college, 65 percent of the residents have had four or more years of college and one-third of adults over 25 have received at least one graduate degree.

Nearby, Stanford University enrolls more than 15,000, including 3,000 foreign students from 96 countries. Because of this association, Palo Alto enjoys international name recognition. People from around the world come for education, research, business, and training.

Palo Alto is proud of its business community and works hard to retain existing businesses. It has always nurtured new businesses and supports the emergence of new growth industries which include software, multimedia, bioscience, and environmental technology. Palo Alto has traditionally been involved in the flourishing of computer, communications,

The Hewlett-Packard Company is now one of the largest and most successful companies in the electronics industry. **Photo by Pat Kirk.**

semiconductor, and aerospace industries. Major Palo Alto employers include:

- Stanford University Medical Center
- Stanford University
- Hewlett-Packard Company
- Varian Associates
- Space Systems/LORAL
- Sun Microsystems
- Palo Alto Unified School District
- Lockheed Martin Missiles & Space
- Palo Alto Medical Foundation
- Watkins-Johnson Company
- Xerox Corporation

Palo Alto also is proud of its university affiliated research park for private industry, Stanford Research Park. Since the 1950s, the Park has provided a special synergistic environment in which industries and the university are mutually involved. A number of faculty members serve on company boards and engage in consulting work. Faculty and students work on joint projects with Park companies, and firms provide employees access to the Stanford Instructional Television Network. This enables individuals to earn degrees by attending classes at their workplace. The result is a scientific and technological cutting-edge exchange of ideas.

Stanford Research Park now has more than 60 tenants, including a number of corporate headquarters.

Santa Clara

Santa Clara, the third most populated city in Santa Clara County, is home to many high-technology businesses. These include Intel, Applied Materials, 3Com, and Synoptics. Fueled by a very strong economy, Santa Clara's growth is driven by high-technology growth, land values, rents, and retail sales within the industrial sector. Recently, NEC located at Scott Boulevard and Central Expressway occupying 275,000 square feet and creating 750 jobs. 3COM occupied 200,000 square feet at Great America Parkway and Highway 237 creating 500 jobs. The Mercado Santa Clara Shopping Center was completed at Mission College Boulevard and Highway 101 occupying 130,00 square feet of retail space and including a 20-screen theater complex. More than 300 jobs were created. S3 built their headquarters at Mission College Boulevard and Highway 101, occupying 300,000 square feet and creating 900 jobs.

Xerox Corporation is a major employer in Palo Alto. **Photo by Pat Kirk.**

Sunnyvale

Sunnyvale is the second largest city in Santa Clara County and is bordered by Mountain View, Cupertino, and Santa Clara. This high-tech city was recognized for its efficient government in 1995 by President Bill Clinton and Vice President Al Gore. It is home to Lockheed Martin Missiles & Space, Amadahl Corporation, Advanced Microdevices, Inc., and hundreds of high-tech firms.

Sunnyvale is home to Lockheed Martin Missiles & Space. **Photo courtesy of Lockheed Martin Missiles & Space.**

A Vibrant Valley

San Jose and the surrounding cities that comprise Silicon Valley have it all. Community and business leaders are on the right track. The area is blessed with an entrepreneurial spirit that nurtures and grows new business ideas. Besides, government leaders are aware of the need to nurture businesses; they continue to do so by providing assistance in the development process.

When companies choose to locate in Silicon Valley, they can expect a well-educated workforce whose members have a desire to do the best possible job. Entrepreneurs with innovative ideas can find help ranging from management assistance to financing.

San Jose and the surrounding cities of Silicon Valley continue to be technology stars that grow brighter every day. In addition to a superior business environment, Silicon Valley is a marvelous place to live and play as well. ◆

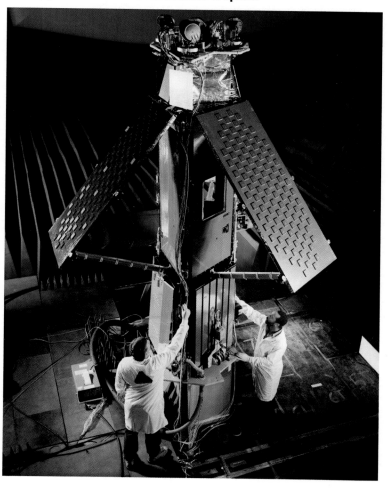

Silicon Valley is a wellspring of technology throughout the nation, a home to dreamers and doers encouraged by an entrepreneurial spirit that generates a powerful business climate. **Photo by Pat Kirk.**

The fearless risk-taking attitude of so many of its residents, along with brainpower and capital, has made Silicon Valley the technological leader of the nation, if not the world. **Photo by Pat Kirk.**

SANTA TERESA

812

Chapter Four

Building a
Transportation System

◆

As we approach the 21st century, Silicon Valley possesses a premier transportation system. However, this was not always the case. If we look back approximately 25 years ago, the transportation problems in Silicon Valley seemed insurmountable.

At that time, Santa Clara County had instituted Dial A Ride, a bus system that required riders to call in and make reservations for transit. The calls began and became a deluge swamping the reservation lines at 80,000 calls per day. Operators told reporters that switchboard bulbs burnt out faster than they could be replaced. Bus drivers depended on computers for their orders. Computers went down and buses drove around the county nearly empty.

The Dial A Ride experiment came in the mid 1970s as Santa Clara County's bus system was converting from private to public operation. The system was in disarray and underfunded; the county had acquired preexisting bus systems and was beginning to consolidate them and develop new maintenance systems.

At the same time, the county's overburdened freeway and expressway system resulted in a commuter's nightmare. Former Santa Clara County Supervisor Rod Diridon, other members of the Board of Supervisors, and many local mayors and city council members began to work with the private sector, as well as with the state and federal governments, to begin the transformation into the premier transportation system that Silicon Valley enjoys today.

The efforts have paid off. As the 21st century approaches, there has been a remarkable change in transportation in and out of Silicon Valley. Today, there are 151,000 riders per day on buses, 23,000 per day on light rail and 30,000 per day on the CalTrain system. The San Jose International Airport has grown to be the fourth busiest airport in California and boasts over 10 million passengers per year. And, the area is laced by six major freeways: Highways 85, 87, Interstates 280, 680, 880, and U.S. 101.

Santa Clara County has a 21-mile-long light rail line that connects South San Jose/Almaden communities north through downtown San Jose to the employment centers of Silicon Valley in North San Jose and Santa Clara. The line operates in the median of Highways 85 and 87 in the south segment. Photo by Pat Kirk.

The Downtown Shuttle provides downtown San Jose with a direct connection to the San Jose Diridon CalTrain Station, the Paseo de San Antonio Light Rail Station on Second Street, and Convention Center Light Rail Station. Photo by Pat Kirk.

The Beginnings of a Transit System

Silicon Valley's preeminent transportation system did not happen overnight. As with downtown San Jose's redevelopment and revitalization into a glittering skyline with a bustling cultural center, funds had to be raised and engineering studies conducted.

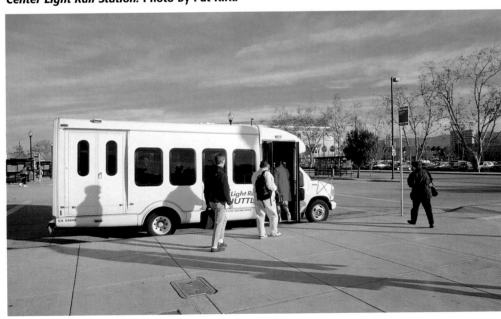

While the bus system was evolving in the 1970's, the county was conducting broad-based engineering analyses of alternative transportation systems for the Santa Clara Valley. Public input was sought to select the most appropriate and fundable transportation options.

Of course, in order to improve Santa Clara County's transit system, necessary revenue needed to be raised. In 1976, Supervisor Diridon chaired the campaign to win voter approval of the first successful permanent half-cent sales tax measure in California to fund transit. The measure was the basis of revenue for the Santa Clara County Transportation Agency. The San Jose Metropolitan Chamber of Commerce played a major role in helping pass this measure. Today, the responsibilities for transit operations lie with the Santa Clara Valley Transportation Authority (VTA), the successor organization to the original agency. The Transportation Authority has a $200 million annual budget and employs around 2,200 people in seven divisions.

A Glance at Public Transportation

GUADALUPE LIGHT RAIL

Santa Clara County has a 21-mile-long light rail line that connects South San Jose/Almaden communities north through downtown San Jose to the employment centers of Silicon Valley in North San Jose and Santa Clara. The line operates in the median of Highways 85 and 87 in the south segment. It moves onto city streets, along First Street and Tasman Drive, in the north segment. Full operations began in April, 1991 and the rail line averages 23,000 current daily riders.

The next expansion of the light rail will be the Tasman West project. Slated for construction in 1997, the rail line will extend from the Old Ironsides Station in Santa Clara into Sunnyvale near Lockheed Martin, then north to the CalTrain Station in Mountain View.

CALTRAIN

This 77-mile-long commuter rail system has served San Jose and the Peninsula for over 130 years. Since July 1992, Amtrak has operated the service under contract to Peninsula Corridor Joint Powers Board, a three-county organization that includes Santa Clara, San Mateo, and San Francisco counties. The commuter rail system operates 60 trains a day between San Jose and San Francisco, including eight "peak period" trains that originate and end in Gilroy/Morgan Hill to provide a reliable commuter rail link for South County residents. CalTrain links with light rail at the Tamien Station in San Jose, and with many bus lines at stations within Santa Clara County.

"THE CAPITAL" INTERCITY SERVICE

Operated by Amtrak under contract with the California Department of Transportation, the approximately 150-mile-long "Capital" system provides intercity rail service between Sacramento and San Jose with six trains a day. Since December 1991, the system has served riders seeking an alternative to highway travel between the South Bay, East Bay and the State Capital. Stations in downtown San Jose and Santa Clara at "Great America Park" offer easy access to this corridor.

SHUTTLES

With the City of San Jose and the San Jose Arena, the Transportation Authority sponsors a bus shuttle carrying light rail riders and other downtown passengers to and from the stadium. This service began in 1993 and is very popular among San Jose Sharks fans and concert and event patrons. The arena shuttle allows San Jose Arena visitors to take light rail into the downtown transit mall, the option of having dinner in many of the fine downtown San Jose restaurants, and taking the shuttle to the arena.

For those that commute to downtown San Jose for employment via CalTrain or Light Rail, the VTA jointly sponsors a Downtown Shuttle

The Transit Mall in downtown San Jose is a 1.5 mile loop that circles the city center and is serviced by 21 bus routes. Photo by Pat Kirk.

with the City of San Jose, Transportation Fund for Clean Air, and the Bay Area Air Quality Management District. The Downtown Shuttle is operated under contract with a private carrier. These mini-busses operate every weekday during commute hours. The shuttle provides downtown San Jose with a direct connection to the San Jose Diridon CalTrain Station, the Paseo de San Antonio Light Rail Station on Second Street and Convention Center Light Rail Station.

SAFETY

San Jose is one of America's safest big cities. In operating a transit system, safety and security are a primary concern. It is not an accident that the VTA's public transit system became one of the country's best protected. In the 1980s, care and money went into setting up an effective policing arrangement and acquainting the county's motorists with the reality of sharing the streets and roads with light rail vehicles.

Instruction in safety has spread into the schools. Entering its third year, the Authority's Youth Outreach and Partnership Programs teach young people about transit operations and safety, and most importantly, to respect transit vehicles or property and guard against vandalism. Youth Partnership links bus and light rail operators with fifth and sixth grade classes for a whole school year. Through this partnership, students have a chance to visit the operator's bus yard or light rail facility, ride the system, and learn first-hand about safety.

EFFORTS TO IMPROVE ROADWAYS

While the bus and rail transit system was being developed, roadways lagged. In 1984, the Santa Clara County Manufacturing Group—supported by the San Jose chamber and numerous other organizations, successfully fought to gain voter approval of another half-cent sales tax, most of which would be dedicated to highways.

With a specific life of 10 years, Measure A raised nearly $1 billion. With the help of some state and federal matching funds, the measure financed construction of Highways 85 and 87, widened major portions of Highway 101, began construction on Route 237, and added many carpool/diamond lanes to major roadways.

In 1992, a new Measure A was developed to replace the original Measure A's half-cent sales tax, which was set to expire due to the 10-year "sunset" provision. While successful at the polls that year, the voters

The commuter rail system, CalTrain, operates 60 trains a day between San Jose and San Francisco, including eight "peak period" trains that link light rail at the Tamien Station in San Jose, and with many bus lines at stations within Santa Clara County. Photo by Pat Kirk.

only gave Measure A a simple majority. A taxpayer group's lawsuit contending that a two-thirds majority was needed was upheld by both a state appellate court and the California Supreme Court.

Undaunted, transportation supporters launched a new campaign in 1996. Now designed as a pair of measures, called A and B, the new effort was approved by voters and will fund highways, transit, and bicycle trails.

The pair of measures create a method of funding vital transportation projects through another half-cent sales tax increase. The specific project list was developed with participation by a broad range of community groups, including the San Jose chamber, and includes:

- Improvements on Interstate 880 and Highways 17, 87 and 101.
- Needed safety improvements on Highways 85 and 152 (Pacheco Pass).
- Expanding light rail service by creating the Tasman East, Vasona, and Capital light rail lines.
- Creation of CalTrain-type service to link Santa Clara County to the BART system in Alameda County.
- Increasing CalTrain service between Gilroy and San Jose and from San Jose up the Peninsula.
- Upgrading and expanding the countywide bicycle network.
- Substantial funding for pothole repair and general street maintenance.
- Signal synchronization on all eight county expressways.
- Diamond lanes at commute hours to encourage car pooling.

Navigating downtown San Jose is relatively easy. To combat commute traffic, light rail transit allows visitors the convenience of leaving their car at home and riding from south San Jose to downtown and north to Great America Parkway in Santa Clara. Photo by Pat Kirk.

SAN JOSE INTERNATIONAL AIRPORT

Perhaps what makes San Jose an accessible city, both on a national and international basis, is the San Jose International Airport. Located minutes from downtown San Jose, San Jose International is the fourth busiest airport in California, serving the travel and cargo needs of one of the nation's most dynamic regional economies. More than half of the world's largest electronic firms lie within 30 miles of the airport. Fourteen commercial airlines depart and arrive over 400 times a day from two terminals. Passenger counts now top 10 million per year and cargo revenues exceeded $273 million.

Recently, San Jose International extended its runway to 10,200 feet for flights to the far east and gained official status as a Port of Entry. What's more the FAA has built a state-of-the-art control tower on-site. The next phase of expansion includes extension of the second runway to full airline length, and a third terminal to accommodate 14 million passengers.

San Jose International is a self-supporting public enterprise requiring no taxpayer assistance. Each year it generates 71,249 jobs in the San Jose area, nearly $4 billion in business revenue, $928 million in personal income and $475 million in local and state taxes. These contributions promise to be direct and non-stop as San Jose International Airport meets the ongoing travel and cargo needs of Silicon Valley.

Foresight Pays Off

Whether traveling by car, light rail, bus, or air, transportation in Silicon Valley demonstrates smart planning. As the region grew, so did the number of drivers, riders, and airport passengers. Key local leaders had the foresight to realize that something had to be done to the infrastructure to accommodate these pressures. Silicon Valley continues to plan for its future transportation needs, and citizens in the area have shown a willingness to fund it. Astute government leaders and enterprising residents make San Jose and Silicon Valley one of the best places to live in the United States. ✦

Located minutes from downtown, the San Jose International Airport is serving the travel and cargo needs of one of the nation's most dynamic regional economies. Photo by Pat Kirk.

The San Jose International Airport has 13 commercial airlines that depart and arrive over 400 times a day from two terminals. **Photo by Pat Kirk.**

The San Jose International Airport has grown to be the fourth busiest airport in California and boasts over 10 million passengers per year. **Photo by Pat Kirk.**

As the 21st century approaches, there has been a remarkable change in transportation in and out of Silicon Valley. Today, there are 151,000 riders per day on buses, 23,000 per day on light rail and 30,000 per day on the CalTrain system. Photo by Dana L. Grover.

During the warm summer months, fully restored antique trolleys share a portion of the Light Rail line, circling downtown San Jose accommodations, attractions, restaurants, and shopping. Photo by Dana L. Grover.

Youth Outreach and Partnership Programs teach young people first-hand about transit operations and safety. **Photo by Pat Kirk.**

San Jose is one of America's safest big cities. In operating a transit system, safety and security are a primary concern. It is not an accident that the VTA's public transit system became one of the country's best protected. **Photo by Dana L. Grover.**

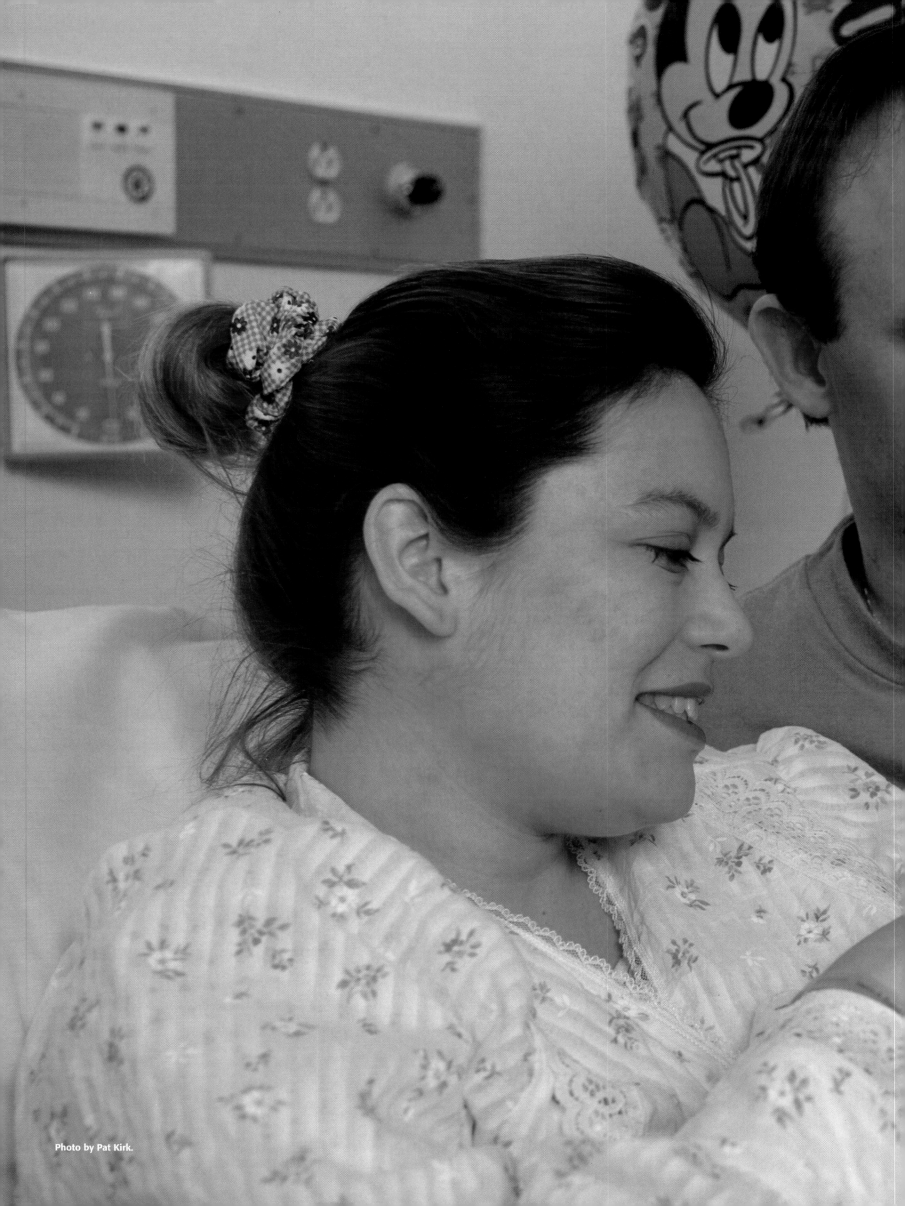

Chapter Five

San Jose & Silicon Valley: Leading Center for Medical Treatment

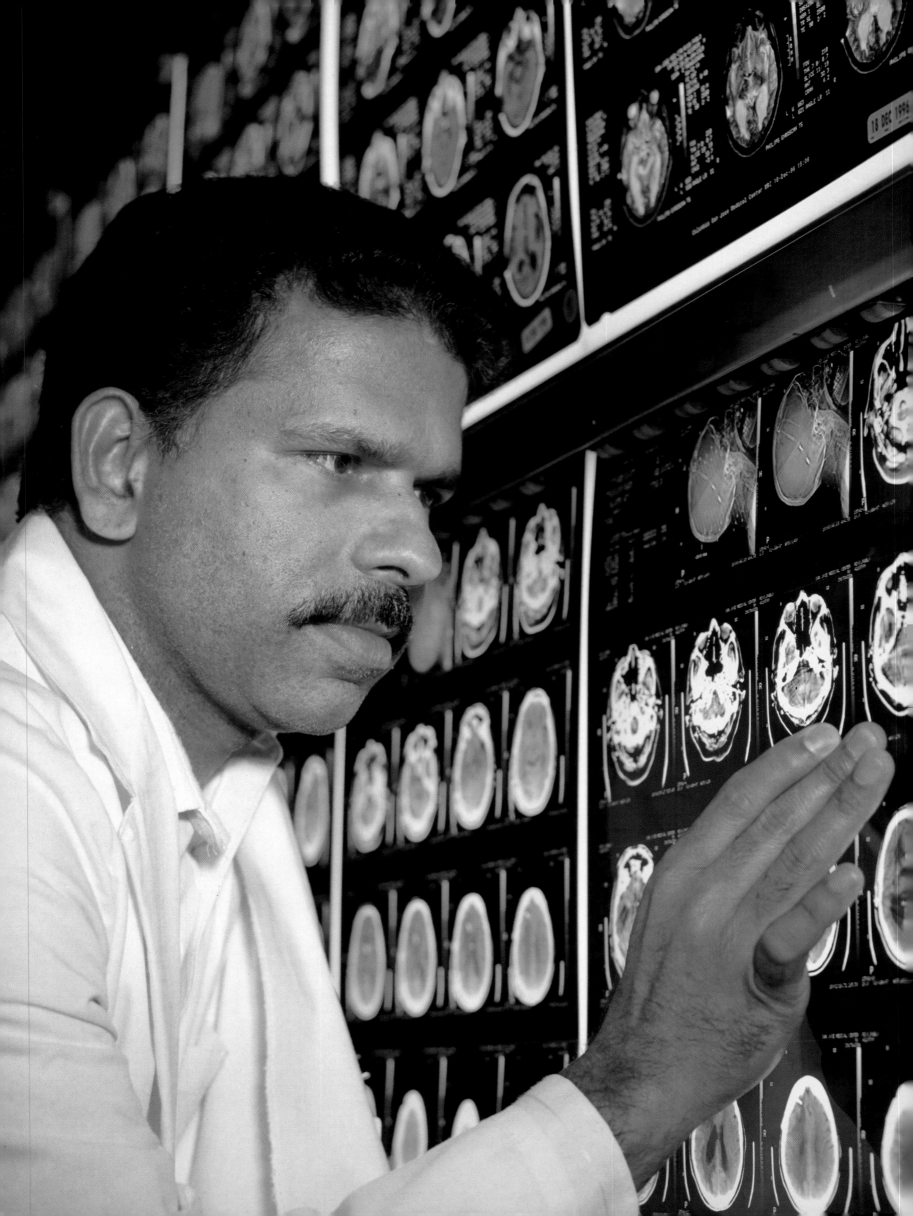

Santa Clara Valley is one of the world's leading centers for medical treatment and research. San Jose and its surrounding areas have one of the highest physician-to-patient ratios, with physicians and surgeons numbering over 3,000. Also, Stanford University Hospital, Palo Alto, about 40 minutes from San Jose, has a world renowned medical school and treatment center.

There are nine general hospitals in Santa Clara County with approximately 3,000 beds offering many specialty medical services. In addition, San Jose has over 30 home health care agencies in its vicinity and more than 1,100 dentists.

Health care has vastly changed through the 1990s. Health care costs were scrutinized by the Clinton administration in 1992. The Clinton health care task force discovered that the cost of health care, estimated at 12-percent of the gross domestic product, outpaced inflation in recent years. Health care costs are expected to continue to rise 11-percent annually, according to recent estimates by the United States Department of Commerce.

As we approach the 21st century, health care is entering a new era utilizing managed care. Managed care encompasses a wide range of approaches that control the unit price of an individual health care service, or package of services. In a recent issue of *Health Policy Newsletter*, an expert defines managed care as "a combined clinical and administrative approach in which ongoing, coordinated health care services are provided, usually for a capitated fee. Capitation, or the payment of a set amount per beneficiary per month, protects the purchaser of services, and allows the provider flexibility in the organization and reimbursement of services."

This change has forced competition among health care delivery systems. Fortunately, competition encourages players in the arena to be the best they can be, and consequently, Silicon Valley hospitals have benefited from this changing climate. They offer a variety of health care delivery systems which include for-profit, not-for-profit, managed care, and a public hospital system.

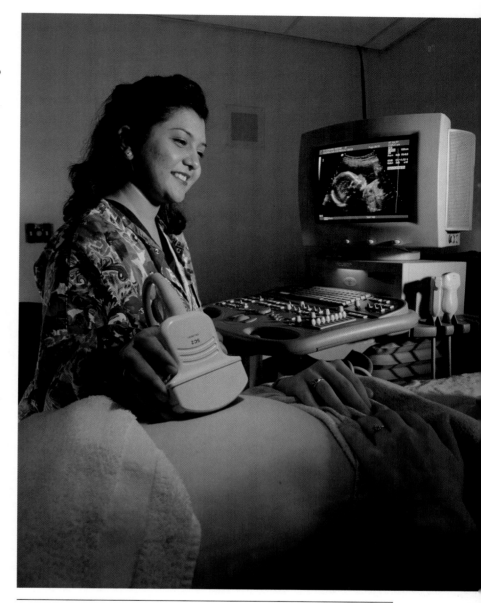

Compassionate care is key to a healthy community. **Photo by Pat Kirk.**

For-Profit Hospital Organizations

COLUMBIA GOOD SAMARITAN HOSPITAL

Columbia Good Samaritan Hospital opened in 1965. It is a general acute-care hospital in two locations: its main campus in San Jose and its Mission Oaks Campus in Los Gatos. Good Samaritan Hospital has a licensed bed capacity of 550. In addition to providing general acute care services, Good Samaritan provides tertiary services that include cardiology, cardiovascular surgery, cancer treatment, obstetrics and gynecology, and psychiatric services.

The Mission Oaks campus offers primarily inpatient and outpatient cancer services, short-stay surgery and ancillary services.

Bay Area parents often choose Good Samaritan as the place to have a baby. Because of high volumes of delivery, staff is extremely experienced and proficient. Good Samaritan provides a full-range of pre- and post-birth educational opportunities. The hospital has become a complete resource for expecting and new parents, even for those delivering in other hospitals. Good Samaritan is also the first community hospital rated

as a Level III Neonatal Intensive Care Unit that allows the hospital the ability to treat high-risk newborns from throughout Northern California.

Good Samaritan's Heart and Lung Institute provides a full range of diagnostic treatment modalities. Every option is readily available to the community, including the latest in minimally invasive procedures and electrophysiology.

In five years, it is projected that cancer will surpass heart disease and stroke as the leading cause of death. Good Samaritan Regional Cancer Center, headquartered at the Mission Oaks campus, offers the latest advancements in diagnoses and treatment. Local residents have access to continuity of care to prevent and treat this debilitating disease.

The Cancer Center is involved in clinical research trials which provide patient's options that are not generally available.

COLUMBIA SAN JOSE MEDICAL CENTER

San Jose Medical Center opened in 1923. It is a general acute-care hospital in a single downtown campus with a licensed bed capacity of 529. In addition to providing acute care services, San Jose Medical Center provides a skilled nursing facility, a rehabilitation center, a center for sleep disorders, a county designated trauma center, a cancer care institute, and cardiovascular services. San Jose Medical Center also offers

It is clear that there is not a shortage of medical services in San Jose and Silicon Valley. The area continues to attract the best and brightest health care providers who continue to assure optimum medical treatment. **Photo by Pat Kirk.**

Planetree, a 36-bed medical/surgical unit dedicated to humanizing, personalizing, and demystifying the hospital experience in a comforting and supportive environment.

San Jose Medical Center has been an integral provider of health care in Santa Clara County for over 70 years. It offers many unique and beneficial services to the increasingly diverse market which it serves. For example, Embracing Diversity is a first-of-its-kind program designed to increase the ability of Columbia Healthcare Delivery Systems to deliver competent health care services to its diverse patient population.

San Jose Medical Center provides a full range of rehabilitation services and has consistently been a market leader treating nearly one-third of Santa Clara County inpatients. On site, the "Easy Street" program provides a unique "real life" environment in which patients can relearn day-to-day tasks such as grocery shopping and driving a car.

State-of-the-art equipment help physicians make accurate diagnoses.
Photo by Pat Kirk.

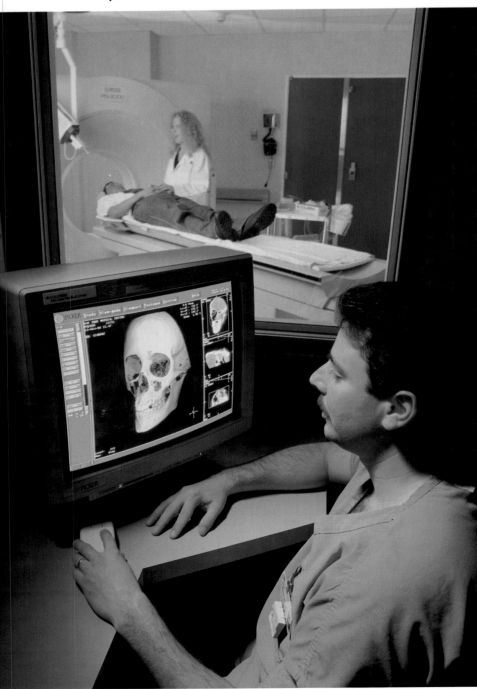

The San Jose Medical Center Trauma Center has been a leader among trauma centers in the county for nearly a decade. It serves approximately 160 patients a year, is supported by two helicopter services drawing from many counties, and is equipped with a campus helipad. Replantation and microvascular surgery is provided as a unique and outstanding service associated with the Trauma Center.

COLUMBIA SOUTH VALLEY COMMUNITY HOSPITAL

Columbia Healthcare Systems operates a third area hospital, 30 miles south of San Jose, in Gilroy: South Valley Community Hospital. Columbia also owns and operates the largest and most experienced home care agency in the South Bay: Good Samaritan Home Care & Hospice (formerly Visiting Nurses Association).

With the proceeds from the sale of Good Samaritan Health System to Columbia, ($56 million), Columbia is establishing the Good Samaritan Charitable Trust where it will manage and operate programs benefiting the entire community.

EL CAMINO HOSPITAL

El Camino Hospital opened in September 1961 as a 300-bed hospital and recently celebrated its 35th anniversary as an acute care facility licensed for 468 beds. The hospital's specialty areas include: general surgery, cardiology, behavioral health, maternal/child care, and orthopedics. Ambulatory or outpatient centers include diagnostic imaging, dialysis, mental health, surgery, physical therapy, and laboratory services. There are approximately 338 contracting physicians associated with El Camino Hospital. This facility is located in Mountain View and serves the communities of Mountain View, Sunnyvale, Los Altos, Cupertino, Santa Clara, and surrounding areas.

COMMUNITY HOSPITAL OF LOS GATOS

Community Hospital of Los Gatos is an acute care, full-service 164-bed hospital founded in 1962. It is located on 11 acres of land in the West Valley of Santa Clara County. It serves patients throughout seven communities in Santa Clara County—Los Gatos, Campbell, Monte Sereno, San Jose, Cupertino, Sunnyvale, and Santa Clara. There are over 500 physicians who represent 51 medical specialties associated with the facility.

Not-For-Profit Hospitals
ALEXIAN BROTHERS HOSPITAL

Alexian Brothers Hospital is a Catholic, 294-bed acute care general community hospital owned and operated by the Alexian Brothers of America, Inc. The hospital opened in 1965 and is located on North Jackson Avenue in East San Jose.

Alexian Brothers Hospital offers many tertiary services such as an accredited clinical laboratory, a corporate health program, diagnostic imaging, diagnostic and vascular ultrasound, emergency department, eye surgery program, family birthing unit, home care services, intensive care unit, transitional care unit, mammography, outpatient surgery program; physical, occupational, and speech therapy; and skilled nursing facility.

Ever since Alexian Brothers Hospital opened its doors, it has supported a number of community outreach programs.

Currently the hospital's Community Benefits program offers services for expectant mothers as well as full health care services for seniors who are on Medicare and Medi-Cal. Alexian Brothers Hospital has a 30-year track record of major accomplishments in the field of community outreach programs.

CATHOLIC HEALTH CARE WEST: O'CONNOR AND ST. LOUISE HOSPITAL

Catholic Health Care West, the largest health care system in California, has two acute care hospitals in Santa Clara County: O'Connor Hospital, San Jose; and St. Louise Hospital, Morgan Hill.

O'Connor Hospital has 360 beds, 978 staff members, and 600 physicians affiliated with the hospital in some way. O'Connor offers many specialty health care services to its patients. These include: the Heart Center, Cancer Center, Recovery Center, Family Center, and a Transitional Care Unit.

St. Louise Hospital has 60 beds, 120 staff members, and 130 physicians. St. Louise provides a family center, cancer care services, a family clinic, and a transitional care unit.

Stanford University Medical Center encompasses Stanford University School of Medicine, the oldest medical school in the Western United States, and is known throughout the world for outstanding achievements in teaching, research, and patient care. Photo by Pat Kirk.

University Hospitals

STANFORD UNIVERSITY MEDICAL CENTER

Stanford University Medical Center is known throughout the world for outstanding achievements in teaching, research, and patient care. Its prominent faculty, staff, and students combine their skills and talents for the advancement of medical practice and science.

Stanford University Medical Center encompasses Stanford University School of Medicine, the oldest medical school in the Western United States, and Stanford Health Services, a University-owned nonprofit corporation providing general acute and tertiary care to local, national, and international patients through three components: Stanford University Hospital, Stanford University Clinic, and Lucile Salter Packard Children's Hospital, an independent, nonprofit pediatric teaching hospital providing general acute and tertiary care exclusively for children.

Managed Care Organizations

KAISER PERMANENTE

Kaiser Permanente is a group practice prepayment plan providing comprehensive medical and hospital services to approximately 2.4 million members in Northern California. It is organized as a unique partnership among three entities–the Kaiser Foundation Health Plan (a nonprofit corporation), Kaiser Foundation Hospitals, and The Permanente Medical Group, Inc.

The Northern California Region of Kaiser Permanente began as a prepaid industrial health care program during World War II serving thousands of workers at Kaiser-managed shipyards in Richmond. Today, Kaiser Permanente, the largest HMO in the country includes 12 regions with 6.3 million members, 7,760 physicians, 66,000 non-physician

Columbia San Jose Medical Center is a general acute-care hospital that provides a skilled nursing facility, a rehabilitation center, a center for sleep disorders, a county designated trauma center, a cancer care institute, and cardiovascular services. Photo by Pat Kirk.

O'Connor Hospital offers many specialty health care services to its patients. These include: the Heart Center, Cancer Center, Recovery Center, Family Center, and a Transitional Care Unit. **Photo by Pat Kirk.**

Health Maintenance Organizations (HMO)

HEALTH NET

Health Net serves more than 1.3 million members in 48 counties in California from San Diego to the Oregon border, giving it the broadest geographic coverage of any HMO in the state. Members are served through a network of more than 33,000 physicians and more than 360 hospitals.

Newsweek magazine recently awarded Health Net with some of the highest ratings of any HMO in California. These included member satisfaction, tracking member health, and overall quality monitoring. Health Net was also noted by *Newsweek* for its innovative diabetes management and asthma tracking program.

LIFEGUARD

Lifeguard was incorporated in 1977 as an HMO by a group of physicians in Santa Clara County with seed money from Blue Cross, four local hospitals, and a federal government loan. Today, it serves 196,000 members through its provider network of 10,000 physicians and contracting hospitals. Currently, Lifeguard operates in 25 counties throughout California with headquarters in Milpitas.

Lifeguard is dedicated to managing health by preventing, as well as treating, disease and illness. Their key strategy is to maintain a successful, high-quality delivery system by managing health through partnerships with its members, employers, and providers.

SECURE HORIZONS

Offered by PacifiCare, Secure Horizons is the largest Medicare-risk plan for Medicare recipients in the nation. Under contract with the federal government, Secure Horizons has more than 383,000 members in California and approximately 20,564 members in Santa Clara County. For little or no plan premium, Secure Horizons arranges for Medicare recipients to receive more benefits than those available through traditional Medicare coverage.

Public

SANTA CLARA VALLEY MEDICAL CENTER (VMC)

Santa Clara Valley Medical Center, founded in 1860, is the oldest and only publicly operated hospital in Santa Clara County. VMC, nationally recognized, is owned and operated by the County of Santa Clara. VMC maintains a philosophy where the needs of the patient are paramount, and where patients are treated in a supportive, friendly, and dignified manner.

San Jose and Silicon Valley's medical community is ready to respond to any situation. **Photo by Pat Kirk.**

employees, 28 hospitals, and 200 outpatient medical offices, with total assets of $4.9 billion. Kaiser Permanente serves all the health care needs of members and their families, with an emphasis on preventative health care. Kaiser Permanente celebrated its 50th anniversary in 1996.

Kaiser Permanente integrates the three elements of health care—physicians, hospitals, and health insurance. In Santa Clara County there are two Kaiser Medical Centers, Santa Clara Medical Center and Santa Teresa Community Medical Center, San Jose.

KAISER SANTA CLARA MEDICAL CENTER

Kaiser Santa Clara is a full service 317-bed hospital and the seventh largest hospital in the county. The hospital has 233 physicians, 728 nurses, and 1,815 other staff members. There are satellite outpatient complexes in Milpitas and Mountain View. The Santa Clara Medical Center and its medical office complexes serve more than 250,000 members in the South Bay.

KAISER SANTA TERESA COMMUNITY MEDICAL CENTER, SAN JOSE

Santa Teresa Community Medical Center is a full service, 222-bed hospital with medical offices in south San Jose. There are 183 full-time physicians and 1,567 other full-time staff members. Santa Teresa Community Medical Center serves approximately 155,000 members.

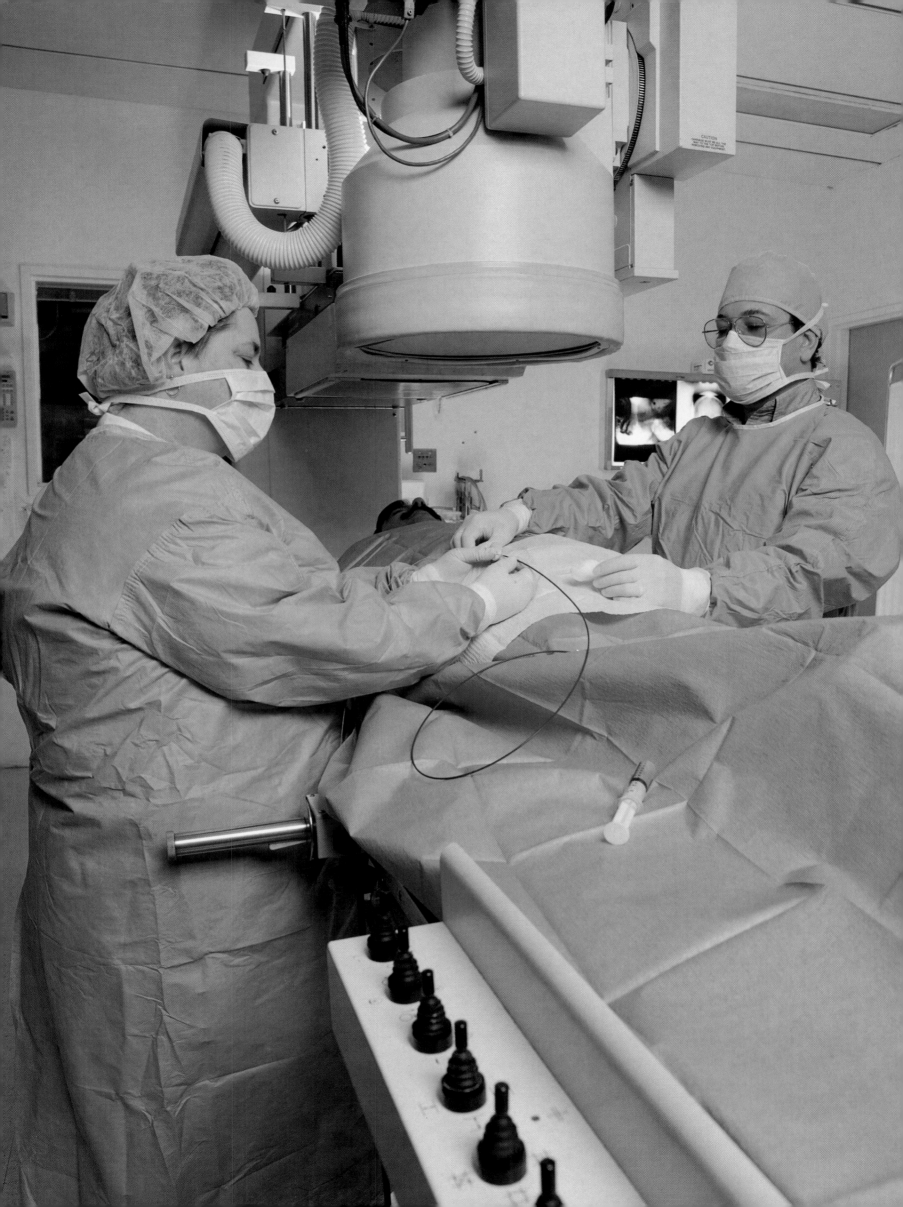

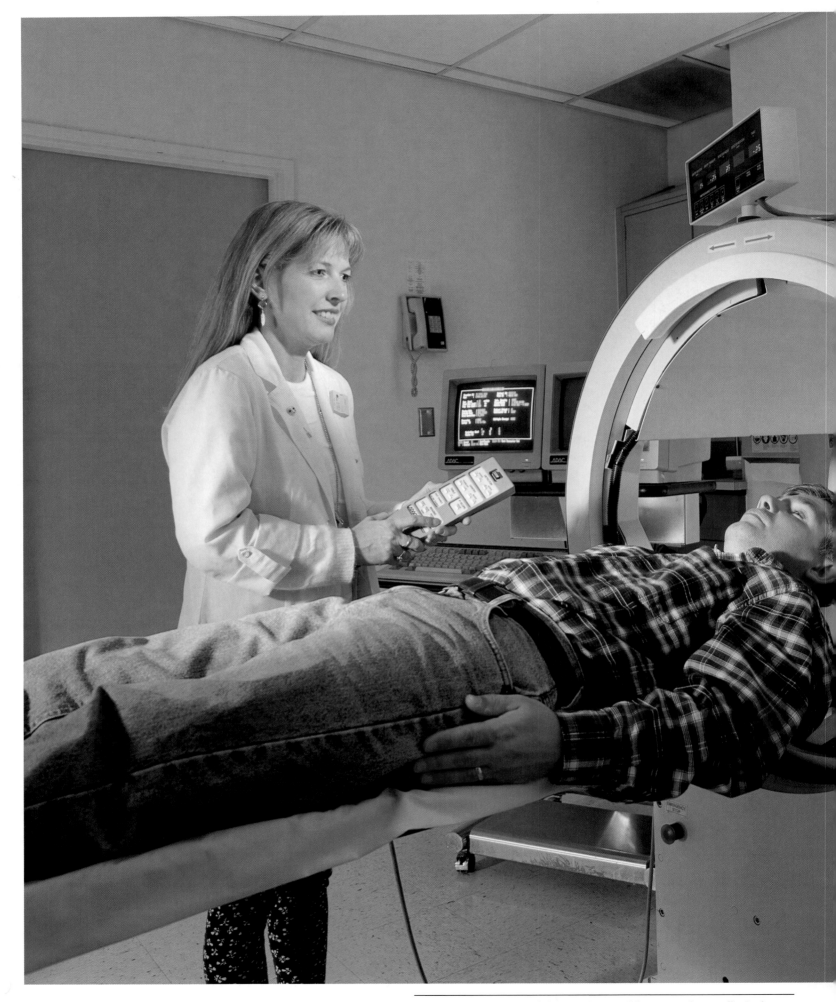

Specialized diagnostic laboratories provide Santa Clara Valley's doctors and patients with state-of-the-art equipment for numerous procedures. Photo by Pat Kirk.

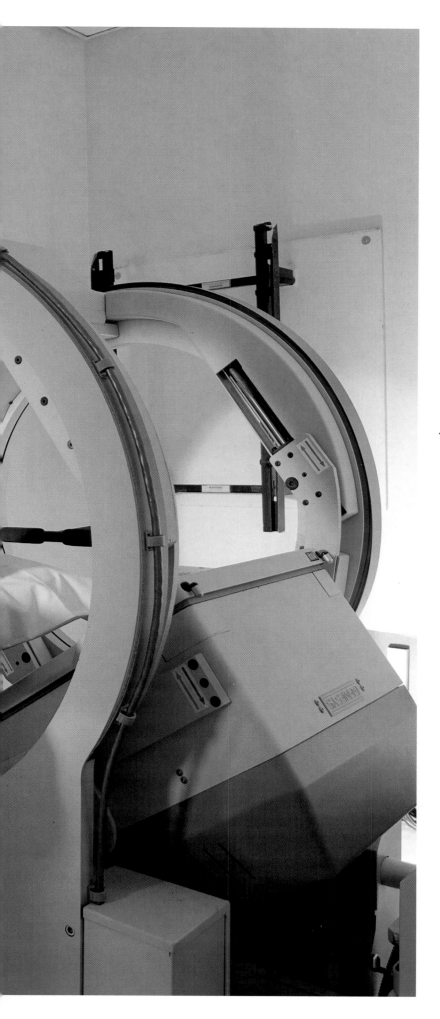

VMC has 441 licensed beds and maintains the highest occupancy rate in Santa Clara County. VMC cares for over 16,000 patients annually. Through its Ambulatory Services Department, VMC offers an extensive array of services at five primary care satellite clinics located in the eastern, central, southern, and northern parts of Santa Clara County.

On a national level, VMC enjoys a reputation for its Spinal Cord Injury and Traumatic Brain Injury programs. Both programs are federally funded and receive research funding from the National Institute on Disability and Rehabilitation. VMC's Burn Center and Level III Neonatal Intensive Care Unit are regional facilities making them invaluable services to residents of Northern California.

VMC is also a designated regional Trauma Center and operates a 24-hour Comprehensive Emergency Department with in-house capability in all major and surgical subspecialties. The medical center also maintains an affiliation with the Stanford University School of Medicine.

In progress is a new wing to replace the hospital's earthquake-prone main wing. VMC broke ground on a new $177 million hospital wing in 1995. The North Tower will add 154 beds to the facility, increase operating rooms from nine to 12, and boost diagnostic rooms from 12 to 22.

It is clear that there is not a shortage of medical services in San Jose and Silicon Valley. The area continues to attract the best and the brightest health care providers who continue to assure optimum medical treatment. ✦

Santa Clara Valley Medical Center (VMC) is the oldest and only publicly operated hospital in Santa Clara County. VMC maintains a philosophy where the needs of the patient are paramount, and where patients are treated in a supportive, friendly, and dignified manner. Photo by Pat Kirk.

Education can often be the best prevention to illness. Santa Clara Valley's health care community takes the time to educate and reha-bilitate its patients. **Photo by Michael Ichikawa, courtesy of El Camino Hospital.**

El Camino Hospital is an acute care facility licensed for 468 beds. The hospital's specialty areas include: general surgery, cardiology, behavioral health, maternal/child care, and orthopedics. **Photo by Michael Ichikawa, courtesy of El Camino Hospital.**

St. Louise Hospital has 60 beds, 120 staff members, and 130 physicians. St. Louise provides a family center, cancer care services, a family clinic, and a transitional care unit. **Photo by Pat Kirk.**

In addition to providing general acute care services, Columbia Good Samaritan Hospital provides tertiary services that include cardiology, cardiovascular surgery, cancer treatment, obstetrics and gynecology, and psychiatric services. **Photo by Pat Kirk.**

Rehabilitative therapy is available for those patients needing special-ized care in the Santa Clara Valley health care community. **Photo by Pat Kirk.**

Columbia South Valley Community Hospital in Gilroy. **Photo courtesy of Columbia Bay Area Healthcare Network.**

Chapter Six

San Jose & Silicon Valley Offer Educational Choices

Besides being a great place to live and play, San Jose is also a leading community in learning. San Jose and Santa Clara County provide a selection of school districts which offer a variety of educational choices. Besides a strong public school system, many private schools in San Jose are rated the best in the nation.

Silicon Valley's technology industry demands a highly educated workforce. Out of 1.5 million adults who work in Silicon Valley, two-thirds are college educated. Consequently, the people of San Jose are concerned about educating their children as well as themselves.

Santa Clara County students surpass state performance levels in a variety of categories. According to data from the High School Performance Reports prepared by the California Department of Education, more Santa Clara County students stay in school. At the state level, 81.1 percent stay in high school while the rate in Santa Clara County is 87.4 percent.

More Santa Clara County students are enrolled in advanced science and math classes. At the state level, 30.3 percent are enrolled in advanced science classes, while in Santa Clara County 40.7 percent are enrolled in these classes. For advanced math classes, 28.9 percent of students in the state are enrolled while 42.4 percent are enrolled in these classes in Santa Clara County.

Traditionally, more males than females enroll in both advanced science and mathematics classes. In Santa Clara County, 41.9 percent of women students are enrolled in advanced science classes while 39.6 percent of men are enrolled in these subjects.

The SAT/ACT scores are higher in Santa Clara County than they are in the rest of the state. Santa Clara County scores average 965, while state scores are 902. In addition, more Santa Clara County students take the SAT. Approximately 42.8 percent of Santa Clara County students take the SAT while 41 percent take the test statewide.

A greater percentage of Santa Clara County students are taking advanced placement tests to qualify for college credit. About 16.7 percent

Because of its high-technology connection, San Jose and Santa Clara County students have more access to computer technology. The Santa Clara County Office of Education offers free Internet access to the schools in the county. **Photo by Pat Kirk.**

complete these tests in Santa Clara County while 11.3 percent do so at the state level.

Finally, more Santa Clara County students attend college. In Santa Clara County, 61.2 percent attend college while in the state only 49.4 percent do.

San Jose and Santa Clara County generally are more affluent than other areas of the state, and students are more mobile. However, there is also a higher percentage of limited English speaking students in Silicon Valley. Even though there are a variety of situations affecting Santa Clara County students, they are achieving at a higher level than the state overall.

Because of its high-technology connection, San Jose and Santa Clara County students have more access to computer technology. The Santa Clara County Office of Education offers free Internet access to the schools in the county. So far, more than 200 schools in 18 school districts have hooked on to the Internet through the Santa Clara County Office of Education.

In Spring, 1996, the high-technology industry held its first Net Day. Employees from industry donated a Saturday from their busy schedules to link hundreds of schools to the Internet.

Business/Education Partnerships

Silicon Valley business and industry leaders take an active role in insuring a partnership with the educational community. Once a year, sponsored by the San Jose Metropolitan Chamber of Commerce, the Principal for a Day program matches more than 275 schools with business leaders. The purpose of the program is to give business and community leaders a firsthand look at education issues and challenges.

Another business education partnership, in which the San Jose Metropolitan Chamber of Commerce is a partner, is Future Connections. Future Connections exposes K-14 teachers, administrators, and school board members to current industry practices. Future Connections coordinates structured, on-site visits to a wide variety of employers throughout Silicon Valley for participating educators. Field trips are tailored to meet the needs of a particular school or district. Future Connections staff also assist companies in designing the experience, briefing employees who will participate, helping to facilitate sessions, and more.

Over 100 corporations and businesses have now adopted schools through San Jose Unified School District's Adopt-A-School program. Adopt-A-School creates partnerships between public schools and businesses. Each individual partnership is unique and developed jointly by personnel from the school and its business partner. The adoption of a school can include a range of involvement from a small classroom project to projects encompassing the entire school student body.

Santa Clara University, one of the oldest colleges in the state, is a traditional university with a good scholastic reputation that offers bachelor's to doctorate degrees. **Photo by Pat Kirk.**

***University of California Extension in Santa Clara County is run by the University of California at Santa Cruz. Each year professional development classes are taken by 30,000 adults through its Santa Clara facility.* Photo by Pat Kirk.**

Adopt-A-School relies on the emphasis of utilizing people—not on donation of funds. Through Adopt-A-School, district students gain industry knowledge by participating in special courses, plant tours, career seminars and much more.

In 1985, Industry Initiatives for Science and Math Education (IISME) was founded by a consortium of San Francisco Bay Area companies in partnership with the Lawrence Hall of Science at University of California at Berkeley. IISME's founders recognized the need for better preparation of Bay Area students so that they will become a competitive global workforce.

IISME provides industry and educational partnerships in hopes of transforming mathematics, science, and technical education. Its programs are focused on teachers as the agents of change. IISME works with companies to develop summer work experience assignments for Bay Area math, science, and technology teachers who are hired for an eight-week paid summer fellowship guided by a company mentor or manager. Teachers learn firsthand the skills and characteristics their students will need to succeed in the workplace. They commit to translating their summer experience to classroom applications with the help of IISME staff and peer coaches.

Nearly 100 Bay Area employers have offered over 900 summer fellowships to teachers through IISME. One quarter of all Bay Area high school math, science, and technology teachers have held IISME fellowships and most importantly, over three quarters of a million students have been reached by IISME teachers. It is no wonder that IISME's Summer Fellowship Program is a national model for Scientific Work Experience Programs.

Challenge 2000, a spinoff of the Joint Venture Silicon Valley Network, actually began in 1992 when 1,000 people wanted to improve the region's sagging economy. The highest priority for action was education. Participants were concerned about the quality of education and they also agreed that education would be the key to Silicon Valley's economic recovery and long-term success.

A small board of local business and education leaders agreed to spend the time necessary to design a new collaborative initiative that would make a major difference in education. They commissioned a public opinion survey that showed 9 out of 10 residents wanted world-class schools.

"To spark a local educational renaissance, a new community commitment to building a world-class educational system that enables all students of Silicon Valley to be successful, productive citizens in the 21st century," continues to be the mission of Challenge 2000. Challenge 2000 focuses on the process of change, not solutions. They are aware that this process will take many years, span kindergarten through 12th grade, and fundamentally change the way we educate our children.

Challenge 2000 has partnered with four teams: the Overfelt Familia (East San Jose), the Blossom Valley Learning Consortium (South San Jose), the Palo Alto Learning Community, and the Family of Schools (Belmont, East Palo Alto, and San Carlos). In selecting and working with these "Renaissance Teams," Challenge 2000 has applied the venture capital model to education. The bottom line for Challenge 2000 is measurable improvement in student achievement by the turn of the century.

For over 40 years, Junior Achievement of Santa Clara County has provided volunteers from the business community to give back to the community by teaching and becoming role models in the classroom. Last year, Junior Achievement reached over 17,000 students through their economics, middle grades, project math, and elementary school programs. Over 500 volunteers visited classrooms approximately 8 to 10 times throughout a semester.

Junior Achievement of Santa Clara County feels that more than half of our young people are leaving school without the knowledge or foundation required to find and hold a good job. That's why their vision is to educate and inspire youth to value free enterprise, to understand business and economics and to be ready for the workforce.

Workforce Silicon Valley (WSV) is an independent nonprofit organization dedicated to enhance the economic vitality of the Silicon Valley community through the development of a world-class workforce. WSV is governed by a 23-member board and a staff organized into seven learning collaboratives which include: advanced manufacturing, information systems, multimedia, health/biosciences, financial services, and fashion technology.

WSV provides many opportunities for students and teachers. It operates a leadership institute to provide 200 teachers with in-depth training in integrated and applied curricula and pedagogy; develops focused school-to-career programs in seven high-skill, high-wage fields through partnerships with 17 high schools and 7 community colleges; engages 6 high schools and 1 community college in the implementation of a school to work curriculum, and provides teachers with internships and site visits to high-performance firms. WSV's goal continues to be preparing students with the knowledge, skills, and attitudes needed to succeed in the world of high-skill work.

There are dozens of business-education partnerships being formed every day. The net result of these efforts is that schools are becoming technically up to date by participating in these programs, and students

Silicon Valley's technology industry demands a highly educated workforce. Out of 1.5 million adults who work in Silicon Valley, two-thirds are college educated. Consequently, the people of San Jose are concerned about educating their children as well as themselves. Photo by Pat Kirk.

will be ready for the workforce—making San Jose and Silicon Valley ready for the 21st century.

In Santa Clara County, there are 33 school districts, with a population of 234,596 students in grades K-12. There are also a number of private schools in San Jose. The largest private school system in Santa Clara County is operated by the San Jose Catholic Diocese, with 28 elementary schools, 1 kindergarten, and 6 high schools.

What is unique to San Jose and Santa Clara County is its diverse student population. The breakdown of Santa Clara County student ethnicity is:

- 43.1 percent   Anglo
- 22.9 percent   Latino
- 23.2 percent   Asian
- 5 percent   Filipino
- 4.3 percent   Black
- 0.9 percent   American Indian
- 0.6 percent   Pacific Islander

Each of the 33 K-12 school districts and the 4 community college districts is autonomous and governed by an elected board of education. The governing board is responsible for setting district policy and hiring a superintendent who administers the district. There are four types of school districts in Santa Clara County, stretching from Palo Alto in the north to Gilroy in the southern part of the county:

- 22 elementary school districts which cover grades K-8
- 5 high school districts which cover grades 9-12
- 6 unified school districts which cover grades K-12
- 4 community college districts which cover grades 13 and 14

The Santa Clara County Office of Education (COE) provides a link between the California Department of Education and the county's school districts. It provides direct and indirect services and programs to students, teachers, staff, schools, and school districts. The COE also provides special education, regional programs, vocational training, and Head Start programs.

San Jose City College is one of eight community college campuses in Silicon Valley that offer two-year programs leading to Associate of Arts degrees in a wide variety of topics—but with special emphasis on the skills desired by Silicon Valley firms. **Photo by Pat Kirk.**

Consequently, a range of educational programs exists for every type of student in Silicon Valley. San Jose Unified School District, the largest of the county's districts, exemplifies the choice and variety of academic and special programs available to students throughout the county.

San Jose Unified School District

After 10 years of court-ordered busing for desegregation, a federal judge recently gave San Jose Unified School District permission to return to its system of neighborhood elementary schools.

As of September 1997, the San Jose Unified School District will redraw boundaries in an effort to achieve a "natural" ethnic balance. And, all busing at the elementary school level eventually will be voluntary. For the time being, the middle and high schools will continue the district's controlled choice plan for student assignments.

San Jose Unified School District dealt with the original desegregation order by offering parents and students a wide variety of program and school choices. Instead of children automatically attending their neighborhood school, parents registered their students for the school of their choice in an open enrollment period that occurred for prospective kindergartners, sixth and ninth graders.

The school choices in San Jose Unified School District are extensive. Parents choose from schools emphasizing science, writing, foreign language immersion, language arts, mathematics, intensive academic studies, visual and performing arts, communications, aviation/aerospace, and a host of other programs and activities.

With choices that are offered through the district, students can choose the area of study they are most interested in. Parents are strongly encouraged to tour any prospective school choice with their students before making decisions.

San Jose Unified School District is located in central San Jose. It has forty-two schools which feature a wide array of magnet and special programs. It is comprised of 28 elementary schools, 7 intermediate schools, 6 comprehensive high schools, and 1 alternative school. It is committed to providing a supportive, integrated environment for student learning. The district serves over 30,000 students.

Private Schools

Here is a sampling of private schools available in Silicon Valley:

NOTRE DAME HIGH SCHOOL

A Catholic college preparatory high school for young women, Notre Dame was established in San Jose in 1851. The school's minimum graduation requirements match the entrance requirements for the University of California and other private and state universities.

BELLARMINE COLLEGE PREPARATORY

Hosting 1,350 students from primary schools throughout Silicon Valley, Bellarmine is a private, non-profit Jesuit high school for young men in San Jose. Students experience a traditional liberal arts education requiring college preparatory disciplines. Historically, more than 95 percent of the graduating class enrolls in a four-year institution.

THE HARKER SCHOOL

A co-educational elementary school for children in junior kindergarten to grade eight, The Harker School is located on a 16-acre campus in San Jose. Harker students consistently score among the highest percentiles in national achievement tests.

Community Colleges

The community colleges in Silicon Valley offer two-year programs leading to Associate of Arts degrees in a wide variety of topics–but with special emphasis on the skills desired by Silicon Valley firms. In addition, many students complete the first two years of work leading to a bachelor's degree at a community college before transferring to a four-year institution.

SAN JOSE COMMUNITY COLLEGE DISTRICT

With three campuses–San Jose City College, Evergreen Valley College and the Institute for Business Performance–and 17 off-campus sites, San Jose Community College District hosts a student population of some 20,000 day and evening students.

Not all learning takes place in the classroom. **Photo by Pat Kirk.**

FOOTHILL COMMUNITY COLLEGE DISTRICT

The Foothill district has two campuses, Foothill Community College in Los Altos and De Anza in Cupertino. The district has about 39,000 day and evening students.

GAVILAN COMMUNITY COLLEGE DISTRICT

With one campus serving the area south Santa Clara County, Gavilan College has 3,700 students.

WEST VALLEY COMMUNITY COLLEGE DISTRICT

West Valley has a student population of 19,000 at its West Valley campus in Saratoga and Mission College campus in Santa Clara.

Universities

Geared to educating students for both the local region and the world, universities serving San Jose and Silicon Valley boast a wide range of degree offerings from bachelor's to Ph.D.'s. In addition, several of the

universities bring students opportunities to participate in research programs, both applied as well as basic.

SAN JOSE STATE UNIVERSITY

Located in downtown San Jose, between Fourth and Tenth streets, San Jose State University has aided the development of the computer industry and the resulting technological advances in our nation by providing the largest source of engineering, science, and business graduates to Silicon Valley companies.

Graduating about 5,500 students annually, San Jose State University also provides the professional infrastructure for the region. From teachers to social workers, artists to law enforcement officers and nurses, San Jose State University educates and prepares the leaders of Silicon Valley.

The university has a student population of 26,000 and is a major employer in Silicon Valley. There are eight fully accredited colleges within the university. These are: Applied Sciences and Arts, Business, Education, Engineering, Humanities and the Arts, Science, Social Sciences, and Social Work. Recently, the San Jose State University graduate and undergraduate business programs have earned an unconditional reaccreditation from the prestigious American Assembly of Collegiate Schools of Business. Out of 2,000 schools in the country, only 325 earn this accreditation.

In 1995, the university appointed a new president, Dr. Robert Caret. Formerly, Dr. Caret served as provost and executive vice president at Towson State University where he served as the chief academic officer and was responsible for the leadership of all academic programs and divisions within the university.

Dr. Caret brings with him new and vital energy for San Jose State University. His vision of the university as it enters the 21st century is to concentrate on serving the entire region of San Jose, Santa Clara Valley, the Bay Area, and the State of California. His goal is to structure San Jose State University as the Metropolitan University of Silicon Valley. By his involvement in the business community and K-18 education statewide, Dr. Caret continues to make San Jose State University "the engine of Silicon Valley."

For many years, the university had an isolated feeling in the downtown area. Of late, the university completed Paseo de San Carlos, a $3.2 million project that connects San Jose State University to downtown San Jose. The project closed to traffic a six-block section of San Carlos Street, uniting the north and south ends of the campus. Today, a brand new pedestrian walkway with grass, fountains, and benches exist on the former San Carlos Street. Now, downtown residents and business people can stroll onto the campus, pause to eat their lunch on a park bench and enjoy the college landscape.

SANTA CLARA UNIVERSITY

Santa Clara University is a Jesuit University located in Santa Clara that was founded in 1851. It is one of the oldest colleges in the state. Enrollment runs at approximately 7,500 students with half being undergraduates. Santa Clara University is the site of one of the California missions which has been rebuilt.

Santa Clara University is a traditional university with a good scholastic reputation that offers bachelor to doctorate degrees. The undergraduate programs include engineering, business and arts, and sciences.

A well-rounded student's education extends beyond the boundaries of education. Photo by Pat Kirk.

More Santa Clara County students attend college. In Santa Clara County, 61.2 percent attend college while in the state only 49.4 percent do. **Photo by Sharon Hall, courtesy of San Jose State University.**

Graduate programs are quite popular at Santa Clara University especially with the over-25 age group. These programs include: Engineering, Counseling, Psychology, Education, Law, and Catechetics-Liturgy-Spirituality.

STANFORD UNIVERSITY

Located in Palo Alto, Stanford University is a private university that has an internationally renowned reputation. Stanford University has 15,200 students in seven schools. These schools are: Earth Sciences, Education, Engineering, School of Business, Humanities and Sciences, Law, Medicine, and continuing studies.

Stanford is a world-renowned institution often credited with being the birthplace of the Silicon Valley. Research partnerships between the university and area industries have led to major technological breakthroughs as well as provide relevant training grounds for future scientists.

OTHER UNIVERSITIES

Silicon Valley residents continue to educate themselves throughout their lives as well as careers. There are a variety of part-time extension courses available for working adults.

University of California Extension in Santa Clara County is run by the University of California at Santa Cruz. Each year professional development

Through the unifying commitment of the Santa Clara County education community, students move ahead with confidence into the 21st century. **Photo by Pat Kirk.**

classes are taken by 30,000 adults through its Santa Clara facility. Courses are offered in computer science, engineering, business and management, environmental sciences, arts and humanities, English language, teacher education, and behavioral sciences. UCSC Extension provides over 1,000 seminars annually and certificates in 25 professional programs.

University of San Francisco, a private Jesuit University, offers bachelor's and master's programs in Silicon Valley at its Cupertino location aimed at working adults. Bachelor's degrees are available in Applied Economics, Information Systems Management, and Organizational Behavior. Master's degrees are attainable in Human Resources and Organization Management. The classes are offered in Sunnyvale, Palo Alto and San Jose.

Golden Gate University, Los Altos, targets working adults. Students may earn a bachelor's degree in Human Relations Management and Telecommunications. Master's degree programs offered include Banking and Finance, Management, Human Resources Management, Information Systems, International Management, Marketing, Taxation, and Telecommunications.

Contra Costa based St. Mary's College offers programs in Santa Clara County through its San Jose facility. The programs are scheduled for working adults. Students may earn their bachelor's degrees in Health Services Administration and Management, and master's degrees in Health Services Administration, Procurement, and Contract Management.

National Hispanic University, San Jose, offers Associate and Bachelor's degrees in Arts, a master's in Education and Business Administration. They also offer courses in English as a second language.

University of Phoenix is the second largest private institution in the United States. The Silicon Valley campus is located in the Golden Triangle of San Jose where 1,500 working adults attend classes per year. Programs offered are bachelor's and master's degrees in Business, Business Information Systems, Management and Nursing. There is also a continuing education catalog published each year that features workshops, seminars and certificate programs. Students can attend classes throughout the Bay Area.

If you desire an educational choice for your child or yourself, San Jose and Silicon Valley is the place to live. Because of its diversity and highly educated population, the area features educators who are on the leading edge of new methods and technology. Santa Clara County continues to surpass state performance levels in a variety of categories. And, Silicon Valley technology industry plays a major role in the affluence of the residents. This affluence and educational level is driving the education infrastructure to be the best it can be. ✦

Located in Palo Alto, Stanford University is a private university that has an internationally renowned reputation and is often credited with being the birthplace of the Silicon Valley. **Photo by Pat Kirk.**

Computer-generated music is a special interest at SJSU. Photo by Sharon Hall, courtesy of San Jose State University.

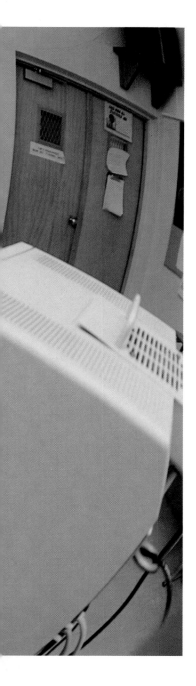

Laboratory practice makes classroom studies come alive. Photo by Sharon Hall, courtesy of San Jose State University.

Because of its diversity and highly educated population, the area features educators who are on the leading edge of new methods and technology—making San Jose and Silicon Valley primed for the 21st century. **Photo by Pat Kirk.**

Once a year the Principal for a Day program, sponsored by the San Jose Metropolitan Chamber of Commerce, matches more than 275 schools with business leaders. The purpose of the program is to give business and community leaders a firsthand look at education issues and challenges. **Photo by Pat Kirk.**

Chapter Seven

San Jose & Silicon Valley: Region of Diversity

The Church of Five Wounds is just one of the many examples of cultural diversity of the San Jose and Silicon Valley area. Photo by Pat Kirk.

S an Jose-Silicon Valley is unique in its blending of cultures and attitudes of a very diverse population. Not only is Santa Clara County diverse but this diversity has carried through in government as well as social and cultural activities. Where other major U.S. cities have racial problems because of diversity, San Jose-Silicon Valley is fairly free of racial conflict. Consequently, residents here enjoy the many ethnic restaurants, festivals, and art that is attributed to a multitude of cultures.

Santa Clara County has a population of more than 1.6 million people. According to the 1990 United States Census, approximately 21 percent are of Hispanic origin, 17.5 percent are of Asian background, and 3.8 percent are Black.

"That's what makes San Jose and the entire Silicon Valley so unique," says Ron McPherson, president of the Santa Clara County Black Chamber of Commerce. "Silicon Valley is a melting pot community. The diversity and the inclusion of all cultures among residents provides a general openness for not only the Black community but all minority groups as well."

Among others, strong ethnic communities in the valley include Hispanic, Southeast Asian/Vietnamese, Japanese, Korean, Filipino, Portuguese, Black, Chinese, Indo-American, and Pacific Islander.

Local government, business, and lifestyle have contributed to making Silicon Valley a haven for cultures from many lands. A recent report, "Who's Planning the Future of the Bay Area?", found that of 272 Bay Area individuals who serve on water boards, transportation agencies, and county planning commissions, only 22 are Latino. However, 12 of them are from Santa Clara County. "Based on how the other counties

were doing, it was surprising that Santa Clara was doing so well in representing Latinos," the report's author, Roxanne Figueroa, said. "Santa Clara County is definitely unique; one of the reasons may be that the board of supervisors seems to be much more in tune with the Latino community in that county," adds Ms. Figueroa.

Santa Clara County Supervisor Blanca Alvarado believes that all government boards should reflect the community they serve. "We're talking about democracy, and we're talking about people from all parts of life being part of the community they serve," says Supervisor Alvarado. In Santa Clara County, three of the seven planning commissioners are Latinos. The same is true at the Santa Clara County Water District. Half of the 12 board members of the Santa Clara County Transportation Authority are also Latinos.

San Jose Rated Number One of the Top 10 Cities for Latinos

"If you're looking to maximize your earning potential, you need to be here," says former Hispanic Chamber of Commerce of Santa Clara Valley President Ernest J. Abeytia. In May, 1996, *Hispanic Magazine* named San Jose number one in its "Top 10 Cities for Latinos" list. The article says if you want to become a mover and shaker in the high-tech business, move to San Jose. And, Abeytia says, "The level of affluence Hispanics achieve is as high as any other big city."

There are over 4,000 Hispanic businesses in San Jose. And, community spokespersons like Abeytia feel that the city's leaders work with minority leaders to insure equality for all minorities.

City Council Member Manny Diaz is the only Hispanic on San Jose's 11-member city council. However, he helped San Jose complete a disparity study in 1994. The study revealed that 97 percent of the city's contracts were being given to white males. Diaz now is helping the Office of Contract Compliance ensure that more of the contracts are given to minority-and women-owned businesses.

Many of the city's Hispanic leaders are optimistic about the future of San Jose. "It's a great place for Hispanics to live," says Abeytia. "You don't find very many cities that can offer the opportunities to live a lifestyle you can aspire to."

Recent statistics from the Hispanic Chamber indicate that all of Silicon Valley is benefiting by the growing Hispanic population. In fact, the Hispanic population grew by 70 percent over the past 15 years. Today, there are over 400,000 Hispanics residing in Santa Clara County with an estimated annual buying power of $4.8 billion. Hispanic businesses in the county total more than 10,000 and have an annual sales of $967 million.

Truly, persons of Hispanic origin living and residing in Silicon Valley present a viable contribution to the business community as well as adding a cultural flair to the area. Throughout the year, there are many opportunities to participate in the Hispanic culture. Each May, a Cinco de Mayo celebration is held in downtown San Jose that attracts over 100,000 participants. An annual Mariachi Festival draws more thousands.

Asian Americans: A Major Component of Silicon Valley's Workforce

One of the largest segments of Silicon Valley's population is Asian American. As previously noted, Asian Americans comprise 17.5 percent of the valley. A recent study, "The State of Asian Pacific America:

Reframing the Immigration Debate," notes that an estimated 15,000 Asian immigrants are employed in Silicon Valley.

The study goes on to say that Asian Americans make up nearly half of Silicon Valley's manufacturing labor force. Asian Americans not only fill critical scientific positions but, as entrepreneurs, create jobs and push technology to new frontiers. Because of their advantage, many Asian immigrants have opened up new markets in Asia and as a result, Asian venture capital funds have invested in start-ups and financial institutions in Silicon Valley.

Asian American entrepreneurs head an estimated 300 high-tech firms in Silicon Valley, the study found. Many started their own businesses after failing to break through a "glass ceiling" at other firms.

At Santa Clara based Intel Corporation, the world's largest semiconductor manufacturer, headed by Hungarian immigrant Andy Grove, about 20 percent of the employees are Chinese immigrants, according to the report. One hundred of the 300 engineers with advanced degrees hired by Intel during the first half of 1995 were on visas, according to company spokesperson, Tom Waldrop.

"When we go to the best schools, the best programs, there they are," says Waldrop. "And these folks don't come cheap because so many other companies want to hire them. If we couldn't hire these people, we wouldn't be so competitive."

Each May, a Cinco de Mayo celebration is held in downtown San Jose that attracts over 100,000 participants. Photo by Pat Kirk.

San Jose: Second Largest Vietnamese Community in the Country

Another very successful component of the Asian American community are the Vietnamese. When the government of South Vietnam fell in 1975, many Vietnamese settled in San Jose. "There were many electronic jobs that required little or no English," recalls Thuan Huu Nguyen, founder/president, Vietnamese Chamber of Commerce of Santa Clara Valley.

Today, there are approximately 120,000 Vietnamese residents in San Jose. "Orange County has the highest concentration of Vietnamese and San Jose is the second largest concentration of Vietnamese in the United States. I've lived in other cities throughout the United States and San Jose is the most open and accepting," says Nguyen.

Besides working in high-technology firms, Nguyen says that many Vietnamese entered the area establishing their own businesses such as restaurants, supermarkets, auto body repair shops, and professional services. Gradually neighborhood communities were formed.

Twenty years later, the Vietnamese community is an integral piece of Silicon Valley. Two years ago, the Duc Vien Temple, a Buddhist Vietnamese Temple was completed on McLaughlin Avenue in San Jose. "This temple represents an area where the Vietnamese community first settled." Today, the Vietnamese community resides throughout Silicon Valley.

Each February the Tet Festival, a Vietnamese New Year's celebration, is held in downtown San Jose. In the Fall, the Vietnamese community stages a children's festival at Guadalupe River Park in downtown San Jose.

Together, Nguyen and his wife, Hanh Giao, operate the Vietnamese Chamber of Commerce. They provide information and opportunity for all business owners to get together. "Our chamber is open to all ethnic groups," says Nguyen.

"There are 7,000 Vietnamese business owners in Silicon Valley. It is important for Vietnamese business people to mingle with not only each other but all business owners," added Nguyen.

Japantown is a Focal Point for Japanese American Community

A strong Japanese American community also resides in Silicon Valley. Its focus is in Japantown, an emerging cultural center near the heart of San Jose. Japantown is a real place with stores, churches and festivals. It is also a symbolic connection that binds the Japanese American community together.

Long a leader of area Japanese Americans as well as the community-at-large, Congressman Norman Y. Mineta retired from public office in 1996. Mineta was formerly mayor of San Jose, the first Japanese American elected to the top political job of any major U.S. city.

Area Japanese Americans are represented on the San Jose City Council as well as in the California Assembly.

City of San Jose Project Diversity

Boards and commissions play an important role in city and county government. They assist in formulating policies and practices and provide a formal avenue for involvement in local affairs. They also provide a training ground for future leaders of the city.

San Jose Mayor Susan Hammer announced Project Diversity at her Unity Breakfast speech in January 1991. She stated that the goal of Project Diversity was to give San Jose residents of diverse backgrounds and ethnic heritages a greater share of decision-making at City Hall through participation on city boards and commissions.

Within a month, Mayor Hammer appointed a Project Diversity Steering Committee to address specific objectives in three areas: recruitment, selection, and training of applicants. Immediately a study was conducted among current board and commission members. What the study found was that 62 percent were male, and that 38 percent were female.

Mayor Susan Hammer. Photo by Pat Kirk.

Each February the Tet Festival, a Vietnamese New Year's celebration, is held in downtown San Jose. Photo by Pat Kirk.

The Duc Vien Temple, a Buddhist Vietnamese Temple, represents an area where the Vietnamese community first settled. Photo by Pat Kirk.

The San Jose America Festival, held each July 4th weekend, allows you to experience the flavor of San Jose and Silicon Valley's diversity. Photo by Mark Leet.

The ethnic composition of the survey revealed that minority women were the most under-represented group. Only 4 out of 93 respondents were women of color. In addition, 15 percent were of Hispanic origin, 12 percent Asian American, 4 percent African American, and 1 percent Native American. Approximately 68 percent of those surveyed were European American.

Current statistics are not yet available. But according to city sources, Project Diversity has had a tremendous effect in increasing the numbers of women and minorities on boards and commissions. The committee gave as its first recommendation a Policy For Diversity which states "The City of San Jose is committed to providing an equal opportunity to its residents to participate on the City's Boards and Commissions. To this end, the City of San Jose shall establish policies and procedures to ensure that the membership of its Boards and Commissions reflects the City's culturally diverse communities."

Today, vacancies are announced in the media, there is a term limit of four years for board and commission members, all city council districts must be represented, and an aggressive recruitment program reaching out to the City's diverse communities is underway.

It has been said that San Jose-Silicon Valley is one of the most racially diverse in the nation. Understandably, people here are mindful of what it means to live and work with others unlike themselves. This blending of cultures and attitudes has created a unique harmonious atmosphere for the entire community.

Just about any weekend of the year, one can experience the diversity of the area by attending the many festivals and celebrations. If you want the flavor of San Jose-Silicon Valley's diversity first-hand, attend the San Jose America Festival, held July 4th weekend. More than 30 performances are presented on two stages with a variety of musical styles that include country, blues, rock, jazz, world beat, mariachi, salsa, reggae, Mexican folk dance, Japanese drumming, and East Indian dance. When you are in the audience, clapping your hands to the music, take a moment to look around. Right away you'll notice the diversity of the crowd and that together everyone is having a great time. ✦

It has been said that Silicon Valley is a melting pot community. The diversity and the inclusion of all cultures among residents provides a general openness for all minority groups. **Photo by Pat Kirk.**

The Chinese altar at the San Jose Historical Museum offers an overview of the area's diverse past and present. **Photo by Pat Kirk.**

The Machu Picchu Gallery and Museum of the America's is a special place where you can look into the world of Mexican, Central, and South American artists. **Photo by Pat Kirk.**

More than 10 cultural festivals are held each year in San Jose, adding to the ethnic pride and diversity that makes the city a truly cosmopolitan community. **Photo by Dana L. Grover.**

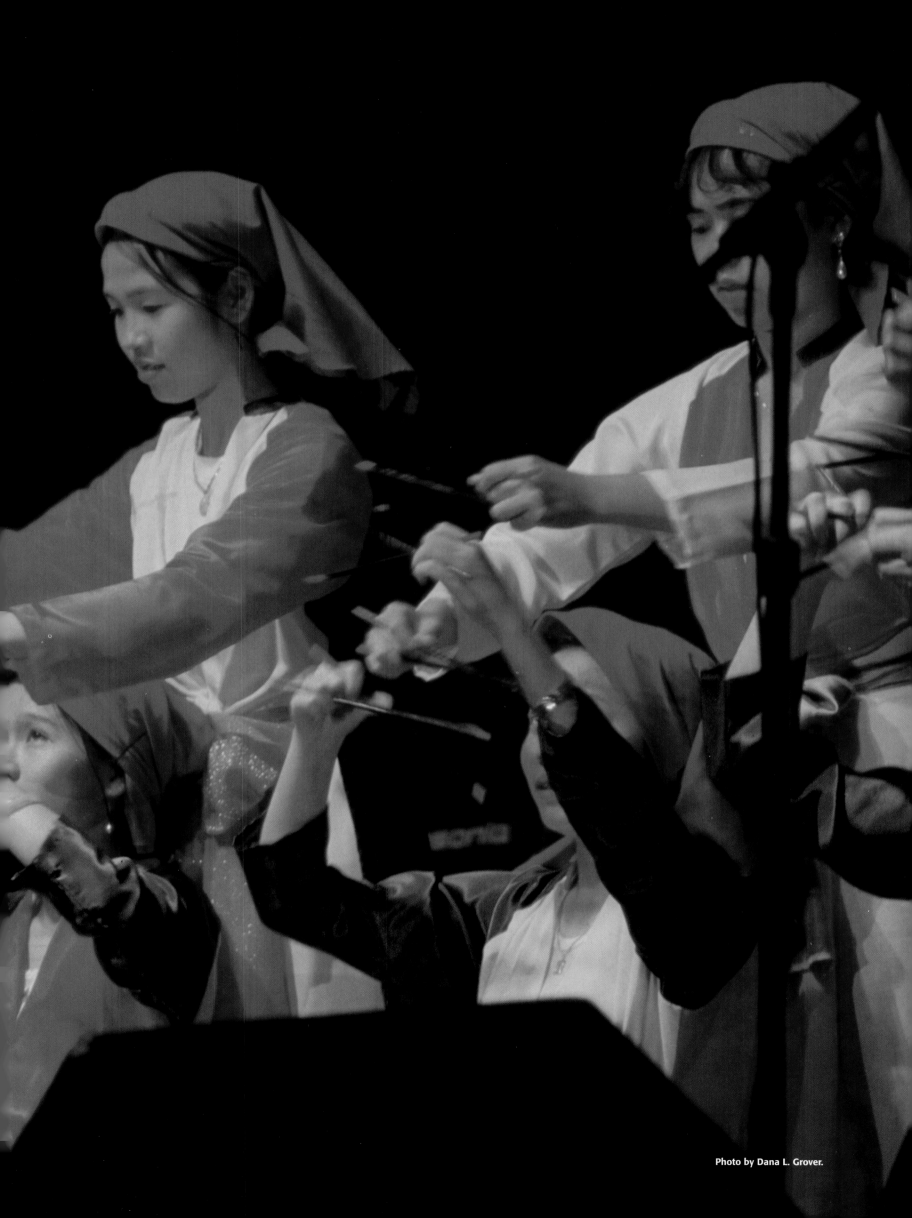

Photo by Dana L. Grover.

Photo by Dana L. Grover.

Chapter Eight

Neighborhoods Create a Sense of Community in San Jose & Silicon Valley

♦

It is hard to pinpoint the center of Silicon Valley. Many view San Jose as the capital and others view the heart as being somewhere between Mountain View and Sunnyvale. A recent *Wall Street Journal* article states that Silicon Valley spans both Santa Clara and San Mateo counties. Wherever the true center lies, we know one fact, Santa Clara County encompasses 15 incorporated cities, with a population exceeding 1.6 million. In addition, there are neighboring cities in San Mateo and Alameda Counties.

Of course, San Jose is the largest city with a population of 849,400 making it California's third largest city. In 1994, *Money* magazine ranked San Jose the fifth most livable city in the United States. In 1995, Zero Population Growth voted San Jose the fourth best city in the state for raising children. In addition, one recent study gave San Jose the lowest crime rate of any metropolis with a population of 400,000 or more in the country.

San Jose is a middle class city with many distinct neighborhoods that give the essence of living in a small community. Some neighborhoods have tree lined streets with New England style homes. Others contain housing from a certain era or contain many residents from a particular ethnic group. However, it is possible to live in the third largest California city and get away from it all.

The Rose Garden area, located minutes from downtown, reaps its name from the Municipal Rose Garden city park. Photo by Pat Kirk.

San Jose Neighborhoods

The Santa Teresa area is located at the very southern end of San Jose. About 30 years ago, you could drive through the area and all you would see were farms and ranches. Today, it is divided into housing, boasts IBM's industrial complex and contains a large county park with a golf course.

There are some homes that were built in the 1950s and 1960s. Most homes were built in the 1970s. Santa Teresa is a well maintained area of San Jose containing many stucco and wood shingled two-story homes.

The Evergreen area is located in Southeast San Jose. It is east of the Santa Teresa area. After the fall and winter rains, Evergreen lives up to its name when the hills surrounding it are lush green. There are many subdivisions that contain three-bedroom homes that were built in the last 12 to 20 years. In the last few years, the Silver Creek Valley Country Club was built and contains a golf course, recreational facilities, parks, and custom homes.

The East Valley area, also known as the "Eastside," spreads out from downtown San Jose and attaches itself to the surrounding hillsides. Most homes are over 20 years old and there are many diverse cultures residing in East Valley.

Above East Valley is the North San Jose/Berryessa area. North San Jose is considered a bedroom community with many middle to upper income residents. Residences consist of four-bedroom homes, townhouses, condominiums, and apartments. The area contains the San Jose Flea Market, and Alum Rock and Penitencia Creek Parks.

Alviso is north of Highway 237. It is a small low-income neighborhood just east of Santa Clara, formerly a seaport and still home to a small yacht club.

Downtown and central San Jose contain many government buildings, hotels, and restaurants. There is a great variety of housing from apartments to bungalows to mansions. San Jose State University is located in the heart and creates foot traffic.

A real jewel east of downtown San Jose and San Jose State University is the Naglee Park district. Bordered by San Jose State University on the west, East Santa Clara Street on the north, Highway 280 on the South, and Williams Street Park at South 16th and Williams Streets, Naglee Park was originally the 140-acre estate of General Henry Morris Naglee. General Naglee arrived in California in 1847. After leading troops as a brigadier general for the United States Army in the Civil War, he settled in San Jose in 1868. Today, Naglee Park is home to many unique Victorian homes and is most likely the oldest neighborhood in San Jose.

The Rose Garden area is just west of downtown San Jose and contains many Queen Anne and Tudor homes. The area reaps its name from the Municipal Rose Garden, a city park located at Dana and Naglee Streets. Located minutes from downtown, the neighborhoods are well kept.

Another small town in the big city is the Willow Glen area. Willow Glen is very quiet and located south and slightly west of downtown San Jose. The homes are old and lovely with tree lined streets. Many were built in the 1930s and contain basements, large gardens, hardwood floors and brick. As the original older residents leave, young families are moving in and adding on to many of the two bedroom homes. Willow Glen has its own downtown that contains many ethnic restaurants, shops, and coffee houses.

Naglee Park is home to many unique Victorian homes and is most likely the oldest neighborhood in San Jose. Photo by Dana L. Grover.

San Jose is a middle-class city with many distinct neighborhoods that give the essence of living in a small community. Photo by Pat Kirk.

The South San Jose area is south of downtown and east of Willow Glen. There are many housing tracts from the 1950s that are mixed with newer housing. The area is accessible by light rail. The commute was vastly improved when the Highway 87 extension opened in 1993.

The Blossom Valley area is located south of South San Jose, north of Santa Teresa adjacent to Blossom Hill Road. The area started developing in the 1960s and derives its name from the blossoming fruit trees that were on the land.

The Almaden Valley area is located west of Blossom Valley and south of Willow Glen. There is a mix of housing that includes homes from the 1960s and many new custom upscale homes. There is a beautiful view of surrounding mountains and downtown San Jose from the hill homes. Almaden Valley gives residents a little bit of country in the big city.

The Cambrian area is located in West San Jose and borders Los Gatos and Campbell. There are many tract ranch-style homes that were built over the last 10 to 30 years. Many original owners continue to live in the area with tree lined streets.

Surrounding Silicon Valley Cities

CAMPBELL

Campbell is a mature suburb that prides itself on being sophisticated yet retaining a small town flavor. Campbell is surrounded by San Jose on two borders. Los Gatos and Saratoga form its southwest border. Highway 880 splits the city of 38,250.

CUPERTINO

Cupertino is home to 43,650 people and 50 high-technology firms. Cupertino enjoys a central location north of Saratoga and west of San Jose. Two of the county's largest employers, Apple Computer and Tandem Computers are located here. DeAnza College, Santa Clara County's largest community college, is also located in Cupertino.

A farm village for most of its life, Cupertino in 1950 had fewer than 500 homes, and then was swept up in the great suburban boom that followed World War II. Census data indicates that three of every four homes were built between 1950 and 1980.

GILROY

If you desire a more rural way of life, then Gilroy is for you. Gilroy is the southernmost town in Santa Clara County and is famous for its annual Garlic Festival each July. A major attraction is the Outlets at Gilroy which features over 150 famous-maker discount outlet stores. The city is the largest in the South Valley area with a population of

Gilroy, garlic capital of the world, attracts more than 300,000 visitors to its annual Garlic Festival each July. **Photo by Bill Strange.**

34,000 and provides an agricultural, rural setting. Gilroy is 28 miles south of San Jose, and is close to beaches on the Pacific Ocean and Monterey Bay.

LOS ALTOS

Home to managers, administrators, professionals, and retirees, Los Altos lies south of Palo Alto and is 20 miles north of San Jose. The community of 27,300 does not allow industry within its limits.

Los Altos has tree-lined streets and a quaint downtown that revels in first class restaurants, bakeries, antique shops, and art galleries. Single homes account for 89 percent of the housing and the majority are built on quarter-acre lots. Such serenity does have a high price tag as home buyers can expect to pay close to $1 million for a residence.

LOS ALTOS HILLS

Perhaps the most prestigious address in Santa Clara County is Los Altos Hills. The town started off as an escape from the fog for San Franciscans about fifty years ago. Today, Los Altos Hills is home to many Silicon Valley CEO's with average house prices over $1 million. If you can afford Los Altos Hills, you do get a lot for your money. Gorgeous valley views, woodsy surroundings, and one-acre lots are included in the price tag.

LOS GATOS

What do actress Olivia De Havilland, Olympic Ice Skater Peggy Fleming, writer John Steinbeck, and violinist Yehudi Menuhin have in common? All of these famous celebrities have called Los Gatos home at one time or another.

As you leave San Jose heading southwest, Los Gatos rests on the eastern slopes of the Santa Cruz Mountains. The Town of Los Gatos is 10 square miles and is famous for its quaint and charming shops along North Santa Cruz Avenue and the Old Town shopping area. Fine restaurants and Victorian style homes surround the town.

Los Gatos, an exclusive address, is home to 28,950. There are many nice homes located on the flatlands that rise to the wooded hills towering

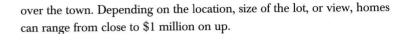

Mountain View's downtown was recently refurbished, encouraging pedestrians to walk along brick sidewalks, dine at numerous restaurants, browse at bookstores, and drink coffee at the many coffee houses. **Photo by Pat Kirk.**

"The Great Mall of the Bay Area" in Milpitas is the largest outlet mall in California, hosting 11 anchor stores and 240 smaller stores. **Photo by Pat Kirk.**

over the town. Depending on the location, size of the lot, or view, homes can range from close to $1 million on up.

MILPITAS

What used to be home to the Ford auto plant, Milpitas now contains many high-tech electronic firms and is a viable part of Silicon Valley. High-tech jobs and low home prices have attracted many professionals to Milpitas. The city has added over 31,000 residents since the 1980's electronics boom and today has a population of 59,700.

Milpitas has a solid commercial base to support its above average amenities. Besides the high-tech industries located throughout the city, retail centers greatly contribute to the city coffers. The Ford Motor Plant, which closed in 1983, was converted 10 years later into "The Great Mall of the Bay Area." The Great Mall is the largest outlet mall in California and hosts 11 anchor stores and 240 smaller stores.

MONTE SERENO

Monte Sereno is a small city between Los Gatos and Saratoga with many custom homes on large lots. Monte Sereno is one of the smallest towns in both population (3,280) and area (1 1/2 square miles).

MORGAN HILL

In 1991, Morgan Hill was identified by the *San Francisco Chronicle* as one of the 16 best family towns in the Bay Area. Located just south of San Jose, Morgan Hill is a city with plenty of open space and country feeling. However, its traditional agricultural economy is giving way to services and residential construction as the city becomes home to more people (27,950) and more businesses.

MOUNTAIN VIEW

Mountain View is a Silicon Valley city that has faced major changes in the past few years. In 1994, U.S Naval Air Station Moffett Field was closed and the airfield complex came under the control of NASA Ames Research Center. Mountain View is close to Palo Alto and Stanford and has over 200 manufacturing plants. Sun Microsystems, the county's eighth largest employer, leads the list of companies. Mountain View is largely a city of apartments and condominiums; and apartments outnumber single home dwellings by two to one. As the county's fourth largest city, population here is approximately 71,300.

Mountain View's downtown was recently refurbished. Pedestrians have the chance to walk along brick sidewalks and choose between 55 restaurants, browse at bookstores, and drink coffee at the many coffee houses.

PALO ALTO

Home of Stanford University and birthplace of Silicon Valley, Palo Alto has a highly educated and cosmopolitan population (58,575). In 1988 and

1991, the *San Francisco Chronicle* ranked Palo Alto the best place to live in the Bay Area in regards to crime, school quality, restaurants, commuting distances, cultural activities, and more.

Palo Alto is the county's northernmost city and a sizable number of Silicon Valley firms are located here. These companies include Hewlett-Packard, Varian, Watkins-Johnson, and Xerox Palo Alto Research Center (PARC).

SANTA CLARA

Santa Clara is the third largest city in the county with a population of 98,200. It is bound on three sides by San Jose with Sunnyvale forming its western border. Santa Clara is a mix of fun, commerce, and education. A major amusement park, Paramount's Great America, is located here. The many high-tech companies located in Santa Clara include Intel, Applied Materials, 3-Com, and Synoptics.

Santa Clara is also home to a Jesuit institution, Santa Clara University, which is the oldest private institution of higher learning in the state.

SARATOGA

Saratoga is a prosperous small town that is home to many professionals. Saratoga is mostly residential and is located on the eastern slope of the Santa Cruz Mountains where 29,600 people reside. It is nestled near the hills and is quite picturesque. Saratoga has its own downtown that boasts many fine restaurants and shops.

SUNNYVALE

Sunnyvale has been recognized by President Bill Clinton and Vice President Al Gore as a city that knows how to make things work. Zero

Sunnyvale was recently rated as the number one city in California for raising children. **Photo by Pat Kirk.**

Population Growth, which analyzes such forces as crime, education, poverty, and pollution, recently rated Sunnyvale as the number one city in California for raising children.

Sunnyvale is the county's second most populous city, with 126,100 residents. The city is also home to hundreds of high-tech firms, and in recent years has been pushing into bio-technology, where there are now about 30 of these firms.

Sunnyvale is home to Lockheed Martin Missiles & Space, Amdahl, Advanced Micro Devices, Westinghouse Electric, and many others.

Alameda County
FREMONT

Fremont is the southernmost city in Alameda County, making it a natural location for expanding Silicon Valley businesses. Apple Computer's manufacturing plant is located here, as well as many other high-tech companies such as LAM Research, Seagate Magnetics, and Logitech. Directly west of Fremont, across the Dumbarton Bridge, are the Peninsula Silicon Valley cities of Palo Alto and Mountain View.

NEWARK

Newark is the site for a growing number of industrial parks and technology centers. Surrounded on three sides by Fremont and on the other by San Francisco Bay, Newark's location near the Dumbarton Bridge links it with the Silicon Valley peninsula.

PLEASANTON

Pleasanton is located strategically near the intersection of Interstate Highways 580 and 680, northeast of Fremont and Newark. Home of the 876-acre Hacienda Business Park and other similar centers, Pleasanton has attracted many Silicon Valley heavy hitters, such as Hewlett-Packard, to expand eastward to its convenient location and open space.

A Regional Housing Market

Besides being the technology Mecca for the United States if not the world, Silicon Valley offers a variety of lifestyles and housing in its cities and towns. However, with the recent technological boom, Silicon Valley's housing costs have appreciated dramatically.

Local efforts to create affordable housing are continuing, and many people are finding a tradeoff between commute distances and housing costs by locating in south Santa Clara and San Benito Counties, as well as in eastern Alameda County, and San Joaquin and Stanislaus Counties in the state's Central Valley.

For people who live in the latter area, there is a major effort to create a commuter rail link between the Central Valley and Silicon Valley. That will truly create a regional housing market for the Silicon Valley and the entire San Francisco Bay Area. ✦

Downtown San Jose offers a great variety of housing from apartments to bungalows to mansions. Photo by Pat Kirk.

Saratoga is a prosperous small town that is home to many professionals. Nestled near the hills of the Santa Cruz Mountains, it has its own downtown that boasts many fine restaurants and shops. **Photo by Pat Kirk.**

Some neighborhoods in San Jose have tree-lined streets with New England style homes. Others contain housing from a certain era or contain many residents from a particular ethnic group. However, it is possible to live in the third largest California city and get away from it all. **Photo by Pat Kirk.**

From single family homes, condominiums, apartments, duplexes, and mobile homes, San Jose is a city where virtually every taste and lifestyle can be satisfied. **Photo by Pat Kirk.**

The world-famous San Jose Flea Market is touted as the largest in the world with acres of bargains and California's largest farmer's market. **Photo by Pat Kirk.**

Home of Stanford University and birthplace of Silicon Valley, Palo Alto has a highly educated and cosmopolitan population that has been ranked as the best place to live in the Bay Area. **Photo by Pat Kirk.**

San Jose's housing market offers opportunities across a wide spectrum from executive housing (shown above), *to low income housing* (above right). **Photos by Pat Kirk.**

Photo by Pat Kirk.

Chapter Nine

Arts & Cultural Affairs

*T*hroughout San Jose and Silicon Valley, arts groups abound. In San Jose, there are over 30 galleries and museums and several performing arts groups. Excitement, diversity, and growth describe the art scene. There is truly education and entertainment for people of different interests, ages, and ethnic groups. As the 21st century approaches, San Jose-Silicon Valley is not only rich in technology but is rapidly becoming Northern California's art and cultural mecca.

In the past few years, two downtown San Jose museums were established, the Children's Discovery Museum and the Tech Museum of Innovation. And the third downtown San Jose anchor, the San Jose Museum of Art, expanded its facility.

Opening in 1990, the Children's Discovery Museum, located at the intersection of Woz Way and Auzerais at Guadalupe River Park, is the largest children's museum on the West Coast. The museum offers changing interactive exhibits and programs that lead children to discoveries about themselves and the world around them. Painted purple and surrounded by an immense lawn area that borders the Guadalupe River, the Children's Discovery Museum is a delight for children of all ages.

Formerly called The Garage of the Technology Center of Silicon Valley, the Tech Museum of Innovation opened in November 1990. The museum was named one of the top 10 U.S. attractions that opened that year. The Tech's hands-on exhibits and labs cover areas of technology such as space, microelectronics, materials, biotechnology, and robotics. Located on West San Carlos Street, across from the Dr. Martin Luther King, Jr., Main Library, The Tech Museum will be moving next year. Recently, ground was broken for a new site around the corner on Market Street.

In June 1991, the San Jose Museum of Art completed a $14 million, 45,000-square-foot addition. The visual arts center's permanent collection primarily features contemporary art, which the museum describes as the art of our times. A partnership with the Whitney Museum of American Art in New York has resulted in world-class art shows. The museum is located at 110 South Market Street.

If you are looking for an historical perspective of the early years of San Jose, check out the San Jose Historical Museum at Senter Road and Phelan Avenue. The San Jose Historical Museum has 21 original and fully restored Victorian buildings including a printshop, candy store, bank, hotel, doctor's office, firehouse, livery, and home. There are also exhibits on early Native American, Spanish, and Mexican influence on the Santa Clara Valley.

The Children's Discovery Museum, the largest children's museum on the West Coast, offers changing interactive exhibits and programs that lead children to discoveries about themselves and the world around them. Photo by Dana L. Grover.

Equally intriguing and unusual is the Rosicrucian Egyptian Museum & Planetarium. The museum contains the West's largest collection of Egyptian antiquities and artifacts, including mummies, statuary, and scrolls. The dramatic building exterior and sphinx are patterned after originals in ancient Egypt. The museum is located on Park Avenue in San Jose's Rose Garden neighborhood.

In early 1995, the American Museum of Quilts & Textiles moved to 60 South Market Street in downtown San Jose. The mission of the American Museum of Quilts & Textiles of San Jose is to promote the art, craft, and history of quilts and textiles. They offer regularly changing exhibits that feature contemporary and historical quilts and textiles from around the world as well as from the museum's own collection.

There are several other art and cultural museums in San Jose that celebrate the diverse culture of the area. One such organization is MACLA, The San Jose Center for Latino Arts. The San Jose Center for Latino Arts is San Jose's leading Latino multidisciplinary arts organization and a key contributor to the blossoming art and culture scene in downtown San Jose. MACLA succeeded in bringing the community's long-held dream for its own Latino arts venue in 1993. Programs at the Center include visual, literary, humanities, and educational services. Since 1993, over 300 professional and community artists and an estimated 450 student artists have presented at the Center.

At a special place in downtown San Jose, tucked away in a courtyard, the Machu Picchu Gallery and Museum of the America's resides. Here you can look into the world of Mexican, and Central and South American artists. Peru native, Olga Encisco Smith, named her gallery Machu Picchu for the Lost City of the Incas, located high in the Andes.

The San Jose Museum of Art's permanent collection primarily features contemporary art, which the museum describes as the art of our times. A partnership with the Whitney Museum of American Art in New York has resulted in world-class art shows. Photo by Pat Kirk.

The San Jose Historical Museum presents an historical perspective of the early years of San Jose. The museum has 21 original and fully restored Victorian buildings including a printshop, candy store, bank, hotel, doctor's office, firehouse, livery, and home. Photo by Pat Kirk.

Besides being able to view works by local, national, and international artists, San Jose is also home to world-class performing arts companies including the acclaimed San Jose Repertory Theater, Opera San Jose, San Jose Symphony Orchestra, American Musical Theater, and the San Jose-Cleveland Ballet.

The San Jose Repertory Theater was founded in 1980. Today, San Jose Repertory Theater is the only fully professional regional theater in the South Bay. The company presents six main stage shows annually and has an extensive community outreach program. Under the direction of Timothy Near, the Rep is committed to responding to the emerging interests of Silicon Valley's diverse population. Soon, a long held dream of the Rep will be realized. Breaking ground in late 1995, the San Jose Repertory Theater will move into its "Magic Box"–its own theater–in 1997.

Previously, most Rep productions have been held at the Montgomery Theater on South Market Street in downtown San Jose. Plans are for the Magic Box to be a 52,000-square-foot building that stands 80 feet tall and contains flexible seating for approximately 600 theater patrons. "The Magic Box comprises an extremely important element in San Jose's growing role as a regional artistic center," says Mayor Susan Hammer.

Opera San Jose was founded by San Jose native, Irene Dalis, a former Metropolitan Opera principal soprano. The Opera and San Jose Repertory Theater share the use of the Montgomery Theater.

The San Jose Symphony, over 116 years old, is the oldest orchestra in California. Over the past two decades, the San Jose Symphony has grown from a half-dozen concerts a year to an orchestra with a budget of $5 million a year performing Signature, Pops, and KickBack Classics series, Family Concerts, special concerts, and collaborations at a variety of other locations. The San Jose Symphony also offers important programs for youngsters and reaches over 15,000 students a year.

Maestro Leonid Grin, a Soviet emigre, succeeded Maestro George Cleve after a 20-year tenure on the podium. Maestro Grin has an international reputation for conducting leading orchestras throughout Europe and North America.

Led by Executive Producer Stewart Slater and Artistic Director Dianna Shuster, American Musical Theater of San Jose, formerly the San Jose Civic Light Opera, recently celebrated its 60th anniversary. AMT is one of the oldest theater companies in the nation and has more than 37,000 season-ticket holders. By changing its name, AMT intends on reaching a wider audience and presenting musicals rather than light opera productions. AMT presents five productions from October through May at the San Jose Center for the Performing Arts.

The San Jose Cleveland Ballet had its San Jose debut over ten years ago. San Jose community leader, Karen Loewenstern, chair of City Center Ballet of San Jose, visited six dance companies throughout the United States and decided to partner with the Cleveland Ballet.

San Jose Cleveland Ballet is the longest running and successful co-venture in the United States. Originally, the San Jose Cleveland Ballet began with a production of "The Nutcracker" in conjunction with the San Jose Symphony. Today, in its second decade, "The Nutcracker," is still performed during the holiday season and three other productions are also offered that begin in October and end in April.

There are several "off downtown San Jose" successful theater companies in the area. The City Lights Theater Company, led by Director Ross Nelson, produces a full season of plays running from October through June. Their goal is to present works that are not found at other theater companies. Plays are usually adventurous, well acted, and above all fun. In 1995, "Praying Mantis," an allegory of South American politics by Chilean playwright Alejandro Slevelking, was named one of the most memorable productions in the entire bay area by the *San Jose Mercury News.*

D.P. Fong Galleries in downtown San Jose. Photo by Pat Kirk.

The Saratoga Drama Group (SDG) began operations in 1963 with the Saratoga Federated Church and presented their early productions in Richard's Hall at the church. Their efforts were so well received that by 1969 the group had outgrown the church and formed a nonprofit community theater corporation. Today, they present their performances at the former Saratoga Council Chambers which they now call the Saratoga Civic Theater.

SDG is unique to the Bay Area because it is entirely a self-supporting non-profit organization with no sponsors or advertising revenue. Only ticket sales defray the cost of staging each show. SDG presents three shows per season from September through June. No roles are pre-cast and all performers are selected in open auditions.

San Jose Stage Company is a community based mid-sized professional theater organization producing contemporary and classical theater in an intimate off-Broadway style setting. Operating in its own theater facility, the company offers six productions per season. The company's goal is to promote a rich ethnic and socially diverse audience composition. In addition to its main stage season, San Jose Stage Company presents the successful "Downtown Arts Series," a 10-week program offering a unique opportunity to experience San Jose's diverse cultural resources.

Northside Theater Company, located at the corner of William and 18th Streets, has produced family-oriented shows with innovation and imagination. The company trains and relies on young adults who care about dramatic theater. Northside Theater Company has received national attention on the CBS TV Show, "Sunday Morning."

Los Lupenos de San Jose is a dynamic, nonprofit institution, that exists to promote the awareness, appreciation, and understanding of the rich and passionate culture of Mexico. Dedicated to education through dance, drama, music, and art, Los Lupenos unites diverse communities, linking the past with the present, with intense energy, an enduring history, and a commitment to artistic excellence. Los Lupenos presents stories, tableaus, suites, or exhibits that use traditional folk dance and art as well as contemporary art forms that have evolved from traditional style.

More than 10 cultural festivals are held annually in San Jose, adding to the ethnic pride and diversity that makes the city a cosmopolitan community. One such festival is Christmas in the Park.

Christmas in the Park has become a San Jose holiday tradition. Each year over 100,000 people make their way to downtown San Jose to view more than 60 magical displays in Plaza de Cesar Chavez. The two acres are transformed into a fantasy toyland with over 30,000 glittering lights, twirling ballerinas, dancing panda bears, singing choir children, Victorian villagers, laughing elves, and Santa's reindeer. Visitors stroll through the magical forests of holiday trees, decorated by local community groups, on their way to visit Santa.

Christmas in the Park actually began in 1950 when San Jose businessman Don Lima began placing animated characters in front of his business on Willow Street at holiday time. Each year there would be a traffic jam as young and old alike came to view this winter wonderland. In 1970, Mr. Lima donated his exhibit to the City of San Jose and for a few years the display appeared on the lawn area of City Hall. In 1982, a committee was established and a joint venture was formed that became known as Christmas in the Park.

Arts & Cultural Affairs throughout Silicon Valley

On a 175-acre pastoral estate at the foot of the Santa Cruz Mountains in Saratoga, Villa Montalvo unites the vitality of the arts and the tranquility

The San Jose Symphony, over 116 years old, is the oldest orchestra in California and performs Signature, Pops, and KickBack Classics series, Family Concerts, special concerts, and collaborations at a variety of locations. Photo by Pat Kirk.

The Tech Museum of Innovation's hands-on exhibits and labs cover areas of technology such as space, microelectronics, materials, biotechnology, and robotics. **Photo by Pat Kirk.**

The City Lights Theater Company presents plays that are usually adventurous, well acted, and above all, fun. **Photo by Pat Kirk.**

The Rosicrucian Egyptian Museum & Planetarium contains the West's largest collection of Egyptian antiquities and artifacts, including mummies, statuary, and scrolls. **Photo by Pat Kirk.**

The American Musical Theater of San Jose is one of the oldest in the nation and has more subscribers than any other in the country. **Photo by Pat Kirk.**

San Jose Cleveland Ballet is the longest running and successful co-venture in the United States. **Photo by Pat Kirk.**

of a woodland preserve. The Mediterranean style Villa has a guest cottage and octagonal Carriage House surrounded by nature trails.

Villa Montalvo is an historic landmark built in 1912 by Cailfornia's first popularly elected U.S. Senator, James Duval Phelan. Villa Montalvo was Phelan's favorite home and a center of artistic, political, and social life in Northern California. Phelan invited leading writers and artists to work on individual projects. Among his famous guests were Jack London, Ethel Barrymore, and Edward Markham. When Phelan died in 1930, he left Villa Montalvo as a legacy for the support and encouragement of music, art, literature, and architecture.

Today, Villa Montalvo is home to an artist in residency program where, since 1942, it has played host to over 600 artists who are awarded the gift of time to actually live there from one to three months to produce their art. Each year, Villa Montalvo hosts a Performing Arts Series that reaches over 40,000 patrons with a broad range of musical styles, dance, and theater; and the Gallery at Montalvo focuses on the work of Bay Area contemporary artists and Montalvo Artist Residents.

To help support Villa Montalvo, the grounds and facilities are available to host weddings, corporate retreats, annual meetings and social events. A jewel of the arts, Villa Montalvo offers well rounded arts and cultural events for all residents of Silicon Valley.

Within the city of Santa Clara, the Triton Museum of Art was founded by rancher, lawyer, and art patron W. Robert Morgan of San Jose. The Triton Museum collects and exhibits contemporary and historical works with an emphasis on artists of the Greater Bay Area. The permanent collection also includes 19th and 20th century American and Southwest Native American art, Pacific Rim, Europe, and beyond.

In Palo Alto, celebrating their 27th year of outstanding theater, TheaterWorks presents 10 productions each year that include innovative plays and musicals that define our culturally diverse Northern California community. The season runs from June through May at two venues, the Lucie Stern Center in Palo Alto and the Mountain View Center for the Performing Arts. TheaterWorks has been awarded an unprecedented 20 Bay Area Dramalogue Awards, 20 Bay Area Theater Critics Circle Awards, and recognition of its student outreach program. For five years running, TheaterWorks received the Arts Council of Santa Clara County's Community Leadership Award for Achievements in Fostering and Promoting Cultural and Ethnic Diversity in the Arts.

Throughout San Jose and Silicon Valley, arts and cultural affairs are a priority in contributing to the vitality of the community. In Santa Clara County, nonprofit arts organizations endow $70 million a year to our local economy. But the arts make a contribution far beyond their positive economic impact. The arts facilitate individual expression and give voice to our rich cultural diversity. They engage and entertain us and provide a creative and educational outlet for ourselves and our children. The arts and cultural affairs of San Jose and Silicon Valley do make a difference—they provide another substantial benefit to living, working, and playing in San Jose and Silicon Valley. ◆

On a 175-acre pastoral estate at the foot of the Santa Cruz Mountains in Saratoga, Villa Montalvo unites the vitality of the arts and the tranquility of a woodland preserve. The Mediterranean-style Villa, an historic landmark, provides well rounded arts and cultural events for all residents of Silicon Valley. **Photo by Pat Kirk.**

***Throughout San Jose and Silicon Valley, arts and cultural affairs are a priority in contributing to the vitality of the community. They engage and entertain us and provide a creative and educational outlet for ourselves and our children.* Photo by Pat Kirk.**

San Jose Children's Musical Theater (SJCMT) is the largest theater for youth in the nation. Known for its unique policy of casting every child who auditions, SJCMT has been applauded for providing a nurturing environment for children to develop self-esteem and to learn communication skills, theater fundamentals, and the pride of accomplishment. **Photo by Pat Kirk.**

San Jose Stage Company is a community based mid-sized professional theater organization producing contemporary and classical theater in an intimate off-Broadway style setting. **Photo by Pat Kirk.**

Christmas in the Park has become a San Jose holiday tradition. Each year over 100,000 people make their way to view more than 60 magical displays in Plaza de Cesar Chavez. Photo by Pat Kirk.

The American Museum of Quilts & Textiles of San Jose offer regularly changing exhibits that feature contemporary and historical quilts and textiles from around the world as well as from the museum's own collection. **Photo by Pat Kirk.**

The Triton Museum of Art collects and exhibits contemporary and historical works with an emphasis on artists of the Greater Bay Area.
Photo by Pat Kirk.

The San Jose Repertory Theater, the only fully professional regional theater in the South Bay, is committed to responding to the emerging interests of Silicon Valley's diverse population. **Photo by Pat Kirk.**

Chapter Ten

Lifestyle—
Sports & Recreation

10

✦

Leisure time, and how to have more of it, seems to be a dilemma facing everyone these days. In San Jose and Silicon Valley, residents and visitors alike need as much leisure time as they can get to enjoy the many concerts, sporting events, attractions, and beautiful park settings.

It is definitely true that San Jose and Silicon Valley offer something for everyone. A major contributor to live sports and entertainment is the San Jose Arena. The arena, located on West Santa Clara and Montgomery Streets in downtown San Jose, opened in 1993. The $140 million, 450,000-square-foot, state-of-the-art building holds 20,000 seats for concert-goers and 18,000 for hockey fans. In its first year of operation, the arena featured concerts by Barbra Streisand and Luciano Pavarotti.

In addition to the many concert and other entertainment programs at the arena, the facility is home to the San Jose Sharks, a National Hockey League team. Now in its sixth season, the team prompted Silicon Valleyites to quickly catch "Shark Fever." The Sharks unique, dynamic apparel of Pacific teal, black, and gray is worn by sold-out crowds at every game in hockey season. In fact, on Shark game nights, downtown thrives with hockey fans sporting the latest Shark attire and patronizing the many dining establishments.

Besides hockey, other sports are played at the arena as well. In 1994, San Jose was awarded an arena football league team, the SaberCats. The SaberCats played their first game at the San Jose Arena in May, 1995. During their first season, the SaberCats drew 85,193 fans to San Jose Arena for an average of 14,199 per game. And in 1996, the SaberCats surpassed the attendance of Bay Area Major League Baseball six out of seven times.

Just to make sure the San Jose Arena is in constant demand, the San Jose Rhinos Roller Hockey Club began in 1994. The game is very similar to ice hockey in its format and rules. In 1995, the Rhinos were the world

A major contributor to live sports and entertainment is the San Jose Arena. The $140 million, 450,000-square-foot, state-of-the-art building holds 20,000 seats for concert-goers and 18,000 for hockey fans. **Photo by Pat Kirk.**

champions of the league, and the average attendance was up 19 percent selling 5,500 tickets per home game. The roller hockey season runs from June through August with post-season play running into early September.

The arena also has played host to an NHL Hockey All-Star game and college basketball teams at the "sweet sixteen" level of the NCAA playoffs.

The nostalgic song, "Take Me Out to the Ball Game," still resonates strong in many Silicon Valley hearts. At Municipal Stadium, the San Jose Giants are in their tenth season as the Class A affiliate of the San Francisco Giants. Prior to the team's affiliation with the San Francisco Giants, the City of San Jose had a storied history of baseball dating back as early as 1891. The Municipal Stadium itself was built in 1942 as a WPA project. Since that time, it has seen many improvements, with one of its biggest attractions, "Turkey Mike's Barbecue," located just off the third base line. The San Jose Giants have won more games than any other minor league team since 1988 and they are the only minor league team out of 116 full-season organizations to post winning seasons for eight consecutive years.

San Jose and Silicon Valley are now experiencing soccer fever. The San Jose Clash became a charter member of Major League Soccer in June, 1994. The Clash play all home games at San Jose State University's Spartan Stadium and have played to sell-out crowds since their opening.

Women's basketball is booming. Basketball is now the number one youth participation sport in the country for girls. Beginning its first season in October, 1996, the San Jose Lasers are Silicon Valley's hottest new start-up. The Lasers are one of eight teams of the newly created American Basketball League (ABL), the world's premier women's basketball league. The season runs from October to February and all home games are played at the San Jose State University Event Center. The team began its inaugural season with 1996 Olympic Gold Medalist and former Naismith Player of the Year, Jennifer Azzi.

University Athletics

The Spartans of San Jose State University, part of the California State University System, recently entered a new era by joining the Western Athletic Conference (WAC), beginning with the 1996-97 season. WAC is the nation's largest Division l-A conference, the WAC includes 16 member schools from 9 states. The new level of competition is challenging Spartan teams in football, women's volleyball, men's and women's basketball, soccer, golf, judo, swimming, and more.

The Broncos of Santa Clara University field a total of 16 athletic programs, all of which compete at the Division One level. Since the 1992-93

Happy Hollow Park and Zoo in San Jose's Kelley Park offers families a unique combination of fun and adventure. **Photo by Pat Kirk.**

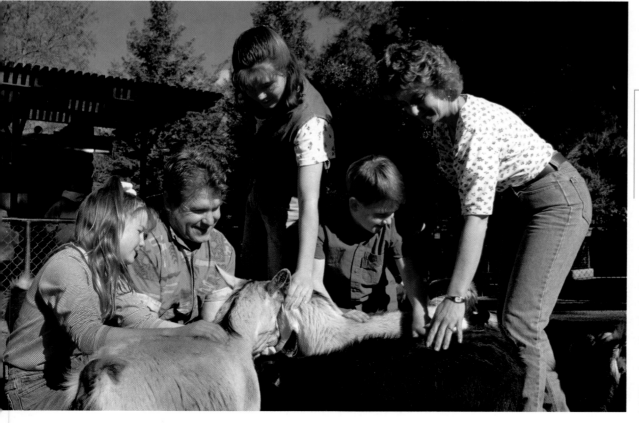

The beautiful and bizarre Winchester Mystery House is a longtime San Jose favorite and is listed in the National Register of Historic Places. With guided tours daily, visitors can see the architectural oddity that was devised by Sarah Winchester, the widow of the rifle heir. **Photo by Pat Kirk.**

academic year, Santa Clara teams have claimed 12 West Coast Conference championships in 6 sports. During that same time frame, 6 Bronco teams (men's basketball, women's soccer, men's soccer, volleyball, baseball, and water polo) have earned national rankings.

Up the Peninsula at Stanford University, the success of its athletic programs was demonstrated by a dramatic 1996 Summer Olympics in Atlanta. Stanford University athletes collected 18 medals—16 gold, 1 silver, and 1 bronze. At Stanford, students have the opportunity to participate in 33 varsity sports and 19 club sports. In addition, over 9,000 students, faculty, and staff participate each year in one of 37 intramural sports. There are also 2,000 students enrolled in 85 physical education classes.

Sporting events are only one resource for San Jose and Silicon Valley. The valley has many attractions that delight residents and visitors alike. Attractions range from mysterious to intriguing and from thrilling to educational.

The beautiful and bizarre Winchester Mystery House is a longtime San Jose favorite and is listed in the National Register of Historic Places. With guided tours daily, visitors can see 110 of the Victorian mansion's

160 rooms containing 47 fireplaces and more than 10,000 windows. The architectural oddity was devised by Sarah Winchester, the widow of the rifle heir.

The world-famous San Jose Flea Market is touted as the largest anywhere. Approximately 2,700 vendors on 125 acres display and sell everything from fruit to furniture. In addition, there is entertainment, food, and refreshments, making a day at the Flea Market an adventure for the entire family.

Happy Hollow Park and Zoo in San Jose's Kelley Park offers families a unique combination of fun and adventure. Amenities include a children's creative amusement park and zoo featuring more than 150 animals. Many of the animals are on the rare and endangered species list and include lemurs, a pygmy hippo, and a jaguar. Children and adults

alike walk through an aviary and a small animal contact area that offer visitors an up-close encounter with both exotic and domestic animals. There are also a variety of play areas, amusement rides for children, and an outstanding puppet theater presenting shows several times a day.

If you are looking for some revitalization during those hot summer months, San Jose's Lake Cunningham Regional Park features Raging Waters, the Bay Area's premier water theme park. Raging Waters has over 30 water attractions including water slides, swimming and diving pools, children's play area, a Polynesian lagoon, a large sandy beach for sunbathing, and much more.

Santa Clara is the home of Northern California's largest family fun park, Paramount's Great America. Open March through September, Great America is a theme park featuring thrilling rides and rollercoasters, the world's largest 3D movie, special rides for tots, and plenty of entertainment for the entire family.

Mission Santa Clara de Asis, located on Santa Clara University campus, offers a good introduction to the Franciscan padres and what they tried to accomplish in pioneer days. Early buildings were destroyed by fire and the mission was rebuilt in 1929.

San Jose Parks

In an area populated by 849,400 residents, San Jose's open space has been thoughtfully planned, and residents can utilize over 3,000 acres of parkland. The city runs 125 developed neighborhood and regional parks, 15 community centers, and seven senior centers. Most centers and park locations offer activities for youth and seniors. Among park amenities are lighted softball fields, soccer fields, basketball courts, public tennis courts, volleyball courts, swimming, barbecue areas, and picnic facilities.

One of the features of driving along Almaden Expressway is Almaden Lake Park. Almaden Lake Park is San Jose's only park featuring an extensive sand beach and swim area, supervised by lifeguards. Visitors can enjoy a range of other recreational activities including fishing, non-power boating, hiking, volleyball, horseshoes, wind surfing, and paddle boating. Adjacent to Almaden Lake Park is the Los Alamitos Creek Trail that features a fitness course that takes you by scenic agricultural lands and riparian communities.

Nestled within the Alum Rock Canyon in the foothills of the Diablo Range, lies Alum Rock Park, California's first and oldest park. Alum Rock Park features 720 acres of natural rugged beauty and provides visitors with outdoor activities such as hiking, horseback riding, bicycling, and family and group picnicking. Residents of San Jose's East Foothills enjoy taking their daily jog as they watch the changing hues of the natural scenery along the 13 miles of trails.

From 1890 to 1932, Alum Rock Park was a nationally known health spa with 27 springs containing seven different minerals. This was the park's most popular period because of its mineral baths, indoor swimming pool, tea garden, restaurant, and dance pavilion. Between World War II and the early 1960s, thousands of visitors came to the park from the booming Santa Clara Valley. The park became so overcrowded that the facilities could no longer be properly maintained and the plant and animal communities were severely endangered. As a result of this overuse, the park underwent a change from a facility with a multitude of uses to a more natural setting emphasizing family outdoor activities.

Offering visitors an opportunity for both recreation and learning about Santa Clara County's agricultural past, Emma Prusch Farm Park sits on 47 acres that were donated in 1962 to the City of San Jose by Emma Prusch. This site was originally the Prusch dairy farm. Upon Emma's death, she deeded the 86-acre farm to the City of San Jose, requesting that the land keep its country feeling, preserving the quality of the Santa Clara Valley. Of the original gift, 11 acres are home to the Police Activities League (P.A.L.) for youth sports, and 47 acres were dedicated in 1962 as the park itself. Today the park features San Jose's largest barn; over 100 community garden plots; acres of open grass for picnicking, kite flying, games, and relaxing; a rare fruit orchard featuring a strawberry tree, wild pear tree, raisin tree, and a grove of international trees; and close encounters with farm animals. In addition, year-round special events that include informative and fun gardening, landscaping classes, cultural festivals, and a seasonal farmers' market are available to the community.

Offering visitors an opportunity for both recreation and learning about Santa Clara County's agricultural past, Emma Prusch Farm Park sits on 47 beautiful acres. **Photo by Pat Kirk.**

Located next to Happy Hollow Park & Zoo in Kelley Park, is San Jose's Japanese Friendship Garden. The Friendship Garden is a lovely, living symbol of the "Sister City" relationship between Okayama, Japan and San Jose. The garden was dedicated in October 1965 and was patterned after Okayama's world famous Korakuen Park. While visiting the garden, take some time to feed the exotic Koi fish.

If you are looking for the perfect setting for walking, reading, nature photography, writing, drawing and painting, or just relaxing, visit

San Jose's Japanese Friendship Garden is a lovely, living symbol of the "Sister City" relationship between Okayama, Japan and San Jose. The garden was dedicated in October 1965 and was patterned after Okayama's world famous Korakuen Park. While visiting the garden, take some time to feed the exotic Koi fish. **Photo by Pat Kirk.**

Nestled within the Alum Rock Canyon in the foothills of the Diablo Range, lies Alum Rock Park, California's first and oldest park. The park features 720 acres of natural rugged beauty and provides visitors with outdoor activities such as hiking, horseback riding, bicycling, and family and group picnicking. **Photo by Pat Kirk.**

The city of Santa Clara is home to the Santa Clara International Swim Center where famous Olympians have trained. **Photo by Pat Kirk.**

Overfelt Gardens. Here visitors enjoy a natural wildlife sanctuary featuring a peaceful pond surrounded by shapely trees, shrubs and flowering plants. The 25 acres were donated to the City of San Jose by Mildred Overfelt in 1959.

Within Overfelt Gardens is the Chinese Cultural Garden, providing a unique opportunity for cultural enrichment. The statuary includes the garden's focal point, an impressive 30-foot bronze and marble statue of the ancient Chinese philosopher Confucius, an ornamental Friendship Gate, and much more.

A hidden treasure in central San Jose is San Jose Municipal Rose Garden. On November 20, 1927, the garden was championed by early members of the Santa Clara County Rose Society when the city council voted to set aside 5 1/2 acres of an 11-acre tract of land at Naglee and Dana Avenues. The Rose Society pledged to provide roses for the new garden.

Today the Rose Garden is one of the most attractive of its kind in the world, drawing thousands of visitors each year from throughout the United States and abroad. The garden is exclusively devoted to shrubs of the rose family and features over 3,500 plants with 189 varieties represented. Every six to eight weeks year-round, there's a new flush of roses with colorful and showy blooms to enjoy. Most of the garden's features have been donated through the years by the Rose Society. The garden now contains a reflecting pool, a structural entrance, an attractive sundial, concrete benches, blue garden vases, a two-tiered water fountain, and miniature rose beds. There is also a natural grass stage surrounded by a cathedral of redwood trees that provides a view of the roses. In May and June, it is common to see school graduations and weddings at this site.

Parks and Attractions around Silicon Valley

Magnificent parks and novel attractions can be found in every city of Silicon Valley. In Campbell, a 30-acre site that was originally Campbell High School has been converted to a community center that features a gym, auditorium, track, tennis courts, and a year-round pool. The Los Gatos Creek Trail bisects the city so that runners, roller bladers, or bicyclists can exercise their way to Los Gatos or San Jose.

Cupertino has 13 parks, a nature preserve, winery, racquet club and many events occurring at DeAnza Community College. Incidentally, DeAnza College also has an art gallery, planetarium, and Flint Center. Flint Center draws many notable Broadway plays, political speakers, and musicians.

Nearby Los Gatos has two parks that are among the nicest in Santa Clara County. Oak Meadow Park has a miniature train and playground that is generally full of children on weekends. Vasona Park has its own reservoir and is part of the Los Gatos Creek Trail. Overall there are 15 parks, 8 playgrounds, 400 acres of open space and plenty of hiking and biking trails in Los Gatos.

Milpitas has more than a solid technological base. It has many family activities that include 21 parks, 11 playgrounds, a new community center and library, and a new aquatics center with four pools. Every sport is offered in Milpitas along with two golf courses and water slides.

Mountain View's location offers Shoreline Park, right on the shore of the San Francisco Bay, where participants can golf, sail, hike, and bike. The Shoreline Amphitheater, located in that same general region, features the top performers in the country for concert performances.

One out of every four acres are parks in Palo Alto. In addition, 1,400 acres in the Santa Cruz Mountains are used by Palo Alto residents only. Palo Alto is also home to Stanford University where the beautiful physical setting and sandstone and red tile architecture are accented by outdoor sculpture.

Besides being the location for Paramount's Great America, Santa Clara has 31 parks and playgrounds. The city is home to the Santa Clara International Swim Center where famous Olympians have trained.

Sunnyvale is home to 17 parks, a tennis center with 13 courts, and Baylands Park. Baylands Park opened in 1993 with 70 acres that link trails to the Bay; picnic tables are available and there is actually a 100-acre wildlife preserve.

With all the work there is to do in San Jose and Silicon Valley, one would surmise that little time is left to enjoy the many concerts, sporting events, attractions, and beautiful park settings. However, in true Silicon Valley spirit, dwellers tend to attack leisure like work. San Jose and Silicon Valley work hard to play hard. Recently, San Jose and Silicon Valley were rated as the nation's number one discretionary income spenders by *American Demographics* magazine. That makes sense with all there is to do and see. The sports and recreation attractions are plentiful and definitely keep San Jose and Silicon Valley on the move. ◆

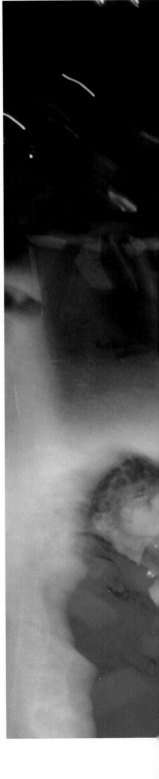

It is definitely true that San Jose and Silicon Valley offer something for everyone. **Photo by Pat Kirk.**

San Jose Sharks hockey team mascot "Sharkey".
Photo by Dana L. Grover.

The San Jose Sharks hockey team prompted Silicon Valleyites to
quickly catch "Shark Fever." The Sharks' unique, dynamic apparel of
Pacific teal, black, and gray is worn by sold-out crowds at every
game in hockey season. **Photo by Dana L. Grover.**

In addition to the many concert and other entertainment programs at the arena, the facility is home to the San Jose Sharks, a National Hockey League team. **Photo by Rocky Widner.**

At Municipal Stadium, the San Jose Giants are in their 10th season as the Class A affiliate of the San Francisco Giants. Photo by Pat Kirk.

The San Jose Giants have won more games than any other minor league team since 1988 and they are the only minor league team out of 116 full-season organizations to post winning seasons for eight consecutive years. **Photo by Ted Orsteen.**

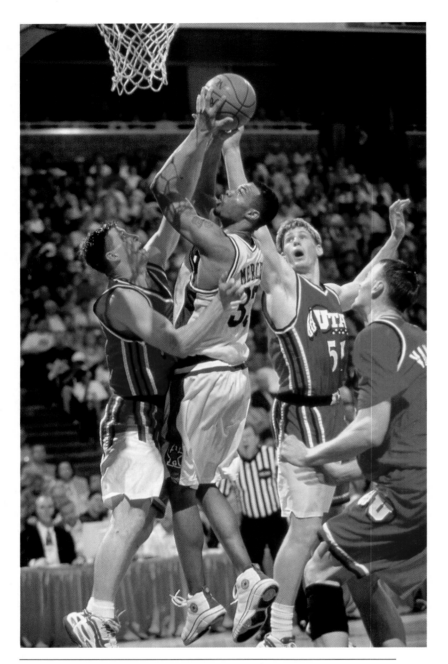

The arena also has played host to an NHL Hockey All-Star game and college basketball teams at the "sweet sixteen" level of the NCAA playoffs. Photo by Rocky Widner.

Magnificent parks and novel attractions can be found in every city of Silicon Valley. In Campbell, a 30-acre site that was originally Campbell High School has been converted to a community center that features a gym, auditorium, track, tennis courts, and a year-round pool. Photo by Pat Kirk.

The San Jose Mercury News *sponsors its annual 10K Run each March, which draws upwards of 10,000 participants and donates a portion of every registration to charity.* **Photo by Pat Kirk.**

Santa Clara is the home of Northern California's largest family fun theme park, Paramount's Great America. The park features thrilling rides and rollercoasters, the world's largest 3D movie, special rides for tots, and plenty of entertainment for the entire family. **Photo by Pat Kirk.**

San Jose's Lake Cunningham Regional Park features Raging Waters, the Bay Area's premier water theme park. Raging Waters has over 30 water attractions including water slides, swimming and diving pools, children's play area, a Polynesian lagoon, a large sandy beach for sunbathing, and much more. Photo courtesy of Raging Waters.

With all the work there is to do in San Jose and Silicon Valley, one would surmise that little time is left to enjoy the many concerts, sporting events, attractions, and beautiful park settings. However, in true Silicon Valley spirit, dwellers tend to attack leisure like work. San Jose and Silicon Valley work hard to play hard. Photo by Pat Kirk.

Photo by Pat Kirk.

Photo by Pat Kirk.

Photo by Pat Kirk.

PART II

Chapter Eleven

Networks

◆

KICU TV 36

Ask most television executives about their stations, and you hear phrases like "market share" and "households reached." But when Jim Evers, president and general manager of KICU TV 36, discusses his station, he talks in terms of *people* and *community*.

Anchor Fred LaCosse interviews a guest on Silicon Valley Business This Week.

"Our station's strength comes from our people and the vibrant Valley we serve," Evers says. "We feel fortunate to live in such a dynamic area and take special pride in the commitment our TV 36 team has to each other, the station, and our community."

An independent, owner-operated television station based in San Jose, TV 36 serves viewers in the Silicon Valley and the Bay Area which comprises the fifth largest television market in the country. KICU's first broadcast aired in October 1967. Since then, it has made its mark with programming that reflects the needs and interests of its diverse audience and a signal that is carried on more than 100 cable systems. KICU offers a variety of programs throughout the broadcast day. Familiar, award-winning off-network shows such as *The Cosby Show, Fresh Prince of Bel-Air, Family Matters, Matlock, Who's the Boss, Dr. Quinn,* and *Family Ties* provide quality fare for family viewing. As the Bay Area's *Eight O'clock Movie Station,* KICU presents a wider range of unique, single-run movies than any other local broadcast station.

Channel 36 is also a serious player in the world of major league sports, offering coverage that includes *Golden State Warriors basketball, San Jose Sharks hockey, San Jose Clash soccer,* and *San Jose Sabercats arena football,* in addition to *local collegiate sports.*

"KICU captures the Silicon Valley audience that wants to be entertained," says Frank Darien, Sr., veteran advertising and marketing executive. "Millions of television advertising dollars are spent each year and nobody knows whether they've done any good or not; but with TV 36, we can see the results and they have been consistently good."

Glenn Hartzheim, president of Capitol Dodge agrees. "I'm a big fan of Channel 36," the long-time San Jose Dodge dealer says, "and so is my clientele. When advertising on KICU, it puts people on my showroom floor. I actually buy more time on TV 36 than an advertising agency would normally recommend simply because the results I get with KICU justify it."

"Besides that," Hartzheim adds, "the TV 36 staff are completely professional and cooperative, their services are excellent, and the station's ownership is local. That means you're talking to people who live and work here, which I like very much."

With its own state-of-the-art, on-site studios and award-winning production crews, KICU produces many of its own programs.

Broadcast live, *High School Sports Focus* features highlights of sports events from more than 140 Bay Area high schools. Studio interviews with players and coaches are also aired. The "Spirit Corner" segment of the program features cheerleading routines and the "Art Wall" segment of the program provides a weekly display gallery of the creative works of high school art students. In addition, once a month, the station awards $1,000 to the general scholarship fund of the high school whose team made the outstanding "Play of the Month."

Darien noted that his client Togo's Eateries recently sponsored a segment of the *High School Sports Focus* program because the chain of

Brian Hall (front) and Robert Gottman at work in KICU Production Control.

KICU Television's management team (left to right) John DuBois, vice president sales; William Beeman, vice president operations; James Evers, president and general manager.

sandwich, salad, and catering shops wanted to increase its exposure to high school-age youth who are both potential consumers and potential employees.

"Recruiting and hiring employees is one of the biggest problems a fast-service franchise has," Darien says. "We did brief sound bites featuring high school kids who work at Togo's, and the reaction has been tremendous." The series of ads has also helped Togo's cement relations with its franchises. KICU tells Darien the school and team they're spotlighting each week. From the 75 Bay Area Togo's, Darien selects the ones closest to the school to be specially mentioned in that week's ad. "Our KICU advertising program has given us much more flexibility in reaching our market, and created a great rapport between franchisee and franchiser."

"*High School Sports Focus* and our other youth-oriented programs help raise public awareness about the positive side of teen activities in the community," says Evers. He and the other local shareholders, John DuBois, vice president of sales and Bill Beeman, vice president of operations, and the entire KICU staff believe so strongly in Silicon Valley's youth that they generously donate their time to such organizations as the Boy Scouts of America, Junior Achievement, Big Brothers-Big Sisters, and many more.

KICU's Community Affairs Program, *Q&A*, helps provide answers to questions about critical issues facing the community. Citizens can ask about issues and have community leaders respond. Throughout the program, the station informs viewers of the names and numbers of governmental and community service organizations that have more information about the topic under discussion.

From its vantage point in the heart of Silicon Valley, KICU understands the global reverberations of local developments in business and

technology. Its program, *Silicon Valley Business This Week*, which has been on the air for over four years is distributed nationally and internationally and is the only Bay Area program entirely dedicated to local high-tech business news. Stories include reports on new technology, mergers and alliances, employment opportunities, as well as newly-developed or introduced products. Each program also offers a personal look at the leadership of some of the country's most exciting companies via face-to-face interview with the Silicon Valley CEO.

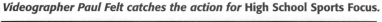

Videographer Paul Felt catches the action for **High School Sports Focus.**

KICU Television's major league sports partners include the San Jose Clash, San Jose Sharks, and Golden State Warriors. **Sports collage photo by Chris Holmes. Soccer photo by John Todd.**

KICU offers complete remote production services. Here, the Creative Services team of Allen Waterous and Steve Dini on location.

"Through Silicon Valley Business This Week, TV 36 has done a lot to give Silicon Valley international visibility," says Armon Mills, publisher of *The Business Journal of San Jose and Silicon Valley*. "Their high-tech news reports and CEO interviews have helped give the world an inside view of what's going on here in Silicon Valley."

"The Federal Communications Commission no longer requires television stations to run public service announcements, so it's hard to get most stations to air them," says Shelly Huff, marketing communications director for the American Cancer Society, Silicon Valley Central Coast Region. "KICU does it without a second thought. By company policy, KICU is active in the community and uses its influence for the public's benefit."

"KICU exemplifies community service in many different ways. They are extremely generous with their resources such as staff time, air time, equipment, facilities, and the KICU Charitable Foundation," says Diane Solinger, development director of the Silicon Valley Chapter of the American Heart Association. "I've lived in other states and have never found a station that gives as much back to the community. They look for long-term projects and relationships because they want to make a significant impact, and then they all work hard to make the project a huge success."

In addition to the American Cancer Society and the American Heart Association some of the other community organizations that benefit from KICU's *volunteer program* are Via Rehabilitation Services, United Way, Salvation Army, San Jose Rotary Club, San Jose Repertory Theatre, and the San Jose Cleveland Ballet.

KICU believes in providing opportunity for growth and advancement for their employees, and today, most of the key management positions are filled with individuals that started their careers with the station. A perfect example is the station's program director, Melissa Tench-Stevens,

KICU's Tammy Ehle creates a sports promo on the AVID editor.

who joined the station as an intern. "She is a key member of our leadership team," says Evers, "and one of the key people responsible for the station's outstanding growth and continued success."

Technology also plays an important role in the operations of TV 36. As part of its plan to transition into digital technology, the station moved into a new 33,000 square foot structure it bought and renovated on Commerce Drive in San Jose.

"The investment in a new facility and state-of-the-art equipment positions KICU TV 36 well for the broadcast industry's conversion to digital technology," says Bill Beeman, vice president of operations. "The speed and flexibility our new digital technology provides has dramatically enhanced the collaborative and the creative process in the station. The new facility includes teleconferencing capability, as well as other services to facilitate the communication needs of the Valley's high-tech community and our advertising clients."

KICU interacts with viewers through such innovations as the TV 36 *Website* available on the Internet, and an *Interactive Voice Response System* that allows callers to receive information as diverse as news and sports and high-tech job openings.

Celebrating its 30th anniversary in 1997, KICU has assembled a team of some of the most talented, creative professionals in broadcasting, many of whom have been recognized with industry awards and corporate honors. Some KICU staff members are also educators, giving back to the community in yet another way, and helping to guide the development of the broadcasters of the future.

"Everyone at TV 36 shares the spirit of volunteerism and service," Solinger says. "I feel really fortunate to have the TV 36 team in our community." ✦

KICU Sports Director Robert Braunstein introduces a local high school football team on High School Sports Focus.

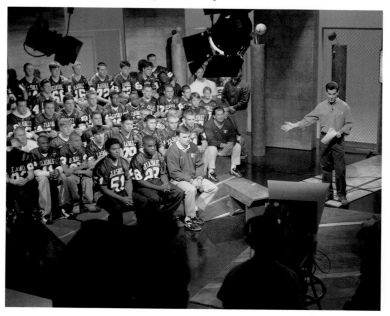

THE BUSINESS JOURNAL SERVING SAN JOSE & SILICON VALLEY

"This business journal started because its founder, Mike Russell, read *Megatrends*," explains Publisher Armon L. Mills. "The book said, 'If you want to be part of something new, go to Silicon Valley.' So he did, and here we are."

When *The Business Journal Serving San Jose & Silicon Valley* was founded in 1983 under the name *The San Jose Business Journal*, Apple Computer hadn't invented the Macintosh, downtown San Jose didn't have much of a skyline, and the amount of computing power you can get today for less than a hundred dollars carried a $5,000 price tag.

The valley was smaller, less diverse, less sophisticated—and so were most of its businesses.

"This newspaper was founded by a feisty Kansas City, Missouri-based startup company called American City Business Journals, the brainchild of a couple of Midwestern entrepreneurs," Mills says.

"As one of the people from corporate to come out to San Jose in the

early days, I remember the palpable sense of excitement in the air. Then, as now, Silicon Valley was one of the cutting-edge places, an area where people turned their dreams from garage ventures to million- and even billion-dollar companies."

From a handful of employees at the start, *The Business Journal* has grown to a staff of about 40. It has expanded its market area from San Jose to the broader environs of Silicon Valley, and now covers all of Santa Clara County plus the southern

The Business Journal has expanded its market area from San Jose to the broader environs of Silicon Valley, and now covers all of Santa Clara County plus the southern part of Alameda County.

All of The Business Journal's reporting and research is done in-house, and its stories are generated by its local editorial staff through their contacts or through legal filings. Pictured are (left to right) Malcolm Maclachlan, Dennis Taylor, Danna Bergstrom, Lorna Fernandes, Alastair Goldfisher, Larry Barrett, and Pete Barlas.

part of Alameda County. It has grown to become the second largest newspaper in the Amerian City Business Journal chain, and one of its most successful.

It has changed locations, formats, features, most staff members, and even its ownership twice. In 1988, the paper was sold to MCP, Inc. Five years later, American City Business Journals bought it back.

The Business Journal has blossomed from a local business upstart to the premier business-focused publication in Silicon Valley, an essential tool for local business providing breaking news and useful information that's just not available anywhere else.

"You can look at the business sections of other newspapers, but for an all-business publication, you come to us," says Managing Editor Bernie Silver. "We cover more industries and a broader area of valley business in order to give our readers what we think they want."

When it comes to learning what its readers actually want, *The Business Journal* doesn't guess. It stays well informed about reader views and preferences by keeping its ears close to the business "ground" and by conducting regular surveys.

"Readers tell us they spend about half an hour each week reading *The Business Journal* because it keeps them abreast of what's happening with Silicon Valley business, and because it gives them practical information they can apply in their own companies," Silver says. "They tell us consistently that they feel obligated to read *The Journal* as a part of running their businesses."

The Business Journal readers are business owners, CEOs, and leading executives of corporations in the valley–a high-quality, influential audience more than 50,000 strong, of whom about 15,000 are paid subscribers. And they renew at an impressive 76 percent rate.

The mission of this publication has always been to provide the best coverage of local businesses anywhere; however, its focus has shifted over the years to reflect the changes in the valley and in its readership.

Some of its reporting beats have been established from the get-go.

One–commercial real estate remains a strong area of coverage, but has evolved and expanded to encompass residential real estate and redevelopment.

Financial services is another "veteran" reporting beat at the journal. But where in the early years its focus was strictly reporting on banks, savings and loans, and traditional financial service providers, today *The Journal*

Armon Mills, *The Business Journal's publisher.*

includes issues of corporate finance and initial public offerings. "We give extensive coverage to the venture capital community, too," Silver says. "Ten years ago that community was practically non-existent here."

Technology is a vital continuing area of emphasis, of course, with two reporting beats–one covering chips and related businesses, the other focusing on the computer industry and its close industrial relatives.

Health care has emerged as an important new area of focus for *The Journal*, as have small business and retail. "Most of our readers are

Throughout the year, the journal puts out a wide variety of special publications—primarily magazines and industry reports.

associated with small to mid-sized businesses," Silver notes. "Although we certainly give thorough coverage to the Apples, the Intels, the IBMs, and the H-Ps, our focus more and more is on small business."

Highly influential in the country's economy, small business has created more jobs than any other sector, and continues to lead the economy in growth. "We feel we owe it to our readers to keep them well informed about what's happening on the small-business front," Silver said.

The Business Journal's focused coverage of two newer areas of growing interest to business readers–education and the not-for-profit community–has made it the leader in reporting on those subjects.

"We're also increasing our coverage of minorities and women," Silver says. "There are more ethnic- and women-owned businesses than ever. We pay close attention to that."

Its constant fine-tuning is something in which *The Journal* takes pride. "We're always reevaluating," Silver says. "Even though the feedback we get says that *The Journal* is highly respected in the valley, we're forever trying to tweak the paper to better serve the needs of our readers."

Its reader-service emphasis is what led *The Business Journal* to establish its own Internet Website. With hyperlinks to the other 35 Business Journals owned by American City, the site is growing fast in reader

popularity. With one of the most sophisticated computer systems of any weekly business journal–and even some major urban dailies–*The Journal*'s technology puts it "definitely at the forefront nationwide," according to former Managing Editor Michael Krey.

Throughout the year, *The Journal* puts out a wide variety of special publications–primarily magazines and industry reports. One of the best known is its *Book of Lists*, which details the top companies in the valley in a growing roster of categories from business services to real estate, from technology to retail. The publication is widely seen as such a useful business development tool

The Business Journal's *editors are* (standing left to right) **Aldo Maragoni, Kat Bryant,** and (seated) **Bernie Silver.**

that it often inspires readers to subscribe so they can receive the focused industry list updates carried in each weekly issue.

Who's Who, Technology Silicon Valley, Silicon Valley Money, Marketing Silicon Valley, Bay Area Market Fact Guide, Entrepreneurial Magazine, Structures, Commercial Real Estate, Small Business Strategies, and *Family Business* are among the notable variety of special publications that attest to the depth of *The Business Journal*'s research capability.

"*The Business Journal* is fairly famous nationwide for putting out one of the biggest, most complete *Book of Lists* of any business journal anywhere," Krey says. "And its special publications–with their meaty content and beautiful look–are among the highest quality published by any business journal."

What's more, every bit of that reporting and research is done inhouse. "We don't rely on wire services," Mills says. "All our stories are generated by our local editorial staff through their contacts or through legal filings."

With such heavy business-to-business visibility, advertisers aren't shy about singing *The Journal*'s praises. "We can cite specific new business from stale prospects that were rekindled as a direct result of our *Business Journal* program," said T.W. Ireland, C.P.A., managing partner of Ireland San Filippo & Company.

Cliff Mohr, fleet manager of Frontier Infiniti, reports a 15 percent increase in business "each time we ran our ad."

Doug Holliday, San Jose Live's marketing manager says, "I am very satisfied with the results generated from our advertising with *The Journal*. Banquet sales are up 23 percent over last year."

And according to William Payson, president of The Senior Staff, "Our classified display advertising in *The Business Journal* is one of the smartest moves we ever made. Currently, we are obtaining five or six solid responses every week, each one of which could pay for the cost of the ad."

"Our real commitment is to the local business community," Mills observes. "That's where it starts with the editorial product–commitment."

The Business Journal *has always strived to be first to bring its readers the news of Silicon Valley's business community, and to present that news fairly and accurately.*

That commitment extends to the entire Silicon Valley community, as well. Through volunteer service on the boards of such organizations as the YMCA, Junior Achievement, Repertory Theatre, Boy Scouts of Santa Clara County, KTEH (the Silicon Valley-based public broadcasting station), and more. *The Journal*'s staff make it a point to give back for the benefit of others.

The Business Journal's donations of time and effort, together with more than $100,000 a year in advertising space and sponsorship of community service organizations and events, make a major difference in the quality of life in the valley. That's why *The Journal* and its publisher have been honored more than once by the nonprofit community for their many contributions to charitable organizations throughout Silicon Valley–most recently with a media award presented by HOPE Rehabilitation Services and the Silver Hope Award presented by the National Multiple Sclerosis Society.

Chip Jones, The Business Journal's *production manager.*

Even with all the changes over the years, there have been two important constants. One is *The Business Journal*'s mission. "We have always strived to be first to bring our readers the news of Silicon Valley's business community, and to present that news fairly and accurately," Mills says. That's what they did when they started out and that's what they do today.

"We like to think we do it better than anybody, and we believe the proof of that is in the growth of our paid circulation, which has increased significantly over the years."

The second constant in *The Journal* story is the people of Silicon Valley. "Sure, many names and faces have changed in the past few decades, but it is our readers and advertisers who have been the key to our success," Mills observes. "Without their support and enthusiasm over the years, *The Business Journal* wouldn't have survived, let alone thrived. And today it is healthier than ever before."

As *The Business Journal* looks toward the future, it pledges to continue with the mission it committed to at its outset–to serve its readers with the best coverage of local business news.

"To that end, we will not rest on our laurels. If anything, we will work even harder as we move forward." Mills vows. "And as Silicon Valley's business community continues to change, our readers will be the first to know about it." ✦

The Business Journal's *managing editor, Bernie Silver.*

THE SAN JOSE MERCURY NEWS

When the first gaslights appeared on the streets of San Jose in 1861, *The San Jose Mercury News* was already celebrating its 10th anniversary under its original name, *The San Jose Weekly Visitor*. That was just one year after California was admitted to the United States, English became the official state language, and the Pueblo de San Jose de Guadalupe became the city of San Jose.

The San Jose Mercury–named in part because of Almaden Valley's thriving mercury mines–became San Jose's first daily newspaper on Election Day, November 5, 1861, three years before the first railroad came to town.

"We've been here from the beginning, recording the history of San Jose," says Jay T. Harris, *Mercury News* publisher and chairman. "More importantly, we share in that history. *The Mercury News* has always made a vital contribution to the community, while the innovative spirit of Silicon Valley shapes our own growth and progress."

Every day, more than a quarter of a million newspapers roll off the presses—and the quality has to match the quantity.

When former New Yorker James Jerome (J.J.) Owen became publisher, the telephone had only just arrived in San Jose. Owen incorporated the newspaper in 1877, on the heels of his personal crusade to bring San Jose into the "electric age." By 1881, his relentless campaigning had worked. San Jose had an instant landmark in its 237-foot Electric Light Tower, and J.J. became a local hero.

By 1942, *The Mercury-Herald*, as it was then known, had become a full-fledged metropolitan daily, with morning and evening editions. Ten years later, the morning *Mercury* and the evening *News* were sold to Northwest Publications, a Minnesota-based newspaper chain headed by Bernard Ridder. Northwest merged in 1974 with Miami-based Knight Corporation to form Knight-Ridder Newspapers (now Knight-Ridder, Inc.), a publicly held company, one of the biggest newspaper chains in America, and owner still of *The Mercury News*.

Bernard's son, Joseph, served as publisher of the two San Jose dailies until 1977, when his nephew P. Anthony (Tony) Ridder was appointed to the position. Tony Ridder now heads up the Knight-Ridder corporation. 1986, the year Tony's successor, William A. Ott, became publisher was also the year *The Mercury News* won the prestigious Pulitzer Prize award for International Reporting, based on its extensive series of articles exposing the graft of the Marcos regime

*The **Mercury News** has been based on Ridder Park Drive since 1967.*

in the Philippines. The paper won a second Pulitzer Prize in 1989 under the leadership of publisher Larry Jinks for its coverage of the Loma Prieta earthquake.

In 1992, without missing a day of publication, the last letterpress was removed and *The Mercury News* switched entirely to state-of-the-art offset presses. The only Linotype machine to be found at the newspaper now is the polished museum piece gracing its lobby.

The next year, the paper launched Mercury Center Online, the first electronic version of *The Mercury News*. Acclaimed as the best newspaper on the Web by *Editor & Publisher* magazine and others, Mercury Center has rapidly grown to become the online "Center of Silicon Valley." Thousands of users from around the world explore complete contents of the paper's daily news, as well as additional features, such as:

"Good Morning Silicon Valley." Aimed at power users who want to jump-start their morning, and updated throughout the day, this service delivers the latest high-tech, stock market, and Silicon Valley buzz, giving users a cutting-edge view of the business of high technology.

"Talent Scout." Silicon Valley's complete high-tech recruitment center and a natural magnet for the area's top talent, includes searchable Mercury News Classified ads, a resume database, and online career advice.

"Digital High." With content created by and for teen-agers, this Mercury Center service attracts a younger, Internet-savvy audience with features that include links to dozens of Silicon Valley high school newspapers.

"Yellowpages." A directory of 16 million businesses nationwide that allows users to search by name, category, and location—and to get street maps and directions to the businesses they choose. Options for advertisers include expanded listings with artwork, hyperlinks to their own Web pages, and direct responses to their e-mail addresses or fax machines.

"Television." TV-related news and features, along with television listings make this the ultimate television guide.

"News Library." A searchable library of *Mercury News* articles dating back to 1985, plus comparable libraries for several other major U.S. newspapers.

The clattering typewriters and teletype machines are long gone, but the newsroom is never silent.

"Newshound." A highly customizable intelligent agent for business professionals and consumers, allows subscribers to search for information they specify from breaking news stories on multiple newspaper and newswire databases. Newshound delivers this information straight to the subscriber's e-mail box.

"Connections." A full service feedback area that puts readers in direct contact with *Mercury News* reporters, columnists, and editors through forums and e-mail.

Mercury Centers also offers a variety of innovative extras, such as "The Last Best Thing," an interactive satire of Silicon Valley, which was published in book form by Simon & Schuster.

Now known as "The Newspaper of Silicon Valley," *The Mercury News* has matched the valley's growth in complexity and maturity. "We've had to broaden our focus to do the job," says Leigh Weimers, a well-known columnist for the paper.

Mercury News *publisher and chairman Jay T. Harris started his career as a reporter. He went on to become executive editor of the* **Philadelphia Daily News** *and a vice president of Knight-Ridder, the newspaper's parent company.*

Despite the computer revolution—or perhaps because of it—sales of the newspaper itself continue to climb. Figures from the Audit Bureau of Circulations, released in 1996, showed daily paid circulation at 288,572 copies, while Sunday paid circulation reached 351,197. *The Mercury News* is one of the nation's ten top-ranked newspapers in circulation growth.

Although the bulk of *Mercury News* readers live in Santa Clara County, the newspaper reaches from San Francisco to Monterey and has a growing presence in southern Alameda County, the Peninsula, and neighboring areas.

Product Distribution, where preprinted materials are added and the finished newspapers are bundled for delivery.

Bob Ryan, director of Mercury Center.

The more than 1,500 employees of *The Mercury News* work at its modern headquarters facility in San Jose and at its 13 bureau offices throughout Northern California, as well as in Hanoi, Los Angeles, Mexico City, Tokyo, and Washington D.C.

As has the paper itself, *The Mercury News* employees have enthusiastically supported the community since its earliest days. Their many thousands of volunteer service hours benefit a long list of community organizations that runs the gamut from the Tech Museum and San Jose Repertory Theatre to Second Harvest Food Bank and United Way, as well as community events from the Silicon Valley Charity Ball to Cinco de Mayo and The Tet Festival.

The Mercury News and its employees "actively support everything from arts groups and human service agencies to small grass-roots programs helping people on a neighborhood level," says Publisher Jay T. Harris.

The Mercury News is one of the valley's major corporate sponsors of community programs and events, and host of a number of its own—including its Gift of Reading program, a literacy project that collects thousands of books for underprivileged children each December; its annual 10K Run, which draws upwards of 10,000 participants and donates a portion of every registration to charity; and its well-known Holiday Wish Book, which invites readers to fulfill the wishes of individuals and groups in need.

Honored with scores of major awards, *The Mercury News* demonstrates its strong sense of community in a number of other ways as well. One example is the paper's coverage of the 1989 Loma Prieta earthquake. Despite the 7.1 tremor that rocked the Bay Area on October 17, *The Mercury News* published and delivered a complete edition the next morning—even to subscribers in the hard-hit Santa Cruz mountains. Through the following days, the newspaper was an essential source of information for the entire region.

"Our goal is to be an information source and public forum that serves all the people of Silicon Valley," Harris says, "a modern version of the town square where everybody can hear and be heard."

This commitment to inclusiveness shows up in the paper's newsroom, too. With nearly one quarter of its professional newsroom staff either Latino, Asian-American, or African-American, *The Mercury News* has one of the best diversity records of any major news organization in the country.

Responsiveness to the needs of the entire community also drives one of the paper's newest initiatives—*Nuevo Mundo*, a free Spanish-language weekly. Launched in May of 1996, this innovative publication targets the large segment of the market who prefer to receive the news in Spanish.

Highlighting "news you can use," as well as local, national, and international news, sports, and features, *Nuevo Mundo* was an immediate hit with Hispanic readers and community leaders, quickly gaining prominence as the Hispanic newspaper of record in the Bay Area.

Nuevo Mundo Editor Larry Romero was a *Mercury News* reporter and editor for 17 years prior to his current assignment. The veteran journalist, son of farmworkers, brings insight as well as knowledge and experience to *Nuevo Mundo*.

The Mercury News has opened new frontiers in journalism for over a century, earning international recognition. "We are the newspaper of Silicon Valley," says Executive Editor Jerry Ceppos, "and our mission is to provide the best coverage of Silicon Valley's business and technology anywhere."

At the same time, the paper is committed to being the best hometown paper in the Bay Area. For example, the Celebrations section of *The Mercury News* helps to preserve the valley's traditional small-town flavor in the face of its big-city size and futuristic technology.

"Even though Silicon Valley is the economic and technological center of the planet, with Celebrations we are capturing why this is the best place in the world to live," Ceppos said. "This section sometimes has more emotion and interest to it than the rest of the paper because readers are telling us what's important to them."

In yet another precedent-setting move, *The Mercury News* created a newsroom-based, full-time position for listening to and talking with readers, and then making the results of those conversations a part of the paper.

The Reader Representative is the voice of the reader within the paper, participating in most newsroom decisions and fostering "dialogues between the journalists and the readers."

For nearly 150 years *The Mercury News* has recorded the day-to-day history of San Jose, charting the city's evolution from a tiny pueblo to the heart of Silicon technological innovation and an unwavering commitment to the community.

Whatever the future holds for Silicon Valley, it's a certainty that *The Mercury News* will have the full story. ✦

Larry Romero, editor of Nuevo Mundo.

Every March, thousands of runners turn out for the Mercury News 10K Run/5K Walk.

SANTA CLARA VALLEY WATER DISTRICT

Silicon Valley is in a part of the world where residents can simply turn on the tap and out pours drinkable water. Most people give little thought to how it got there, where it came from, or how it was made safe for their use.

But one agency in the valley–the Santa Clara Valley Water District–works full time on these issues. Established by voters in 1929, the district today reflects the consolidation of four geographical districts into a single countywide agency. It is governed by a seven-member board of directors–five elected and two appointed by the county board of supervisors.

The work of the district centers on the county's supply of water: getting it, managing it for beneficial uses, making sure it's safe to drink, and preventing its doing damage–as a result of flooding, for example.

Water Supply and Water Quality

The district manages 10 local reservoirs, two major groundwater basins, three drinking-water treatment plants, three pumping stations, a hydroelectric plant, hundreds of miles of improved creeks and rivers, 18 percolation facilities, and an extensive in-county water distribution system.

In a normal year, rainwater captured by local reservoirs and the area's groundwater basins provides less than half of the county's water supply. As a result, the district must also import water from sources outside the region. Surface water originating in northern and eastern California rivers is purchased and transported through the State Water Project and the federal Central Valley Project for use in Silicon Valley.

Because groundwater is naturally cleansed as it moves through the soil, well water is considered safe to drink without disinfection or artificial filtration. Even so, the district operates a groundwater monitoring program to check for pollution and track changes in quality.

Surface water, on the other hand, must be purified. Applying a complex treatment process, the district's three water treatment plants transform raw surface water into high-quality water that's safe to drink.

As Santa Clara County's wholesale water supplier, the district delivers and sells its treated water to retailers, including city water departments and private water companies, which, in turn, sell water to residential and business consumers.

In 1995, the district purified and delivered approximately 107,000 acre-feet of water suitable for drinking. (One acre-foot represents about

The Guadalupe River Flood Control Project will help protect downtown San Jose from floods and is also the site of a beautiful river park.

326,000 gallons–the amount of water it takes to cover one acre to a depth of one foot.) About 161,000 acre-feet of groundwater was pumped; and water retailers obtained and distributed another 76,000 acre-feet from San Francisco's Hetch Hetchy system. Santa Clara County thus used roughly 345,000 acre-feet of water in 1995.

Traditionally, Santa Clara County's groundwater has been of very high quality. However, although soil filters out bacteria and most other pollutants, society now knows that soil can't filter out everything. Man-made chemicals can seep into the groundwater from a variety of sources: illegal dumping, surface spills, landfills, septic systems, leaking underground storage tanks, and improperly built or maintained wells.

That's why prevention and elimination of groundwater contaminants through ongoing programs of education and action have become an important part of the water district's work. In cooperation with government agencies, private industry and the public, the district helps lead efforts to monitor, protect and, as needed, to restore the purity of the county's groundwater.

Flood Protection

Floods along the county's 700 miles of creeks and rivers and high tides along the 12 miles of San Francisco Bay shoreline have periodically wreaked costly damage on homes and property. Protecting the county from floods is another major concern of the water district.

The valley floor is a natural plain that has flooded many times. As industrial development unfolded in the South Bay, the area was quickly

Uvas Reservoir is one of the district's 10 water supply reservoirs.

carpeted with shopping centers, housing developments, roads, and industrial complexes. Still, only a trickle of money was available through the 1950s to address issues of flood control and channel improvements.

It took a huge flood in 1955 to make the need for greater funding painfully apparent. On Christmas Eve, a massive storm deluged the valley's creeks. The resulting flood overran hundreds of homes. It uprooted trees and clogged waterways. It swept away cars and blocked countless culverts. That disaster helped the community understand the enormity of the flood problem in the valley. And the district began getting the funds it needed to take action. Major floods since then, in 1963, '69, '72, '83 and '86, have reminded residents of the valley's vulnerability to too much water.

Over the past 25 years, the district has worked with public committees in five flood control zones to complete more than $100 million in flood protection projects—more than any local flood control agency in California. A key project currently under construction is the $139 million Guadalupe River Flood Control Project. This project will help protect the San Jose downtown area from flood damages that could reach into billions of dollars. In addition, the project is a highly innovative design that incorporates a beautiful river park and recreational uses.

While an estimated $600 million in flood protection work remains, the 1990s have ushered in an era of funding cutbacks. The district has therefore launched a Comprehensive Flood Management Project that will asses the future direction and priorities of its flood protection work.

Water Resource Management for Today and Tomorrow

In managing the county's water resources, the district attempts to satisfy many diverse objectives, including water reliability, high-quality drinking water, water recycling and conservation, flood protection,

Ozonation is one alternative way to disinfect water.

environmental protection and accessible recreational areas.

Through innovative programs like "Adopt-A-Creek," which invites hands-on help from the public in creek cleaning projects, the district seeks and values the public's role in its water management strategies. Indeed, many district programs—particularly water conservation—are dependent on public understanding and participation. During the 1987-1992 drought, the public responded to the need for conservation by cutting back on water consumption by as much as 30 percent.

Looking to the future, the district has developed a process for mapping out Santa Clara County's long-term water supply program. Called IWRP (Integrated Water Resources Plan), this approach updates the district's 20-year-old master plan, incorporating input from all major stakeholders: the general public, businesses, community and environmental groups, water companies, farmers and water district professionals. Ways to enhance water conservation and recycling, more effective means for surface and groundwater storage, and viable approaches to water transfers—all these options and more are explored in the IWRP process.

As this century comes to a close, the Santa Clara Valley Water District remains committed to meeting these water management challenges so that county residents can continue to enjoy protection from flooding and a safe, reliable water supply. ✦

The Alamitos Groundwater Recharge Pond is one of more than 75 recharge facilities managed by the water district.

KNTV-TV Channel 11

is a perfect fit for Silicon Valley, which is known throughout the world for its entrepreneurial spirit.

"In market after market, our stations have built the number-one or number two news operation," says Granite chairman and CEO W. Don Cornwell. "All our stations compete effectively in their markets, routinely beating competitors from larger broadcast companies."

In a part of the world as kaleidoscopic as Silicon Valley, home to the headquarters or corporate office of nearly every high-technology company on earth, the importance of daily news simply can't be understated. And day in, day out, 365 days a year, award-winning KNTV-11 broadcasts such a comprehensive line-up of news programming from early morning to late at night that it has become the dominant news and information source for the 530,000 homes in this sophisticated region.

Known as The San Jose NewsChannel, KNTV is the only full-service network-affiliated VHF television station in San Jose, the eleventh largest city in the United States and the "capital" of Silicon Valley.

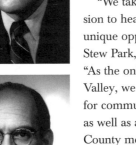

"We take our news mission to heart and see it as a unique opportunity," says Stew Park, the station's president and general manager. "As the only television news service focusing on Silicon Valley, we are an important public information vehicle for community service and community programming, as well as a vital advertising resource for Santa Clara County merchants."

KNTV's roots in this vibrant region span more than four decades. In fact, the station's site has been designated a San Jose Historic Landmark.

Started by Sunlight Bakery owner A.T. Gilliland and his son, Allen, KNTV signed on the air September 12, 1955–a time when Santa Clara County was strictly an agricultural area populated with approximately 100,000 households.

Sold to Landmark Communications in 1978, the station sharpened its emphasis on local news, maintained its strong commitment to the community, and enjoyed impressive growth. In 1990 KNTV was sold to the current owners, Granite Broadcasting Corporation.

Granite, a young, minority-owned company based in New York City, owns and/or operates eleven stations throughout the U.S. The highly entrepreneurial approach of Granite and KNTV to station management

W. Don Cornwell (top) Granite Broadcasting's chairman and CEO; Stuart J. Beck (center) Granite Broadcasting's president, acquired KNTV in 1990; Stewart B. Park (bottom) KNTV's president and general manager, has been with the station since 1962.

The KNTV sign and studios are familiar sights at the corner of Park Avenue and Montgomery Street. The location has been named a historic landmark as the site of San Jose's first television station.

"The broadcasting industry is steeped in grand traditions. Enormous opportunities await those who can build upon those traditions, enlarging the boundaries which limit the industry's growth," he said. "By continually creating forums for innovation, that's just what we're trying to do."

Among those innovations is "11 Online," KNTV's web information site–one of the first television interactive sites in the country.

Debuting February 1, 1996, 11 Online lets the growing legions of Internet surfers easily access local news headlines, weather forecasts, sports information, news features, health tips, recipes, program schedules, and much more. Via "The Homework Home Page"–a valuable educational tool–kids can tap into links providing information and resources in subject areas including English, math, science, literature, government, social sciences, and lots more.

Future plans for 11 Online include a Silicon Valley Mall to serve as a cyberspace shopping place offering everything from automobiles to supermarkets, real estate to restaurants, home entertainment to financial institutions–and keeping KNTV on television's cutting edge of technology.

11 Online is also an easy way for viewers to communicate with the station. "Up to now, television has been a one-way form of communication. The only feedback we got was from the ratings," says Roberto Munoz, managing news editor. "Now we can actually get feedback and story ideas directly from viewers."

KNTV's innovations aren't limited to technology, either. Its proud record of commitment to the region's various communities has spawned a host of innovative, community-focused programs and events. "KNTV has a history of producing news documentaries and specials that tackle local issues like education, transportation, and the valley's economy," Park said, "and supporting community efforts through nonprofit and civic activities."

When it comes to community, KNTV has always taken a leadership role. In a series of specials, for example, KNTV has chronicled the rebirth of San Jose's downtown core including the Grand Opening of the Fairmont Hotel, a Grand Opening Preview of the Children's Discovery Museum, the Dedication of the refurbished St. Joseph Cathedral, the Grand Opening of the new wing of the San Jose Museum of Art; among others.

KNTV's "Share The Spirit" program makes it possible for local businesses to bring many special local television programs to the community, including the "Fujitsu/KNTV Run For The Kids," coverage of an annual 8K race that has raised hundreds of thousands of dollars for local children's charities; "Packard Children's Health Van 11," a special reporting on the accomplishments of a mobile pediatrics clinic for children in need operated by the Lucille Salter Packard Children's Hospital at Stanford in conjunction with KNTV; "Portraits of Success," saluting outstanding citizens in the Hispanic community; and more.

KNTV's main control room is the hub of on-air operations during the production of local programs, including more than 1,700 local newscasts each year.

KNTV has also promoted and focused public attention on such valuable projects as the Second Harvest Food Bank's "Holiday Food Drive," Alpha Cab's "Life Rides" program, and "Volunteer Line 11," an innovative part of 11 Online that allows people to review volunteer jobs and sign up on line.

All that quality and commitment hasn't gone unnoticed. KNTV's local programming has distinguished itself with many local and national awards, including "Best Newscast" in the local Emmys, the Associated Press Awards, and the Radio and Television News Directors Association Awards, as well as the prestigious Iris award for "Best Local

The San Jose NewsChannel is the only television news organization headquartered in Santa Clara County. KNTV reporters are at work 365 days a year reporting local news.

Magazine Program" given by the National Association of Television Program Executives.

"Over the past 40 years, this once-agrarian valley has been transformed into the technology center of the world, and KNTV has been in the center of it all," Park says. "As Silicon Valley's leading television news organization, we get great insight into where technology, and therefore much of society, is going."

KNTV's niche in one of America's most affluent television markets is much envied—and well deserved. "We attribute our success to our dedication to the local community," observes Park. "Lives are touched by what we do; businesses and organizations are affected. That's why we feel our special community obligations so keenly."

KNTV is more than Silicon Valley's preferred source of community news—it is one of the valley's truly extraordinary community citizens. ✦

EMPIRE BROADCASTING

A t a time when locally owned radio stations are being gobbled up by large national corporations, Empire Broadcasting is one of the few companies whose principals are permanent residents of the community in which they own stations.

Empire Broadcasting, which owns and operates radio stations KLIV-AM (all news format), KARA-FM (soft pop music), and KRTY-FM (country music), was born in 1967 in Rochester, New York. That's when a group of executives of an AM-FM radio-combine in that city tried to buy a station of their own. Based on their successful track record, they succeeded in raising money for a radio station purchase in Rochester—but the deal fell through.

Instead, they found themselves considering a radio station 3,000 miles away, "in some place called San Jose, California," says Bob Kieve, president and co-owner of Empire Broadcasting, who, at 74, has been called "the dean of San Jose radio."

The executives liked the radio station and discovered they could afford it. So they bought it and began to run it. That station was KLIV.

Five years later, they bought a second station in Santa Clara. Christening it "KARA in Santa Clara," they turned it into a commercial and broadcasting success.

In five more years, they bought two additional stations in Auburn, California, renaming the FM station K-HYL (because it was on a hill overlooking Sacramento). Acting quickly, they increased K-HYL's power, and converted it into a Sacramento station.

About that time, California's economy took off, and so did the fortunes of its radio stations.

By 1983, Empire's Rochester stockholders decided to cash in on their investment. In a "split-off arrangement," they traded their stock in Empire's Silicon Valley radio station holdings for ownership of the Sacramento arm of the business, which they later resold. "We had originally bought the Sacramento stations for $500,000," notes Kieve. "And when the Rochester investors sold the stations just three years after their split-off from Empire, they got $8 million."

One of Empire Broadcasting's four mobile units in front of the broadcasting headquarters.

Today, almost 70 percent of Empire Broadcasting's stock is owned by people who run and work at the radio stations. Of the stockholders, Bob Kieve; Vince Lopopolo, executive vice president of Empire Broadcasting and general manager of KLIV; and John McLeod, vice president of programming, have been associated with Empire Broadcasting for nearly three decades. And they've been active residents of the San Jose area for the same period of time.

Do they believe in locally owned radio? They sure do! What's more, they're all deeply involved in the community as volunteers for such beneficial groups as the Symphony, the San Jose Metropolitan Chamber of Commerce, the Salvation Army, the Convention/Visitors Bureau, the American Musical Theatre, and others. As a result, they feel they know what the needs of the community are...and what their stations can do about those needs. If history is any judge, they're absolutely right. ✦

The morning broadcasters gather for a group picture. From left to right are: Kim Vestal, 15-year wake-up deejay on KARA; Gary Scott Thomas, one of the KRTY morning personalities; Jane McMillan, long-time morning anchor on KLIV-News; and "Jungle Doug" Griffin (seated), the other member of the KRTY team.

SAN JOSE INTERNATIONAL AIRPORT

In 1939, Hewlett Packard Company began manufacturing electronic devices in David Packard's Palo Alto garage. That same year, Ernest Renzel, Jr., a young San Jose businessman and aviation enthusiast, orchestrated the purchase of 483 acres as a site for the planned San Jose Municipal Airport.

Those two independent events initiated the technology revolution that is transforming the world. Over the ensuing decades, Santa Clara Valley would evolve into Silicon Valley, the global center of high technology. And the land Ernie Renzel optioned would become home to San Jose International Airport, Gateway to Silicon Valley.

Because technology requires transport, San Jose International Airport serves as a business partner to the world's leading technology companies. As the fourth busiest Airport in California, San Jose International's two terminals host 13 commercial airlines that arrive and depart on its three runways more than 400 times a day. Approximately nine million passengers pass through its terminals each year.

The Airport's growth over the past decade has been nothing short of spectacular. Cargo shipments have increased by an astonishing 2,040 percent, and passenger totals have increased 113 percent. Even the most conservative estimates project equally explosive growth for the Airport into the new century.

Last year, San Jose International extended its commercial runway to 10,200 feet to accommodate flights to the far east, and built a state-of-the-art control tower.

In 1995, San Jose International achieved official Port of Entry status—a designation which gives Silicon Valley companies a competitive edge, saving them hundreds of thousands of dollars in transportation costs each year.

The Airport is home to two award-winning Fixed Base Operators—ACM Aviation and San Jose Jet Center. These state-of-the-art facilities offer first-class amenities for corporate flight crews, business jets for charter, and space for 120 planes, from Gulfstreams to Bonanzas.

San Jose International is more than a thriving Airport. Completely self-sustaining and highly profitable, it is also one of the region's most dynamic and successful businesses, generating more than 70,000 jobs in the San Jose area—some 3,560 at the Airport itself. Tens of thousands of jobs in hotels, restaurants, shops, entertainment, and ground transportation businesses have been created to support the millions of visitors traveling through San Jose International each year.

In turn, the income of these resident employees supports even more jobs and local businesses—pumping billions of dollars in direct business revenue and personal income into the economy, and generating millions of valuable tax dollars for the benefit of all.

Today San Jose International Airport is the hub of a global economic force and a leader in commercial aviation. The next technological advancement to spring from the collective genius of Silicon Valley will no doubt be introduced to the world through the gates of San Jose International Airport, Gateway to Silicon Valley, Gateway to the Future. ✦

San Jose International Airport is the hub of a global economic force and a leader in commercial aviation.

CALIFORNIA WATER SERVICE COMPANY

"**W**e like to think that the Silicon Valley entrepreneurial spirit has rubbed off on us," says Jim Good, vice president, Corporate Communications and Marketing for California Water Service Company. That's a pretty unusual thing for a public utility to say—especially one that celebrated its 70th anniversary in 1996. But then, Cal Water is a pretty unusual public utility.

Faced with rising competitive pressures driven by: (1) entry of large European water utilities into the U.S. market, (2) consolidation of U.S. water utilities, and (3) the growing number of federal environmental mandates, many utilities would have fought or resisted the changes. But Cal Water has chosen to capitalize on them. It has developed new business by partnering with public agencies and providing them specially contracted services through a separate corporate arm that conducts unregulated activities.

Under such a "customer service" contract with the City of Menlo Park, for example, Cal Water provides meter reading, billing, and other non-operational services for a fee. Both parties benefit from this partnership. Menlo Park is able to offer its residents enhanced service at a reasonable price and California Water is able to generate income, free from the vagaries of water supplies, interest rates, and regulatory actions. From 1993 to 1995, the company's income from such public-private partnerships tripled to nearly $1 million out of $14.7, and the upward trend is expected to continue. "We see a lot of potential growth for the Company in this area over the medium term," Good said.

This is not to say that Cal Water de-emphasizes its traditional core business as a company regulated by the State Public Utilities Commission.

Cal Water serves 1.5 million people throughout the state, including residents of the Silicon Valley communities of Los Altos, Los Altos Hills, Cupertino, Menlo Park, and parts of Mountain View and Sunnyvale.

"We've operated as a traditional utility, with steady earnings and dividend growth, for many years," Good said, "and we plan to continue."

Founded in 1926 and now the state's largest investor-owned water utility, California Water Service Company moved to San Jose in 1931, where it is headquartered today. It serves 1.5 million people throughout the state, including residents of the Silicon Valley communities of Los Altos, Los Altos Hills, Cupertino, Menlo Park, and parts of Mountain View and Sunnyvale.

Founded in 1926 and now the state's largest investor-owned water utility, California Water Service Company moved to San Jose in 1931, where it is headquartered today.

In spring 1992, the company completed construction of its 15,800 square foot water quality/engineering complex in San Jose, delivering equipment and facilities that are among the industry's most technically advanced. This sophisticated new facility has allowed Cal Water to fully computerize its water engineering, testing, monitoring, and control systems. It's another link in Cal Water's long established chain as one of the state's finest potable water purveyors.

Mention the phrase "public utility," to most people, and the words "institutional," "impersonal," and "imposing" come to mind. But here again, Cal Water is an exception, and the "people-friendly" tone is set at the top.

The office door of Peter Nelson, President and CEO, is glass, not thick wood to keep people out. His desk is a simple table, not an intimidating monument to mahogany and power. And, other than a few family photos, the walls of his office remained unadorned for many months because Nelson had no time for office decoration. During his first three months on the job in 1996, his focus was on meeting each of the company's 630 employees personally, even to the point of joining them on service calls and meter reading visits to get a "customer's-eye view" of business.

Community is important at Cal Water, too. "Our employees and the Company actively support our community," said Jim Good, "by donating considerable time and money to support charitable and community services activities such as the Tech Museum, San Jose State, Rotary, United Way, and many more."

People…community…innovation…quality service—that's what Cal Water is all about. "We're focused on helping the customer," Good says. "We go to great lengths to support the communities and districts we serve, and to assure customers that their tap water is not only safe, but of the highest possible quality." ✦

Chapter Twelve

Professions

◆

Photo by Pat Kirk.

ERNST & YOUNG LLP

Leadership is not a word usually associated with audit, tax, and management consulting firms, even large international ones. Nonetheless, leadership best describes Ernst & Young, the market leader in virtually every segment of the high-technology industry—computers and peripherals, semiconductors, software, telecommunications, and life sciences.

Ernst & Young's Silicon Valley practice, for example, works with approximately 40 percent of the Silicon Valley high-tech market—more than twice as many technology firms as its nearest competitor. And more than 80 percent of the San Francisco Bay Area's top biotechnology/biomedical companies are clients of Ernst & Young.

Ernst & Young's Silicon Valley practice is a part of Ernst & Young LLP, the world's leading professional services firm.

In Silicon Valley's early years, this firm had the foresight to recognize technology as the wave of the future, and to commit its staff and resources to meeting the needs of that market. Ernst & Young was the first to understand and meet the special needs of technology-based companies. Hence its dominant position today.

The firm's client roster reads like a "Who's Who" of electronics and life sciences. Through its offices in San Jose, Palo Alto, San Francisco, Walnut Creek, Sacramento, and Reno, Ernst & Young serves one-third of the top 100 high-technology companies ranked by revenue, and nearly half of the 50 fastest growing companies in the valley.

More than 30 percent of Silicon Valley's public companies look to Ernst & Young for accounting and professional services—among them such high-tech pioneers as Intel, Sun Microsystems, and Genentech. "We've been with these leaders through every step of their growth, from the start-up phase to becoming multi-billion-dollar global corporations," says partner Dave Ward.

"No other audit, tax,

Ernst & Young is the fastest growing of the 'Big Six' firms in their field. They are the dominant practice in Silicon Valley, and are well positioned to bring value to their expanding base of clients.

and management consulting firm has taken more companies public, helped more manufacturers establish international operations, or been involved in more Silicon Valley business deals than Ernst & Young," he explains. "That's the experience that translates into competitive advantage for our clients."

Ernst & Young's Silicon Valley practice is organized around high-technology market segments, with extensive resources focused on understanding and meeting the needs of those segments.

The firm's information systems specialists work with major high-tech companies in every industry segment, creating information strategies from clinical trials and analytical data management to distribution and after-sale service. Its professionals consult on networks and communications, technical systems, database software, and more.

Over the years, Ernst & Young has developed a rare consulting capability to help technology companies become world-class manufacturers. Design for manufacturing, quality management systems, just-in-time processes, and other proven initiatives help client companies gain the know-how to achieve lower costs while maintaining high quality.

"We know your business because we track the trends and issues that shape your industry," Ward observes.

The reason for Ernst & Young's popularity among the valley's high-tech leaders is simple. No other firm offers comparable depth and variety of services and has as many top, specialized professionals located in Silicon Valley—nearly 600 people.

The Ernst & Young approach to client service is markedly different from the norm. A collaborative style, it is characterized by personal involvement, integrated team effort, and multidisciplined advisors, allowing the firm to anticipate—and meet—client needs.

With decades of experience guiding Silicon Valley companies from infancy to global market leader, the Ernst & Young team has developed insights into the dynamics of high-tech growth that its less experienced competitors lack. That edge has enabled the firm to forge an outstanding referral network of venture capitalists, attorneys, and underwriters for the benefit of its clients.

Ernst & Young's Silicon Valley practice is a part of Ernst & Young LLP, the world's leading professional services firm. Encompassing a base of more than 71,000 people in 600 cities in 100 countries, its global resources and international business expertise are unmatched.

That kind of premier international network allows clients to tap the specialized knowledge of Ernst & Young professionals serving high-tech and other manufacturing businesses in Eastern and Western Europe, the Soviet Union, plus Australia and the Pacific Rim.

These professionals can help clients understand and plan for the complexities of offshore manufacturing, as well as how to appropriately establish and manage operations in foreign countries. For companies with international operations, Ernst & Young can advise on the most advantageous forms of organization. They can serve as resources for clients in planning international tax strategies, plus dealing with issues of foreign exchange, currency, regulations and reporting, customs and duties, market entry options, and transfer pricing.

Of special benefit to its clients are Ernst & Young's consulting skills in key technical areas like electronic commerce, Internet security, internal audit, and outsourcing—as well as its substantial capabilities and experience with mergers, acquisitions, and initial public offerings.

Of special benefit to its clients are Ernst & Young's consulting skills in key technical areas like electronic commerce, Internet security, internal audit, and outsourcing—as well as its substantial capabilities and experience with mergers, acquisitions, and initial public offerings.

Roger F. Dunbar (left), area managing partner and David P. Ward (right), office managing partner of Ernst & Young.

Ernst & Young also has unsurpassed real estate consulting capabilities. "Cost segregation work, operational planning facilities, operational efficiency, buy-sell lease options—our consulting resources run virtually A through Z in the world of domestic and international real estate," Ward says.

The entrepreneurial spirit that put Silicon Valley on the global technology map and drives it today continues to inspire Ernst & Young's Silicon Valley practice. As the valley grew, so did the practice. And so did its expertise in helping high-tech companies get started and stay on course, address complex issues and meet new challenges, develop strategic business plans and effective management systems, understand industry issues, and help develop creative solutions.

"We are the fastest growing of the 'Big Six' firms in our field," Ward says. "As the dominant practice in Silicon Valley, and given the premium we are placing on continued growth, we are well positioned to bring value to our expanding base of clients."

So, why does leadership best describe Ernst & Young? Because in Silicon Valley—as elsewhere in the world—Ernst & Young is 'The Leaders' Choice^{SM}.' ◆

HOGE, FENTON, JONES, & APPEL, INC.

"There's not a day the courthouses are open that a Hoge Fenton attorney isn't in court on behalf of a client," says Michael McSweeney, a partner in the 44-year-old law firm of Hoge, Fenton, Jones, & Appel, Inc.

All firms litigate, but at many that means conducting discovery, filing legal motions, and negotiating settlements in order to resolve cases, without going to trial. Hoge Fenton's 50 attorneys do all those things too, but, when it's in their client's best interest, they don't shy away from taking a case before a judge or jury. Some of the firm's members have each tried well over 100 cases.

Hoge Fenton counts among its partners some of the best trial lawyers around. Take Charles Brock, a senior partner in Hoge Fenton— "Clients, judges, and lawyers who have fought cases against him say he is the epitome of legal skill and integrity," comments a San Francisco Daily Journal feature article about Brock. Attorney Allen Ruby, who has argued cases against Brock, has observed, "Among people who know, Charlie is the best." What's more, he says, "Charlie Brock never made a promise he didn't keep. That's how good his reputation is."

Hoge Fenton partner James Towery, who served as the 1995-96 president of the California State Bar admits "Some of the most satisfying moments in my career have been in representing clients and getting good jury verdicts for them."

Hoge Fenton enjoys a formidable reputation for excellence and high professional standards in virtually all areas of civil law. Several of its partners have "graduated" to the bench, including one who sits on the U.S. District Court. Other Hoge Fenton partners are Fellows of the American College of Trial Lawyers, a national organization of lawyers representing the best of the legal profession based on peer ratings and a minimum of 15 years of trial experience.

Founded by J. Hampton Hoge in 1953, Hoge Fenton's roots are in insurance defense work. Over the years, however, the widely respected law firm has enlarged both its client base and its areas of legal expertise. Today, the firm is organized into specialized units that address a broad scope of contemporary legal issues for a diverse group of corporate, government, and not-for-profit organizations, as well as partnerships and individual clients. Employment Law, Estate and Trust Planning and Litigation, Professional Malpractice, Tax Law,

Located in the heart of downtown San Jose, Hoge Fenton has its finger on the pulse of the ever-changing business facing the Silicon Valley. **Photo by Sam Geraci/SFG Photography.**

Environmental Law, Appellate Law, Intellectual Property Law, and Alternative Dispute Resolution are among the areas in which the depth and diversity of Hoge Fenton's knowledge have helped establish its reputation for competence, creativity and commitment to serving its clients.

Intellectual property matters involving trademarks, unfair competition, copyrights, trade secrets, patent infringement, and technology licensing, as well as the acquisition of technical equipment, have long been handled by Hoge Fenton. After all, the firm is based in San Jose, the technology center of the world, where innovation is a way of life and intellectual property is the lifeblood of its businesses.

Hoge Fenton's attorneys have represented companies in insurance, real estate, and professional malpractice litigation, business disputes, and product liability matters involving products as diverse as surgical instruments and steam rollers, tires and microfilters, ball valves, lollipops, and mechanical bulls. They have handled cases involving injury and death, as well as substantial claims for property damage and economic loss. Members of the firm have impressive records and experience.

Corporate concerns are a driving force in the Silicon Valley, and Hoge Fenton is at the forefront of this arena as well. For over four decades, the attorneys have counseled clients in numerous industries such as banking and finance, health care, retail, construction, consumer goods, real estate, engineering, consulting, computers and computer software, and more. As a result, they bring a collective expertise to clients' transactions and litigations in areas such as loans, mortgage banking, loan workouts, trusts and fiduciary issues, secured transactions, environmental concerns and employment law.

With early expertise in litigation, Hoge Fenton has built one of the finest business litigation practices in the state. "Although our trial attorneys

A friendly and respectful working environment fosters an open exchange of ideas. **Photo by Sam Geraci/SFG Photography.**

principally practice in Silicon Valley, we appear with increasing frequency in courts throughout the country," says Lewis Fenton, a founder of the firm. From its initial detailed case analysis and preliminary budget, through its strategic consulting and representation in court, or in alternative dispute resolution forums, Hoge Fenton incorporates state-of-the-art litigation support techniques such as witness databases and document retrieval equipment.

"Hoge Fenton can represent either side in a legal dispute. This prevents us from slipping into a fixed mindset," says Fenton. "Our ability to analyze the facts and issues from the other side's point of view often enables us to achieve a better result for our client."

However, clients aren't the only beneficiaries of Hoge Fenton's commitment to service. The community has gained as well. For many years, members of the Hoge Fenton team have volunteered their services for the benefit of such public benefit groups as the San Jose Arena Authority, City Team Ministries, the San Jose Repertory Theater, the Julian Street Inn Homeless Shelter, the San Jose Leadership Counsel, the San Jose Museum of Art, the YWCA, the San Jose Symphony and more. In fact, Hoge Fenton is one of the organizations singled out for special recognition for raising more than 8,000 pounds of food for low-income families in a single campaign, and members of the firm have given a presentation to the National Bar Association on how to conduct a successful food drive.

In the four decades since its founding, Hoge Fenton has made many changes in order to maintain its expertise at the cutting-edge of legal knowledge, systems and practices. But one thing that hasn't changed is the firm's philosophy. It centered on clients and their needs in 1953, and it remains there today. "With a lot of attorneys, you get the sense that they're standing over the telephone with a stopwatch so they can bill you for every second," says Mark Geredes, chief operating officer of First Franklin Financial Corporation. "But with our Hoge Fenton legal team, we always get the sense that they're looking out for us, keeping us informed, talking things through on the telephone and helping us find ways to achieve the best results. They even advise us on ways we can cut down on our bills with them!"

First Franklin is one of Hoge Fenton's hundreds of satisfied clients. According to Geredes, in 1991 alone, Hoge Fenton helped his company recover in excess of $1 million against insurance companies in litigation involving sub par appraisal work. As Geredes says, "Results always speak the loudest." ✦

The attorneys at Hoge Fenton draw upon their extensive litigation experience to represent the interests of their clients. **Photo by Sam Geraci/SFG Photography.**

Hoge Fenton attorneys and staff prepare and serve meals at the Julian Street Inn. **Photo by Sam Geraci/SFG Photography.**

PRICE WATERHOUSE LLP

Smart technology companies know how important the right team of advisors is to their success. As engines of growth in today's fast-paced global economy, technology companies can't afford to make mistakes. That's why two-thirds of the top technology companies in Silicon Valley look to Price Waterhouse, a leading global professional services organization, for cutting-edge advice and practical, innovative solutions to complex business problems. Price Waterhouse, one of the select international consulting firms known as the "Big Six", is a widely respected name in audit, tax, corporate finance, and management consulting circles. Established more than 150 years ago in London, Price Waterhouse brings to its clients a wealth of experience that strengthens their decision-making capabilities—helping them anticipate and manage change, transition more smoothly, reduce their global tax burdens, generate growth and stability, and gain a competitive edge in today's dynamic global marketplace.

Price Waterhouse serves top-tier global technology companies, technology-based joint ventures, and emerging technology companies through its leading *Technology Industry Group*. This specialized Group provides a broad spectrum of services tailored to the unique needs of technology companies, reflecting Price Waterhouse's in-depth understanding of the industry and the challenges it faces. To best focus on the needs of individual clients of all sizes, Price Waterhouse has created

Donald A. McGovern, vice-chairman of Price Waterhouse's U.S. Technology Industry Group and managing partner of the firm's Silicon Valley office. Photo by Andrew Cohen.

multidisciplinary operating groups within the Technology Industry Group to serve specific industry sectors: Semiconductors, Software & Internet, Systems & Peripherals, Networking & Communications, Life Sciences, and other technology-related companies.

Technology Industry Group professionals provide advice and assistance in several key areas, among them tax planning and compliance.

Pictured left to right are Don McGovern, Jim Henry, Bill Pfann, and Larry Hupka of Price Waterhouse LLP. Photo by Andrew Cohen.

Price Waterhouse's Multistate Tax Consulting is the leading group of its kind among the Big Six. Further, the firm is a leader in providing International Tax Services. The Group also advises on new business alternatives related to capital formation, including venture capital, corporate acquisitions, mergers, and joint ventures. Management Consulting Services include Change Integration, Business Process Reengineering, and Information Technology—including systems integration and software implementation. Price Waterhouse is the preferred services provider of SAP and is a leader in Oracle implementations as well.

Price Waterhouse takes a risk-based, business approach to auditing, which provides added value to its clients. Other services related to annual audits include securities registration (IPOs and secondary offerings); regulatory issues and manufacturing requirements; intellectual property and licensing; technology investments; operations benchmarking; accessing capital markets and facilitating strategic relationships; and maximizing R&D investments—all customized for technology companies.

Technology Industry Strength in Silicon Valley

More than 35 partners and 400 professional staff are based in the Price Waterhouse Silicon Valley office, which specializes exclusively in serving technology clients—from Fortune 500 firms to brand new ventures. Established in 1963, the growth of the firm's practice has skyrocketed—along with the growth of many of its clients. "Many of our largest technology clients began their relationship with us as start-ups," says Don McGovern, vice-chairman of Price Waterhouse's U.S. Technology Industry Group and managing partner of the firm's Silicon Valley office. "We know first-hand that tomorrow's multinational technology stars come from today's successful start-ups. That's why we make long-term commitments of time and effort in companies with extraordinary potential." For technology companies in the start-up phase, Price Waterhouse Technology Industry Group professionals can help their clients obtain financing through a variety of sources—from venture capitalists and

Standing left to right are Don McGovern, Mark Rubash, Jon Gochoco, Larry Hupka, Greg Franceschi, Bill Ramsden, Jim Cigler, Mark Singer, Dave Zechnich, Ginny Gates, Jim Dezart, Mike Patterson, Chris Nolet, Jeff Dearinger, Marshall Mohr, Doug Morgan, and Jim Henry. Sitting left to right are Bruce Bothwell, Susan Gore, Chuck Robel, Bill Pfann, Vince Ostrosky, Dorene Neel, and Larry Gillis. **Photo by Andrew Cohen.**

"angels" to public offerings and private placements, from strategic partners to government funding programs. They can help establish an accounting and tax infrastructure that takes maximum advantage of tax regulations, set up executive compensation strategies that attract and retain the best management, and develop the most effective strategies and systems for every business process and need–both domestic and international.

With such an extensive base of industry-experienced professionals putting the firm's leading-edge tools and techniques to work, Price Waterhouse is well-positioned to match its services to a client's stage of growth. The same business advisors who handle a client's financial management and tax needs can mobilize Price Waterhouse's vast global resources to ensure that employee benefits strategies are beneficial yet cost-effective, that international operations are optimally structured for tax savings, that complex multistate tax laws are understood and complied with, and that acquisition strategies are structured for success.

Active at the forefront of the Industry

Technology is transforming the world of business so dramatically that creating strategy without a knowledge of the potential and future directions of technology is virtually futile. That's why Price Waterhouse's industry expertise is so important to its clients. "One of the areas where we bring the greatest value to clients is in helping them leverage new technologies into strategic advantage," McGovern says. "We bring our clients knowledge of industry best practices and trends gained in serving technology leaders such as Adaptec, Applied Materials, Hewlett-Packard, LSI Logic, Raychem, and many others–as well as many of the industry's youngest, most promising companies." Active at the forefront of the industry, the Technology Industry Group is in close contact with the industry "movers and shakers." With its finger on the pulse of the industry, Price Waterhouse publishes a number of specialized reports to keep its clients abreast of the latest industry trends:

Software Business Practices Survey: This annual survey is a comprehensive review of company operating practices, plans, and industry trends.

Computers & Peripherals Financial Benchmarking Study: This annual study quantifies best-of-breed financial performance in multiple industry subcategories on multiple financial measures.

National Venture Capital Survey: This quarterly survey tracks U.S. venture capital investments in emerging companies and new technologies destined to shape the industry.

The Technology Forecast: To keep Price Waterhouse professionals and clients abreast of new findings and tools, Price Waterhouse also produces the Technology Forecast, a leading document overviewing trends in the technology industry.

"With the knowledge gained from our comprehensive, industry-focused surveys, our extensive international network, and our exceptional staff expertise, we have the vision needed to see how technology will revolutionize industries," McGovern said. "And by sharing that vision with our clients, we help them create competitive advantages."

The *Leader In Serving Technology Companies and Multinationals*

Successful firms go by the numbers, so it's no surprise that Price Waterhouse has won the "triple crown" of client satisfaction. Emerson Research–the widely respected, independent market research company that conducts regular, exhaustive client satisfaction surveys involving all of the Big Six firms–asked high-tech, multinational, and emerging public companies in 1995 which firm best met their growing, ever-changing needs. When the results were in, Price Waterhouse had swept the field: Number one in overall client satisfaction; Number one serving with multinational companies–thanks to the responsiveness of its global network; Number one in serving emerging public companies; Number one in knowledge of the business; and Number one in market share–auditing. "Price Waterhouse was the only firm where delivery met expectations. The firm continues to do an excellent job of 'walking the talk'," wrote Emerson's research analysts in their final report. "Price Waterhouse had more five-star ratings than any other firm–including audit/accounting, knowledge of the business, responsiveness of the partner. From the client's perspective, Price Waterhouse is truly 'King of Multinationals'." ✦

JOHANSON & YAU ACCOUNTANCY CORPORATION

Business and individuals looking for an alternative to large accounting firms often find their way to Johanson & Yau Accountancy Corporation. "We work with many of the Silicon Valley area's most established closely-held businesses, as well as many new start-up companies," says Anthony Yau, managing partner. "While we provide the highest standard of traditional accounting and tax services, we also offer vital one-on-one attention."

Their "Partners in Profitability" approach allows the firm's skilled professionals to develop a deep understanding of their clients' businesses. As a result, they can tailor their recommendations to help their clients make the most effective—and most profitable—decisions.

Founded in 1979, Johanson & Yau provides a wealth of diverse knowledge and experience. "Our four partners have a combined 104 years of professional experience between them," says founding partner Darrell F. Johanson. "We have worked with many of our clients for years, dating back to well before the firm was formed."

Based in San Jose, the heart of Silicon Valley, Johanson & Yau has positioned itself to be especially sensitive to the needs of both small and medium-sized companies. Its clients tend to have sales ranging anywhere from $100,000 to $75 million a year—everything from small professional practices to corporations with over 100 employees.

In addition to servicing private businesses of many sizes, the firm's industry coverage is quite broad, and includes real estate developers and operators, high technology companies, light manufacturing, construction contractors, wholesale distributors, service businesses and professionals such as doctors, attorneys—even athletes.

The firm's tax compliance and planning expertise is not only directed at businesses, but also to individuals. "Particularly here in Silicon Valley where huge fortunes can be made practically overnight," says Yau, "people need expert advice to protect their estates and ensure a secure future for their families. That's an important part of what we do. We not only work with the owners and key employees of our client businesses. We also work closely with executives of local high technology companies who require careful financial planning related to their stock options as well as retirement and family education matters."

The firm's expertise in a variety of consulting areas is a vital focus of it activities. "Many of our clients initially came to us just for financial statement or tax preparation," says partner Frederick U. Leonard. "They soon found out

The firm's staff are pictured **(seated left to right)** *Cheryl L. Hinshaw, Byron J. Ishiwata, Joni Archer, Frederick U. Leonard, Bunny Chuah,* **(standing left to right)** *David R. Davis, Sara E. Kelley, and Anthony S.C. Yau.* **Photo by Pat Kirk.**

that our greatest value is the additional help we provide, whether it be the everyday advice to routine business problems, or performing specific engagements such as a review of a company's accounting system and controls, assisting with projections or performing due diligence on an acquisition target and helping the owner to structure the deal. Our ability to provide this level of service has been the key to our success."

Another specialized niche Johanson & Yau has developed comes from working with many clients from Taiwan and Hong Kong. Anthony Yau's ability to speak both Mandarin and Cantonese has attracted a large number of Chinese businesses and families. "People coming to the United States have special needs relating to federal tax laws," says Yau. "We have helped many Chinese investors, as well as many other clients from Asia and Europe."

Community support is another key value at Johanson and Yau. Partners and professionals are active in community service organizations, including the Lions Club, Rotary, Children's Discovery Museum of San Jose, and more. Frequently they have served as an organization's officers and board members, contributing even more of their volunteer time for the benefit of the community.

The firm has grown, since its inception, to a staff of about 20 professionals. In 1988, it moved to its present downtown San Jose location. "We provide our staff an environment where they can learn and advance at a steady pace," says partner David R. Davis. "Every staff person works directly with the managers and partners. Our firm cannot grow unless our staff grows along with it."

Johanson & Yau built its reputation on the concept of top professional skill and prompt, responsive, personal service. "We work hard to help our clients succeed," says Davis. ◆

Johanson & Yau's partners are pictured **(left to right)** *David R. Davis CPA, Anthony S.C. Yau CPA, and Frederick U. Leonard CPA.* **Photo by Pat Kirk.**

ALLAN ADVISORS, INC.

Lon Allan, an attorney with more than 20 years of experience in Silicon Valley, has developed an innovative way to deliver corporate legal services–one that turns back the pages of history. "Three decades ago when I graduated from Stanford Law School, attorneys served as trusted advisors and counselors," he says. "But in the years since, the legal profession has become the law industry, and what was once a close working relationship is now seen as a business commodity."

"Contemporary demand for volume in client count and billable hours has forced senior partners at large law firms to almost become account executives," he says. "Yet, business executives still need the personalized advice and counsel that was once an attorney's stock in trade."

Allan's response to this need has been to establish himself as a consulting firm of one–Allan Advisors, Inc.,–providing a service he terms Contract Inside Counsel[SM].

Under his business model, Allan spends one day a week at the offices of each of his three public company clients, meeting with the CEO and senior staff, serving as onsite legal resource and advisor addressing a variety of issues and needs. For a number of clients, he also serves as an outside director, bringing his broad legal and management perspective to their boardroom.

Lon Allan serves as a trustee of this community performing arts venue.

Allan's approach to legal services is personal rather than institutional, based on relationships instead of transactions. As a result, his select roster of clients includes those who began with him at the start of Allan Advisors in 1992. They are a diverse group, ranging from "no-tech" to "high-tech" firms, from $1-$2 million start-ups to established public companies with sales in the hundreds of millions.

Lon Allan is an outside director of this public company.

Allan has developed an equally innovative system of payment–one that directly aligns his financial interests with those of his clients. Instead of charging the top hourly rate a lawyer of his expertise commands in today's market, Allan sets a flat annual retainer: he is paid half the market billing rate in cash and the remaining half in stock. "When you don't charge by the hour, it's amazing how much more readily people accept your advice," he says.

By having a financial stake in the companies he serves, Allan's financial interests mirror those of his clients. Such an insider perspective makes him especially useful in helping clients get the most from the other legal specialists with whom they need to contract. "I can negotiate on their behalf out of 20 plus years of experience," he says, "and assure that their rates are cost-effective and the advice is practical."

Relationships are important in Allan's personal life, too. He and his wife, Mary, a busy realtor at Alain Pinel Realtors, first met in high school and are celebrating 30 years of marriage. They both contribute actively to the community, donating not only money, but also their energy. Many arts and public service organizations have benefited from the Allans' commitment to quality community relationships and board service, including KTEH, the local public television channel; the National Conference of Christians and Jews; the San Jose Metropolitan Chamber of Commerce; the YWCA; the San Jose Museum of Art; Opera San Jose; and Villa Montalvo Center for the Arts.

Their combined commitment to clients, community, and family keeps the Allans on the go, but they don't seem to mind. "Our television antenna broke in the 1989 earthquake," Allan says with a smile, "and we haven't fixed it yet." ✦

GASSETT, PERRY, & FRANK

A diverse group in many ways, attorneys at Gassett, Perry, & Frank have also run the Boston Marathon, served as a mayor, gone fly fishing (and even managed occasionally to catch a fish or two), played the mandolin, trained horses, gone scuba diving, and more. "One of our attorneys is grandmother to her attorney daughter's daughter," Noel Gassett says, "proving that we attorneys are human after all!"

The offspring of a law practice established in San Jose in 1947, Gassett, Perry, & Frank represents both insureds and self-insureds. The firm has developed a client base over the years that includes numerous insurance companies and businesses, along with governmental and quasi-governmental agencies.

"We've grown as the valley has grown," says Gassett. "Take the small to mid-size entrepreneurial company in Silicon Valley—a typical client for us. We have the same excitement about this unique part of the world as they do. This valley is a fun place to be, because so many new legal issues are developing." Telecommuting and solo business operations are two such areas where cutting-edge litigation is taking place and Gassett, Perry & Frank is at the forefront.

"Gassett, Perry & Frank is—first and foremost—a litigation firm, with a distinct defense orientation," says Gassett. "It's our business, and we've done it for nearly 50 years."

The firm's attorneys include graduates from top universities and law schools, and professionals with experience in business, economics, insurance, politics, and the sciences. They specialize in public and governmental entity litigation, construction defect litigation and mediation, professional negligence litigation, including attorney malpractice actions, white-collar criminal defense, environmental and hazardous waste compliance and litigation, business and commercial transactions and litigation, insurance matters, and employment law, and mediation of all kinds of business-related suits.

Client service is an important watchword at this law firm. "The world is filled with good lawyers, but not everyone is able to provide our level of responsiveness to client needs at all stages," Gassett said. "Our goal is to give quality service at reasonable rates, as efficiently, as quickly, and as cost-effectively as possible." To achieve that goal, members of this firm work with clients from the start to establish the desired outcome for the litigation, and to then determine the most efficient, cost-effective way to achieve that outcome.

Contributing to the community is another part of what Gassett Perry, & Frank is about. "We devote significant time to community service," Gassett says. Firm members are actively involved in the arts and education, as well as such professional organizations as the Association of Defense Counsel of Northern California, California Manufacturers Association, Defense Research Institute, Northern California Fraud Investigators Association, and the International Association of Insurance Counsel.

With roots that stretch back decades, Gassett, Perry, & Frank is firmly committed to Silicon Valley. "If you want to work for us, you have to believe in the future of this valley," Gassett says. "We want people who are connected here and have a strong sense of community." ✦

A diverse group in many ways, attorneys at Gassett, Perry, & Frank have also run the Boston Marathon, served as a mayor, gone fly fishing (and even managed occasionally to catch a fish or two), played the mandolin, trained horses, gone scuba diving, and more.

*I*t's been nearly half a century since we first opened our doors in downtown San Jose," says Paul Pugh, senior partner of Petrinovich, Pugh, & Company, CPAs. "During that time, we've watched both the Santa Clara Valley and the Bay Area go through remarkable changes."

Petrinovich, Pugh, & Company is poised to meet the challenges of the next century with a wide range of dynamic, creative, tax, and financial solutions. Even so, unlike the region it services, its approach to business hasn't changed since its founding.

"We understand that the fundamental element of success is knowing our customers–their businesses, their markets, their worlds," Pugh says. "We do that by establishing a true partnership with each client. This allows us to look beneath the surface and deliver truly innovative solutions."

PETRINOVICH, PUGH, & COMPANY

This is not a typical compliance firm, but rather one that searches for innovative and practical solutions that will be sound today and tomorrow. "We ask tough questions and welcome challenging answers," he says. "That's because our perspective is global–from tax minimization all the way to systems and management consulting."

Petrinovich, Pugh, & Company believes its job is to manage the financial world of its clients, so they can concentrate on running their businesses. The ultimate goal is to help clients get the most out of every dollar spent–and every dollar earned.

Experience counts always, and Petrinovich, Pugh, & Company has an abundance of it. They've partnered with some of the most successful Silicon Valley companies in distribution, manufacturing, the legal and medical professions, advertising, construction, real estate development, and a host of others.

"We helped one of our clients–with a family-run side business–mature that business into a thriving corporation," Pugh says. "In another case, we took an electronics distributor from early growth stages, and helped it develop into a million-dollar company."

And, for one of the largest placement advertising agencies in the country, Petrinovich, Pugh, & Company formed a viable growth-to-exit strategy. "After their early success, we advised the company against a possible buyout," he explained. "When the firm reached its full potential five years later, they received a much more lucrative financial deal."

Without exception, clients find that Petrinovich, Pugh, & Company's belief in partnership gives them a formidable competitive advantage. "By blending our basic commitments to service and partnership with technological savvy and know-how, we're able to be there with our clients every step of the way," Pugh says. "And you can take that to the bank!" ✦

The four partners of Petrinovich, Pugh, & Company pictured are (seated left to right) **Paul Pugh, Thomas Wagstaff,** *(standing left to right)* **Jerome Bellotti,** *and* **Marc Parkinson.**

Petrinovich, Pugh, & Company is poised to meet the challenges of the next century with a wide range of dynamic, creative, tax, and financial solutions.

This timeless, effective approach allows Petrinovich, Pugh, & Company to effectively guide a local business as it develops into a national corporation, or support a start-up company with everything from systems development and tax planning all the way through to stock option strategies.

Because it's based on open communication, mutual understanding, and respect, the partnership Petrinovich, Pugh, & Company forms with its clients is exceptional in many ways.

For one thing, there are no surprises. Fees are clearly outlined and agreed upon before work begins. "We think of ourselves as controllers who function alongside our client companies, while remaining responsive to their needs," Pugh says.

MCCAHAN, HELFRICK, THIERCOF, & BUTERA

McCahan, Helfrick, Thiercof & Butera (MHT&B), a large San Jose-based accounting firm, is well known in the Silicon Valley business community. "We are consistently ranked in *The Business Journal*'s 'Top 25' accounting firms," says J. Bruce McCahan, CPA, "and recognized by *Money* magazine as one of the best tax practitioners in the nation."

With 22 employees and over 40 years of experience, the company has the expertise and resources of a much larger firm, yet the ability to give small-company attention to its clients.

"The biggest complaint we hear from clients about their former accountants is, 'My CPA waited until the last minute to tell me things,'" McCahan says. "That's why we make it a point, not only to give our clients advance information, but to anticipate and project their future needs. We make it our mission in life to see that our clients don't get unpleasant surprises."

Well established as a source of expert witnesses in Santa Clara County Superior Court cases, the firm is a leader in the area of litigation support. This involves assisting attorneys in matters such as computation of damages, valuing businesses, and tracing missing funds or other assets. "We were one of the first to enter this field in the 1970s at a time when other CPAs weren't interested," McCahan says. "Now, it's one of the hottest specialties."

Another fast-growing specialization for MHT&B is computer consulting–helping clients get properly equipped and online with hardware and software customized to meet their accounting needs." It boils down to absolute service to the client," McCahan says. "Whatever they need from us, we try to provide."

That "go the extra mile" philosophy extends to the community as a whole, too. Members of the MHT&B team volunteer for a number of community groups and activities including the San Jose Police Crimestoppers program, the Shelter Foundation, and the Notre Dame High School.

With 22 employees and over 40 years of experience, MHT&B has the expertise and resources of a much larger firm, yet the ability to give small-company attention to its clients. Photo by Robert Sondgroth.

Since its founding in 1971 as a full-service CPA firm, MHT&B has met the needs of clients in a variety of industries, including manufacturing, medical, dental, and other professionals, non profits, real estate, restaurants, retail, wholesale, technology, and others. MHT&B provides the entire range of services one normally expects from a CPA–tax preparation, planning, and representation; accounting and auditing, litigation support, management consulting, crisis management, succession planning, fraud investigations, retirement plan evaluations, mergers and acquisitions services, and more.

That the firm has grown so well with virtually no advertising is testament to the quality of service it provides. Referrals from satisfied clients have, in fact, been a major source of new business for MHT&B.

"To ensure that we maintain the highest level of expertise, each partner and member of our professional team is required to take at least 40 hours of continuing education every year," McCahan said. "With emphasis on technical expertise and quality service, we can be more than mere historians. We can broaden our focus to include planning, and really help our clients know where they are going–not just where they have been." ✦

McCahan, Helfrick, Thiercof, & Butera, a large San Jose-based accounting firm, is well known in the Silicon Valley business community. Pictured are (seated left to right) Raymond J. Thiercof and J. Bruce McCahan, (standing left to right) James F. Butera and Charles W. Helfrick. Photo by Robert Sondgroth.

Photo by Dana L. Grover.

Chapter Thirteen

High Tech & Manufacturing

◆

SIEMENS BUSINESS COMMUNICATION SYSTEMS, INC.

Santa Clara-based Siemens Business Communication Systems (formerly ROLM) is the North American arm of the world's largest provider of business communications solutions–Siemens, a true global powerhouse.

With wireless phones, workers on the move are instantly accessible to callers, saving time and reducing support staff requirements.

"For some 150 years, the name Siemens has been synonymous with innovation," says Albert Hoser, president and CEO of Siemens Corporation, headquartered in New York City. "We ushered in a new communications era with the pointer telegraph, and the electric age with the first dynamo, and we've never stopped building on this strong foundation."

The multi-billion-dollar Siemens U.S. operation employs nearly 50,000 people at its plants and facilities throughout North America. The Bay Area is home to other Siemens operations besides the 6,000-employee Siemens Business Communication Systems: Siemens Components, Inc., in Cupertino and its subsidiary, Crystal Technology, Inc., in Palo Alto; the Oncology Care Systems Group of Siemens Medical Systems, Inc., in Concord; Siemens Corporate Purchasing in Sunnyvale; and Siemens Pyramid Information Systems, Inc., (formerly Pyramid Technology) in San Jose.

Siemens helps customers move vast volumes of information quickly and intelligently throughout the world. "From switching systems to networks to the Internet, we provide advanced integrated global communications solutions that turn increasingly diverse technologies into practical applications," says Karl Geng, president and CEO of Siemens Business Communication Systems. "As a result, we help our customers cut costs and increase efficiency, flexibility, service and profits, giving them the means to thrive."

Enhancing its strengths in computer-telephony integration (CTI) and wireless communications,

Siemens tailors solutions for such major business sectors as health care, education, utilities, retail, public sector, and finance; and forms strategic alliances with industry leaders such as MCI, Newbridge, and Cisco, among others.

"Offering comprehensive call-center solutions worldwide, we are the leading technology provider for the largest market segment–centers of between 100 and 250 agents," Geng says. "Our RésuméRouting call center product directs calls in real-time to agents who are knowledgeable about customers' needs and ready to help." Considered the most sophisticated call center offering on the market and designated "Product of the Year" by *Call Center Magazine*, RésuméRouting raises the benchmark for all call center applications.

Recently Kansas City schools asked Siemens Business Communications, as an established force in Internet service, to create a wide area digital network capable of handling everything from data to voice to videoconferencing. The infrastructure Siemens developed for this school district allows high-speed access via computers–one for every two students–to myriad applications, including the Internet, E-mail, multi-media and virtual reality. And the distance learning made possible by the Siemens system enables children at remote locations to attend class and share resources.

Now, whether communicating directly with NASA's Spacelink, or with schools as far away as France, thousands of students and teachers are enjoying classrooms as big as the world–thanks to Siemens.

This company's pioneering of intranet solutions has earned it the coveted BOTI (Business on the Internet) award from *Communications Week* magazine for its RouteOne intranet, which moves mission-critical and corporate data to web servers on a global network.

In 1996, it became the first U.S. telecommunications company to earn

---

Siemens Business Communications equips customers with the tools they need to streamline operations, reduce costs, and generate revenue through scalable, cost-effective communications systems.

Siemens videoconferencing solutions can make the promise of non-traditional education delivery methods such as distance learning, collaborative learning, and resource access, a reality.

complete ISO 9001 certification, encompassing its headquarters office as well as its R&D, manufacturing, sales, service, and support centers.

As a company built on breakthroughs and innovation, Siemens sets high standards for its employees, and provides an outstanding level of compensation and support to them in return. "In my time with Siemens Business Communications, I have been very impressed by the team atmosphere," says Tania Henderson, a technical support analyst at the Santa Clara facility. "Everyone is willing to give each other support and advice."

Rick Riggan, hardware systems engineer, began his career at Siemens as a co-op student in the product test department. After graduating from college, he joined the hardware development group full-time as a systems engineer.

"I chose to work for Siemens because I am able to participate in the development of new and creative technologies," he says. "Recently I had the opportunity to work on a new solution for our flagship product line. I set up a technology demonstration that showcased our results and personally presented this demonstration to both customers and some of our top executives. I was able to meet and discuss the project with several influential people—an opportunity I never thought I'd have as an engineer."

Fred Cardina, vice president of human resources, says Siemens' employees are at the center of the company's success. "They continually demonstrate their resilience and adaptability to change, knowing that change is a necessary fundamental of the 21st century corporation."

In 1996, Siemens was recognized for its flexible rewards program, for encouraging employee self-development, and for raising the bar to world-class standards of performance with the Optimas award. Considered the "Oscar" of the corporate human resources world, the Optimas award celebrates the nation's biggest, brightest, and smartest successes in corporate management of human assets.

Siemens has also worked with key educational and community agencies to pioneer a unique approach to apprentice training. In the process, the company has set new standards for helping workers to master job skills and created new career opportunities for the many young people who participate. Its company-supported internship program, established in partnership with Sequoia High School and Mission College, enables students to receive on-the-job technical skills training and a college education. The result? Employment opportunities in a high-demand, fast-growing technical field for students.

"Siemens Business Communications is at the forefront of a particularly exciting industry that is continuing to expand in scope, with new frontiers looming in networking, voice, data, and convergence," Geng says.

From the seeds of its start-up in 1847, Siemens has grown to become a truly global enterprise with almost 400,000 employees all over the world. What links the past and the present, and Siemens Business Communication Systems with the Siemens worldwide corporate network, is the innovative team spirit of its employees—and their dedication to leading the industries Siemens has helped create and shape for 150 years. ✦

ProCenter™—a comprehensive, integrated portfolio of call center resources—builds on Siemens' long history of innovation in server-based telecommunications systems, automatic call distribution (ACD), computer-telephony integration (CTI), and virtual representative groups.

THERMA, INC.

A relaxed corporate culture, even a husband-wife management team, aren't all that unusual in Silicon Valley. But even here where "company casual" is the norm in dress and attitude, not many firms can boast a resident company dog. However, at San Jose-based Therma, Inc., Basil, a much-loved Yorkshire terrier, has full run of the hallways, offices, and workshops.

"From the start, we never had any intention of being a traditional mechanical contractor, or even a traditional company," says Nicki Parisi, co-founder and chief financial officer.

Given the Parisi's unconventional approach to business—which is characterized by a rare level of employee freedom and close, flexible working relationships—it's no surprise that this 30-year-old precedent-setting firm has been called the "ultimate family company."

Not that it's a small operation, mind you. Therma is the largest mechanical contractor in Santa Clara County, and one of the largest in the Bay Area.

"We have installed more than 30 percent of all the commercial and industrial air conditioning systems in this county," says president and

The mechanical pad for Komag Building #9 is a 200,000 square-foot Fab Facility. Therma is state-of-the-art in every significant way, using the latest technologies to produce the most efficient and trouble-free results.

co-founder Joe Parisi, "and we have built more electronics, semiconductor, and biotech/pharmaceutical plants in our area than any other mechanical contractor." That translates into mechanical systems in hundreds of millions of square feet of buildings—all the result of Therma's expertise.

An acknowledged leader in cleanroom technology for submicron geometry semiconductor manufacturing, Therma consistently wins major contracts throughout Northern California and has even been commissioned by overseas businesses for work in Ireland, Italy, Korea, Singapore, and Taiwan.

"No question, Therma does great work on every level of the project," says one customer. "But the real issue for me is that I know I'm absolutely going to have a validated system when they're done."

The company specializes in the programming, design, construction, installation, and service of such mechanical systems as air conditioning,

process piping, plumbing, refrigeration, special exhaust systems, cleanrooms, acid neutralization, energy conservation, and controls.

"Therma has the expertise and experience to handle a single project or provide a total turnkey package—and we know how to do it right the first time," Joe Parisi says. "Customers tell us that's a big advantage for them, one that improves their bottom line."

Therma's primary customers are industrial users of mechanical contracting services—a broad group that includes the leading semiconductor, electronics, biotechnology, and pharmaceutical companies, as well as large real estate developers.

Joe and Nicki started Therma in San Jose in 1967. Originally, Joe had planned to become an electrical engineer. However, after working one summer with a mechanical engineering firm, he changed his major at San Jose State University. Afterwards, Joe worked at Fereday Mechanical as a minor partner before deciding to strike out on his own.

Nicki was born and raised in Idaho, the third generation of her family to work in the construction industry. Her grandfather was a local plumbing contractor, and her father owned a mechanical contracting business. As a young girl, Nicki would visit job sites with her father; later she worked in his office.

The Parisis have been a professional management team since Therma's inception. "The reason it has worked so well," says Nicki, "is that we started off small, so Joe and I were able to establish our individual areas of responsibility early. And as the business has grown, we have each stuck to those responsibilities."

Joe oversees Therma's sales and manufacturing operations, while Nicki manages the firm's finances.

In its youth, Therma focused on meeting the special needs of the valley's emerging high-tech companies, assuming a wide variety of contracting projects for those firms. "During our first six months in business, we took on all kinds of odd jobs just to make ends meet," Joe recalled. "We were electrical contractors, sprinkler contractors—anything anybody needed, we jumped in and tried to give it to them."

That's how Therma was able to develop its special expertise in designing and installing some of the most essential elements of semiconductor manufacturing, such as exotic gas piping, fume exhaust, and acid neutralization systems. As the young high-tech companies evolved, so did Therma's knowledge and skill.

Back then, Therma also manufactured clean benches and other cleanroom accessories, eventually developing a separate company—Modulair—which

Nicki Parisi, co-founder and chief financial officer of Therma, Inc. Photo by Russ Fischella, SF.

manufactures cleanroom modules. That company was sold in 1985.

Joe and Nicki set up their first offices on Burger Drive in San Jose, in cramped quarters that are legendary among company old-timers. As the firm grew and more people and equipment had to be crammed into the limited spaces, Joe says the size of his drawing table was gradually reduced— "courtesy of the company power saw."

"One day I returned from a sales call and my desk was standing out in the parking lot with a phone on it," Joe remembers. "That's when I knew it was time to move."

The way the move

President and co-founder Joe Parisi of Therma, Inc., the largest mechanical contractor in Santa Clara County, and one of the largest in the Bay Area. Photo by Russ Fischella, SF.

was handled is typical of the Parisi style of building a sense of fun and family within their company. "We decided it would be fun not to tell the employees about it," Nicki says. "We just moved everything over on Thanksgiving weekend, and when the employees reported for work on Monday, they found a note on the door with maps to the new building."

The Parisi's written instructions led employees to a 60,000-square-foot facility a few blocks away. Fifteen times larger than Therma's original 4,000-square-foot offices, the new building had plenty of room for everyone's needs—for at least a few more years.

Today, Therma occupies an 87,000-square-foot facility on Ringwood Avenue in San Jose. Providing work space for approximately 1,200 employees, it includes the most modern sheet metal shop in Northern California, where spiral and rectangular duct work is manufactured on automated equipment, a prefabricated piping facility, the most extensive cleanroom trailers in the industry for on-site fabrication; a modern garage for servicing the company's 400 vehicles; and an in-house restaurant for the convenience of employees, who work shifts staggered over a 12-hour day.

It doesn't take long to see that the Therma is, first and foremost, customer driven. One of the first fully computerized companies in the mechanical contracting industry, Therma is state-of-the-art in every significant way, using the latest technologies to produce the most efficient and trouble-free result.

In addition, Therma maintains field service offices for the convenience of its regular customers—several in San Jose, one in South San

A view of the rooftop HVAC & Process Komag Building

Francisco, one in Santa Clara, and one in Oakland—the list of whom encompasses the global leaders in the electronics, semiconductor, biotechnology, and pharmaceutical industries.

What's even more telling, though, is the attitude of Therma's staff. Therma's people just work harder and more creatively. A project can be as small as $50 or as large as $100 million—but you can't tell which if you're trying to gauge by the enthusiasm and commitment of the employees.

"Therma didn't become one of the largest mechanical contractors by focusing on the bottom line," Joe says. "Everybody here is more interested in building long-term relationships with the customers and with each other." Those values show up in the exceptional quality of Therma's finished product.

The key, of course, is Therma's people. Right from the start, Joe and Nicki established a culture that valued people above all else. And it's resulted in one of the lowest rates of turnover in the industry. In fact, just about everyone who started with Therma 30 years ago is still there—except for two employees who retired.

The Parisis have always insisted on the finest quality of work and total honesty on all levels, but they also wanted to eliminate the traditional chain of command. They wanted to establish an environment so free that limits to thinking and performance didn't exist. What's more, they've done it. "Working at Therma is the best job I've ever had. It's fun to come to work," says 13-year-employee Anthony Steimle, operations manager. "My only regret is that I didn't get here sooner."

Steimle says that Therma's workers are given considerable independence. "We're empowered to create a niche and a working environment that suits our skills," he says. "We're almost treated like we're independent business people, with a lot of latitude to sell, to do things, to design and estimate things, to create. And Therma provides the resources to back us up."

As Joe puts it, "We try and stretch their imagination." That kind of freedom and support is one reason why Therma attracts and keeps the

best. Another reason is that Therma doesn't skimp—it provides the best in tools, equipment, and facilities for its employees. The facilities are clean, bright, cheerful, and well-organized.

"When people come by for a tour, they say they've never seen a sheet metal shop that's so clean and neat and quiet," Joe says. "We take a lot of pride in our facilities."

Therma's employees respond in kind, with a rare dedication to meeting the operating needs of customers, no matter what. In the aftermath of the October 17, 1989 Loma Prieta earthquake disaster, for example, Therma employees rushed to repair broken pipes and failed systems. They put in about 5,000 hours of overtime to get Therma's customers back up and running, even though many of them had sustained major quake damage in their own homes that had to wait.

"None of us are thought of as just pipefitters or plumbers or engineers," says mechanical engineer Steve Rusconi. "We're encouraged to think and act creatively. We're treated like artisans. And you know what? That's exactly what we are. Our customers really appreciate that."

At Therma, there are no pat answers, only creative solutions. There is a free, ongoing exchange of ideas and a noticeable lack of jealousy or competition among employees. There are virtually no walls, not even cubicles, to divide employees or signify status. Engineers and designers interact directly with architects and clients—and freely with each other. The door to the president's office is always open. Anybody can walk in, and often do.

That kind of open, innovative approach to business has led to the development of a number of industry standards. Like the area's most extensive cleanroom trailers—the first portable cleanroom modules anywhere.

Therma designed and installed the first large airconditioning systems with variable speed motors for energy conservation. And upon hearing of the problem Stanford University Medical School students were having with formaldehyde fumes in their anatomy classes, Therma's engineers designed a new stainless steel dissection table that exhausts fumes completely.

Therma's team attitude extends to its worksites. This company makes no attempt to call attention to itself on the job site or anywhere else. Its people are quite content to be a part of their customer's team. "When you focus on giving your customer the best possible service, you are concentrating on what's really important," Joe says. "And that is getting the job done right, on time, and within budget."

Joe and Nicki support both their industry and their community with the same kind of team spirit. Active in the Santa Clara Valley Contractors Association and the local Sheet Metal Contractors National Association, Joe works consistently for the betterment of the industry. And Nicki volunteers her services for the benefit of such important community organizations as the American Cancer Society and the San Jose Ballet.

"There are a lot of reasons for our success, but it really boils down to one simple fact," Joe says. "Therma just isn't like any other company." Over the decades, it's that difference that customers of all sizes have come to value. ✦

The Genetech Building #7 Pilot Plant is a 11,000 square-foot R&D facility. Therma is one of the first fully computerized companies in the mechanical contracting industry.

MITSUBISHI ELECTRONICS AMERICA, INC.

In 1996, James Gosling, Sun Fellow at Sun Microsystems and chief architect of the Java™ platform, described what was then a new semiconductor integrated circuit (IC) as his "personal winner for the coolness category for hardware. ...you've got 100 megahertz in something about the form factor of your fingernail. Once you've got stuff like this, it really changes the type of things you can build. You could build a complete speech recognition system into a doorknob."

What Gosling described was the world's first system on a chip—a combination of dynamic random access memory (DRAM) and microprocessor in the same piece of silicon—Mitsubishi's M32R/D. Until 1996, no semiconductor supplier had been able to combine these two critical system functions in the same IC. With this technology breakthrough, Mitsubishi launched its *eRAM-enabled*℠ business strategy and ushered in the final phase of system integration on silicon as we know it today.

As emerging multimedia and peripheral applications continue to require ever-more massive amounts of data processing, traditional technology—including separate ICs for memory (DRAM), processor, and

Mitsubishi's M32R/D microprocessor, the world's first system-on-a-chip, uses Mitsubishi's eRAM™ process technology to combine dynamic random access memory, static random access memory, and microprocessor functions in the same piece of silicon. It's like taking several different kinds of chips and fitting them into a piece of silicon the size of a fingernail.

other logic functions—has given way to system-on-a-chip technology. With traditional semiconductor technology, the processor and memory portions of a system were each implemented as separate ICs.

Mitsubishi's *eRAM*™ technology and products include intellectual property (IP), systems design expertise, and the ability to integrate major separate system components, such as DRAM and microprocessor, as "cores" into one piece of silicon. *eRAM* capabilities also encompass the integration of software—such as Sun Microsystems' Java platform, and operating system and application software—on a single chip, and the ability to reuse or scale the cores across a wide range of system designs. *eRAM* technology and this new way of designing systems on a single chip using cores significantly enhances functional compatibility between system hardware and software, and creates an extraordinarily wide and reliable data pathway—known as bandwidth—between the microprocessor, memory, and other complex system functions.

The result was a new paradigm for electronic system design—a new way to create radically new categories of powerful, fast, handheld computing and communications products that are easy to use, offer long battery life, and are cost effective. These new products include: Information Appliances (application-specific home appliances that can access information from the Internet), Internet televisions and telephones, digital cameras, portable medical patient care systems, remote utility maintenance systems, mobile sales force systems, mobile executive decision support systems, wireless electronic mail devices, and global positioning system (GPS) satellite navigation products.

Here in the Silicon Valley, Mitsubishi Electric Corporation's North American semiconductor business units—Electronic Device Group and VSIS, Inc.—are leading the way in establishing this new cores-based design paradigm. Their work with North American electronic systems original equipment manufacturers (OEMs) has led to the design, development, and delivery of innovative and affordable new classes of consumer and industrial products.

In addition to *eRAM*-based systems design, the 300-employee Electronic Device Group, established in 1980, also provides North American OEMs with systems design integration, application engineering, marketing, and sales support for Mitsubishi Electric's wide range of proprietary and licensed IP cores, including M32R, ColdFire™, and 68EC000; for system software, such as Diba's Information Appliance software and Sun Microsystems' Java platform; as well as for separate semiconductor ICs and related system products.

The Electronic Device Group spun off VSIS, Inc., in 1996 as a separate, entrepreneurial organization that now has 35 employees. The establishment of VSIS was a critical component of Mitsubishi Electric President Takashi Kitaoka's "transnational" business strategy, which is characterized by three key attributes.

First, Mitsubishi's transnational business strategy enables the development of assets and capabilities—or core competencies—in diverse local markets where specific technologies are quickly emerging, as well as the distribution of those assets throughout other Mitsubishi global market areas that require them. For example, 3-D graphics hardware and software technologies are developing fastest in the USA. In 1995, Mitsubishi Electronics America announced its partnership with Evans & Sutherland Computer Corporation to develop real-time, full-featured 3-D graphics chipsets for the personal computer (PC). The first product resulting from the partnership has been introduced across the globe.

Second, transnationalism enables Mitsubishi Electric's overseas operations to develop the business strategies and technology core competencies

Mitsubishi's Electronic Device Group supplies its North American OEM customers with a broad base of advanced semiconductor technologies and products for emerging computing, communication, and consumer markets.

that make sense for their specific local or national markets, and to integrate those core competencies into the company's worldwide operations. This is in contrast to traditional, centralized global companies which allow their subsidiaries to implement only the parent company's strategies and use only the parent company's centrally developed technologies.

Third, the Mitsubishi Electric companies share and diffuse their knowledge across global business units, versus retaining IP within separate business units, or retaining it in a centralized headquarters.

As a key player in Mitsubishi's transnational business plan, VSIS's strategy is to develop IP in North America for profit via diverse methods, including partnering, technology sharing, and investment with other leading technology companies.

The Electronic Device Group and VSIS, both located in Sunnyvale, work in tandem to implement Mitsubishi Electric's mission of creating semiconductor-based solutions for customers' future applications requirements. Both business units are wholly owned subsidiaries of Mitsubishi Electronics America, Inc., which is one of 10 members of the Mitsubishi Electric America, Inc., family of companies.

Electronic Device Group

The Electronic Device Group division of Mitsubishi Electronics America develops custom and semicustom ICs as well as semiconductor IP cores that meet customer requirements for specific applications. It also markets, sells, and provides application engineering support for a broad line of semiconductors and related electronic components, including:

microcontrollers; dynamic, static, flash, and application-specific memories; gate arrays and embedded cell arrays; application-specific standard products; microwave and radio frequency products; optoelectronic products; contact image sensors; color thin-film-transistor liquid crystal displays; and disk drive storage products, including those based on LS-120 and DVD-ROM technologies.

Markets for Mitsubishi Electric's semiconductor-based technologies are expanding dramatically. They include computers (mobile PCs, network-centric computing devices, desktop and portable PCs, workstations, and high-end 3-D graphics PCs and workstations); office equipment (printers, copiers, scanners, and facsimile machines); wired and wireless communications (cellular phones, base stations, and satellites); consumer products (televisions, set-top boxes, audio equipment, and 3-D game products); networking products (routers and hubs); and communications and connectivity (ATM, ISDN, switching equipment, terminal, digital cross connect, and transmission equipment).

"Foremost among Mitsubishi's technological contributions is its exclusive world leadership in the *eRAM* embedded memory technology," said John Zucker, executive vice president of Mitsubishi's Electronic Device Group. "The *eRAM* technology will radically increase the intelligence and performance of consumer products while making them affordable to the masses."

Mitsubishi Electric's renowned quality has been an important factor in Electronic Device Group's market growth. Among the many awards Electronic Device Group has received for Mitsubishi Electric's products and performance, three in particular stand out—the first two underscore Mitsubishi Electric's well-earned reputation as a technology innovator; the third highlights its uncompromising commitment to customer relations, service, and support.

In 1994, *Electronic Products* magazine recognized Mitsubishi with its Product of the Year award for Mitsubishi's innovative 3D-RAM frame buffer memory. According to the magazine's publisher/editor, Frank Egan, *Electronic Products* began giving out these awards in 1976 as a means of recognizing significant contributions to the electronics industry. Although there is no limit to the number of awards that can be presented each year, 3D-RAM was one of only seven singled out for such recognition that year. Mitsubishi won the award again in 1996 for its M32R/D microprocessor-DRAM chip.

Mitsubishi's 3D-RAM frame buffer memory improves workstation and PC 3-D graphics rendering performance by a factor of 10 as a result of integrating logic and memory together in the same piece of silicon. The 3D-RAM was one of only seven products throughout the industry recognized by Electronic Products magazine for its Product of the Year award in 1994.

With 3DPro™, Vsis's flagship product, Mitsubishi ushered in real-time workstation-level 3-D graphics cost effectively on the PC platform. (Fire demon image created with Softimage® 3D and provided courtesy of Softimage. ©1996)

Also in 1996, Sun Microsystems honored Mitsubishi with its prestigious Excalibur for Excellence Award, which is given each year to a single Sun supplier. "Legend has it that the sword Excalibur could only be drawn from the stone by one who had proven worthy through exemplary acts of honor and courage," the award reads. "That's why we'd like to applaud Mitsubishi Electronics America, Inc., as this year's recipient—application-specific integrated circuits (ASICs) were delivered 100 percent on-time with world-class lead times, and were 99.99 percent defect free. They qualified packaging and process technology more than seven months ahead of schedule—so we salute Mitsubishi for their efforts this past year, going above and beyond the call of duty."

In the presentation, Mel Friedman, Sun Microsystems' vice president of Worldwide Operations, observed, "We're going to have to change our standards for this award from now on because Mitsubishi's performance broke all records and has, therefore, raised the bar for all future contenders."

Vsis, Inc.

In July 1996, Vsis, Inc., Mitsubishi Electric's first semiconductor systems design spinoff, was formed to address the emerging systems-level applications requirements of North American customers. Vsis handles leading-edge "system-on-a-chip" designs, leveraging Mitsubishi Electric's R&D and fabrication facilities, as well as IP from both inside and outside the company, to combine silicon and software in next-generation ICs for 3-D graphics acceleration and imaging, consumer embedded applications, network-centric and Java-based computing, telecommunications, and other emerging markets.

"Vsis is structured as a nimble and autonomous design company to respond quickly to emerging customer needs," said Yasutaka Horiba, president, CEO, and chairman of Vsis. "For the level of integration we want, a strong systems focus is absolutely necessary."

Designed to remain a small, entrepreneurial company, Vsis is managed by a board of directors as a profit-making venture, with 100 percent of its stock owned by Mitsubishi Electronics America. The company employs several business models to create IP, business opportunities,

end-products, and bottom-line income. These business models include augmenting Mitsubishi Electric core technologies with internal research and development, codevelopment, and strategic alliances—as well as whole or partial company acquisition, technology transfer, and technology licensing. Bottom-line revenues come from marketing consultation, design and development work, technology licensing, royalties, and manufacturing.

Mitsubishi's flagship family of 3-D graphics and imaging products, *3DPro™*, was introduced in August 1996—the result of a technology partnership between Mitsubishi Electric and Evans & Sutherland. *3DPro* combines Mitsubishi Electric's innovative 3D-RAM frame buffer memory and Cached DRAM texture memory technologies with Evans & Sutherland's *REALimage™* technology, an outgrowth from nearly 30 years of expertise in 3-D graphics acceleration.

"*3DPro* was the genesis of the next paradigm in 3-D computing for the personal computer," said Stephen Hester, Vsis's executive vice president. "In the late 1970s and early 1980s, we began to see computer-generated 3-D graphics on the 'big screen.' These were created with extremely expensive supercomputers. Then, in the early to mid 1980s, we saw the emergence of workstations to generate faster, better, and much less expensive 3-D graphics and animation. In the 1990s, with *3DPro*, Mitsubishi ushered in real-time workstation-level 3-D graphics cost effectively on the PC platform."

A key Vsis objective is to drive Mitsubishi's *eRAM* technology and M32R/D microprocessor plus DRAM chip as a means of enabling consumer embedded applications. In concert with this objective, Vsis teamed with Silicon Valley start-up, Diba, Inc., to develop a complete, integrated hardware-software technology platform for Information Appliances—a quickly emerging class of consumer products that provide easy, convenient, and affordable access to the Internet via traditional consumer appliances. The Diba-Mitsubishi Information Appliance platform combines Mitsubishi's hardware—M32R/D microprocessor and a "super I/O" application-specific integrated circuit (ASIC)—with the Diba™ Application Foundation software. A future version of the platform will integrate the M32R/D and super I/O ASIC on the same chip, lowering costs even further and making it possible—for the first time—for consumer electronics manufacturers to deliver portable Information Appliances at affordable prices.

At Mitsubishi, customers come first. Mel Friedman, Sun Microsystems' vice president of worldwide operations, declared that Sun would have to change its standards for this award from now on "because Mitsubishi's performance broke all records and raised the bar for all future contenders."

Mitsubishi Electric Corporation

Mitsubishi Electric Corporation was established in 1921 under the stewardship of Koyata Iwasaki, the last president of the original Mitsubishi organization started by his uncle, Yataro Iwasaki, in 1870. It was Koyata Iwasaki who enunciated the principles that are still practiced by Mitsubishi Electric: "Corporate responsibility to society, integrity and fairness, and international understanding through business."

Mitsubishi Electric employs more than 111,000 people worldwide and achieved sales of $33 billion in 1996. As a critical part of its transnational philosophy, Mitsubishi Electric is placing market development activities, research and development, and production facilities as close as possible to end-product markets throughout the world. The company is giving these decentralized business units the power to make decisions necessary to thrive in their local markets as well as to develop core competencies the company can leverage throughout its worldwide operations. Based on projected industry requirements in the year 2010, Mitsubishi Electric established its *Vision21* plan, which is designed to lead the company in the six business domains considered most appropriate to serve society and the planet in the 21st Century: environment, energy, wellness, amenity, security, and transportation and communication.

Concern for the environment is not just a slogan at Mitsubishi Electric. In 1991, the corporation established its Environmental Protection Department, dedicated to the environmental management of the entire corporation. In 1993, the company drafted an environmental plan and within two years had implemented procedures designed to protect the ozone layer, reduce industrial waste, and promote resource conservation and recycling. Goals for the year 2000 include revising the corporation's basic environmental philosophy, achieving ISO 14001 compatibility for its Environmental Management System (EMS), and establishing specific goals to prevent global warming, enable conservation, recycle natural resources, and manage chemical substances.

Mitsubishi Electric is equally committed to its employees and their communities, and fosters a philosophy of local support for the communities in which it conducts business. Corporate volunteers have hosted children at nature-discovery camps for orphans and single-parent families, and they have participated in community cleanups. Donations have been made to scholarship and student-exchange programs, to environmental research, and to other public-interest endeavors.

In 1991, Mitsubishi Electric and Mitsubishi Electric America established the Mitsubishi Electric America Foundation to identify and support national and local agencies that are committed to helping physically challenged young people experience a full, active, and productive life. The Sunnyvale activities of the foundation and company are managed through the Community Active Responsive Employees (CARE) committee, staffed by local Mitsubishi Electronics America volunteers. Local non-profit organizations and charitable activities receiving foundation and/or company contributions through the CARE committee include: Via Rehabilitation Services, Inc., formerly known as Crippled Children's Society; Timpany Center; Make-A-Wish Foundation of the Greater Bay Area; Eastfield Ming Quong; Children's Cancer Research Institute, San Francisco; Project Open Hand; Union Bank "Heart of the City" 10K Race, benefiting the American Heart Association; Hope Rehabilitation Services; Juvenile Diabetes Foundation, Greater Bay Area Chapter; and Books Aloud, Inc.

Mitsubishi Electric and its Silicon Valley business units are dedicated to providing customers with innovative, high-quality semiconductor products and technologies. The corporation is just as dedicated to being a good corporate citizen internationally and locally by protecting the environment and supporting physically challenged young people. Technological and service excellence, integrity, and corporate citizenship remain driving forces at Mitsubishi Electric Corporation, helping to ensure the global success of its customers and employees, and the enhancement of societies throughout the world. ✦

- *eRAM is a trademark and eRAM-enabled is a servicemark of Mitsubishi Electronics America, Inc.*
- *Java is a trademark of Sun Microsystems, Inc.*
- *ColdFire is a trademark of Motorola, Inc.*
- *Diba is a trademark of Diba, Inc.*

Vsis and Mitsubishi teamed with Silicon Valley start-up, Diba, Inc., to create a complete, integrated technology solution—both hardware and software—for Information Appliances. Information Appliances combine the power of computers with the ease-of-use, convenience, and affordability of traditional consumer appliances.

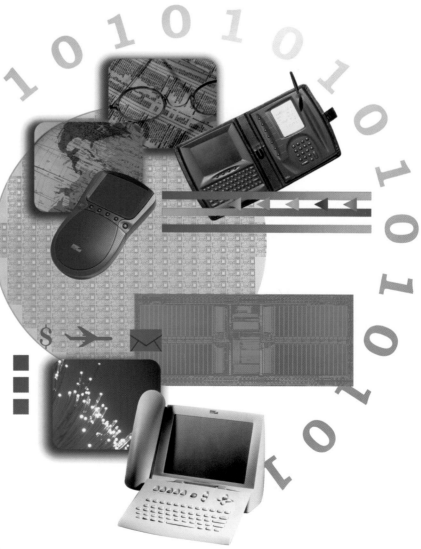

HEURISTICS SEARCH, INC.

Heuristics is known for practicing the same kind of teamwork in its operations that its clients do in theirs. Instead of assigning a single representative to each account, Heuristics assigns a highly trained team of people.

Money isn't the fuel that powers the Silicon Valley engine; it's people–talented, trained, top-notch, technical people. Without them, there is no innovation, no ability to attract investment. Without them, there is no Silicon Valley.

Helping Silicon Valley companies attract the world-class talent they need to continue leading the global technology revolution is what Heuristics Search, Inc., is all about.

Heuristics is America's largest professional recruitment firm that focuses exclusively on placement of software development engineers. Established in 1979 by company president Elizabeth Patrick, its clients range in size from start-ups to multinational giants. One thing they have in common, though, is a pressing need for the best and the brightest of software engineers. Unlike firms that take a standardized, "cookie-cutter" approach to business, Heuristics' placement and consulting services are custom-tailored to the specific needs of each client's hiring managers. These specialized services include regular salary surveys drawn from a population of computer scientists' special showcasing opportunities for clients to assure that Heuristics' recruiters understand the client's business in depth–even giving clients access to the firm's offices for professional, disturbance-free, off-site candidate interviews.

"It's our job to provide the right technical talent and interviewing environment for the company," Patrick says. "Managers in charge of the projects usually know best what technical expertise is needed for present and future projects. And we want to meet–better yet, exceed–their expectations."

Because things get done in Silicon Valley primarily through teamwork, interpersonal chemistry is important, too. "The personality that will best fit in with the client's work group and management style is what we look for," she said.

Written job specifications detailing required knowledges, skills, and abilities, convey only a part of what's needed in a job. Likewise, a candidate's resume presents only a part of what that person has to offer.

Heuristics is America's largest professional recruitment firm that focuses exclusively on placement of software development engineers.

Adding-in personality, people skills, and the experiences and expectations formed over a lifetime of work completes the picture.

"To achieve a good match, compatibility of personality and style between the candidate and the hiring manager is critical," Patrick said. "By working closely with the managers, we learn the specifics of what they need from their employees in order to accomplish their goals."

Heuristics' clients and candidates work with leading-edge technology, but the business of Heuristics is people and relationships. "Our goal is to establish a mutually satisfying, long-term relationship in which each party utilizes the strengths and talents of the other," Patrick explained.

Rather than wait until an opening materializes before recruiting to fill it–a process that can take as long as three months–Heuristics takes a proactive approach. "We maintain a continuous dialogue with the market," Patrick says. "Our extensive networking process allows us to respond quickly and effectively to our clients' needs."

One of the newest additions to Heuristics' cache of networking tools is its site on the World Wide Web. The site takes a tongue-in-cheek approach, using cartoons, jokes, "brain games," and other light-hearted techniques to convey its message and attract site visitors.

"Candidates, clients, and the Heuristics staff all have a good sense of humor, and we wanted to tap into that," Patrick says. "It's hard work here in the valley, but it's also fun."

Typical of Heuristics' business style, its website not only draws out useful information from visitors, it also gives out a wealth of pointers–career tips, access to the annual Heuristics Search Salary Survey, key advice on high-technology career decisions, and more.

Heuristics is known for practicing the same kind of teamwork in its operations that its clients do in theirs. Instead of assigning a single representative to each account, Heuristics assigns a highly trained team of people.

"Our team concept is vital to the quality of our service," Patrick says. "Clients don't have just one account executive representing them at Heuristics; they have every person in the company. This approach assures our clients the best possible service from our entire firm."

In an industry known for its high staff turnover, Heuristics turnover is surprisingly low. "We have staff members who have been with us 15 years, 17 years, and more," Patrick said. That kind of stability is a boon to Heuristics' clients, who don't have to start from "Ground Zero" with each new staffing order.

Heuristics takes its responsibilities as a corporate citizen seriously, too–as evidenced in part by its support of the San Jose Cleveland Ballet, the San Jose Symphony, San Jose public television, and other community service causes and groups.

And the firm feels a real kinship with the companies it serves. "We've grown up here in Silicon Valley, just as they have," said Patrick. "Our knowledge and appreciation of this valley's high-tech industries is personal and extremely deep."

The Heuristics team knows firsthand how much the performance and productivity of the valley's high-technology companies contribute to the economy of the entire region–for that matter, to the entire country. That's why its expert recruiters work so hard to find and place the right people–the people who will help client companies maintain their spectacular innovation and technical excellence. After all, Heuristics' client companies are technology leaders in a region that is the technology leader of the world.

"What keeps us working 50 and 60 hours a week is the endlessly exciting technological breakthroughs of our clients. We love technology and we love people." Patrick says. "We've prospered because our local industries have prospered. And we work hard to give back the highest value we can to our client companies, to our candidates, and to the entire Silicon Valley community." ✦

Heuristics' recruiting teams review more than 50 resumes, and personally interview an average of 40 people each week.

The staff of Heuristics Search, Inc., help Silicon Valley companies attract the world-class talent they need to continue leading the global technology revolution.

SILICON GRAPHICS

Silicon Graphics, headquartered just north of San Jose in Mountain View, is one of Silicon Valley's high-tech success stories. In 1981, a Stanford professor and six of his graduate students decided to start a company and market products based on their graphics chip design. With a minimum of resources and a lot of dedication, this team pioneered 3D computing technology and founded what has become the computer industry's fastest-growing company.

In the early 1980s, most computer users were accustomed to viewing flat, two-dimensional images on their display screens. Only the most expensive computer systems (costing millions of dollars) had the horsepower to display and manipulate realistic-looking three-dimensional images. The original Silicon Graphics team set out to introduce a computer system that more closely resembled the human approach to problem solving–with a visual, intuitive view of the object or situation being analyzed. The company's revolutionary silicon chip–the Geometry Engine processor–provided the processing power necessary to make visual computing a reality even with affordable desktop computers. This first-generation Geometry Engine processor has evolved into the advanced processors used in the company's current high-performance visual computing workstations, servers, and supercomputers.

From its beginning, Silicon Graphics has inspired everyone to rethink how computers are applied–to let people create, capture, and communicate ideas visually and naturally. The company's innovations have made it possible for a broad spectrum of customers to more intuitively and efficiently attack a wide range of challenges. Silicon Graphics systems realistically move 3D objects on a computer screen to simulate–or even predict–characteristics of the real world. With these types of on-screen prototyping and realistic design capabilities, scientists, engineers, and

From a handful of employees, Silicon Graphics has grown to an international organization of nearly 11,000. Since Silicon Graphics engineers are constantly exploring new territory, they depend upon creativity and innovation to get the job done. The corporate headquarters environment and company management style foster individual contributions and encourage imaginative thinking. **Photo courtesy of Silicon Graphics, Inc.**

creative professionals can more quickly develop and test new products or ideas.

The company's products–from desktop workstations to servers and supercomputers–have not only become the standard within the traditional technical fields such as engineering, science, and medicine. Real-time visual computing technology from Silicon Graphics has redefined the way that we experience entertainment. Many computer-generated images, made affordable with Silicon Graphics innovations, are commonplace in today's media. Advertisements, movies, television, video games, and theme parks all use graphics and imaging from Silicon Graphics to generate virtually real depictions of places, objects, and events.

The executive team at Silicon Graphics also breaks from traditional thinking. Committed to delivering total solutions to the market, the company teams up with other industry leaders rather than attempting to acquire in-house expertise for every business segment. In the financial arena, Morgan Stanley worked with Silicon Graphics to apply visual computing to its Global Risk Management System. The resulting visual models speed analysis and provide Morgan Stanley with a competitive advantage. Boeing reduced design changes, errors, and rework by more than 50 percent by managing the design and mock-up of the new Boeing 777 entirely inside Silicon Graphics computers, achieving unprecedented precision in the completed aircraft. Silicon Graphics' collaboration with Nintendo, the world leader in video games, has produced a 64-bit home

Silicon Graphics is a leading supplier of high-performance interactive computing systems. The company offers the broadest range of products in the industry–from low-end desktop workstations to servers and high-end supercomputers. **Shown from left to right: Brake Disc Assembly, designed with CATIA/Dassault Systemes; Stress Analysis on an Aircraft Steering Wheel, image courtesy of TRW; St. Peter's Cathedral, courtesy of ENEL SpA and Infobyte SpA; Underwater Camera, courtesy of Katz Design. Photo courtesy of Silicon Graphics, Inc.**

game system, Nintendo 64, which opens the door to a truly immersive 3D world.

"The confluence of the different types of digital media—computers, television, telephones—is creating a wealth of new applications for computer users," said Edward R. McCracken, chairman and chief executive officer of Silicon Graphics. "And Silicon Graphics is leading the way in helping people to see the possibilities."

The list of still-to-be-explored opportunities is long, as Silicon Graphics designers continue to make combined graphics and computing technologies even more affordable. The company helps leading technology providers around the world deploy innovative solutions to new and emerging markets. Strategic areas for the future include applications for the World Wide Web, enterprise computing solutions, and digital media applications that fully incorporate text screens, voice-overs, animated graphics, and virtual reality applications for unprecedented human interaction.

The human brain processes thoughts visually. Silicon Graphics has proven that computers and visual processing can enhance any business where thinking is required. Just think of the possibilities! ✦

Silicon Graphics computers enable digital artists and designers to unleash their creativity and explore the possibilities. Zebra image created by Christine Lo. Photograph of girl courtesy of Lisa Hoffner. **Photo courtesy of Silicon Graphics, Inc.**

The Silicon Graphics Visionarium shows visitors how Silicon Graphics computer systems help customers, educators, and scientists bring products and projects to market in a timely and realistic fashion. The facility allows participants to interact with real-time, three-dimensional environments. Visitors not only view data, but also move around it, drive it, walk or fly through it, hear it, and experience it, just as they would in the real world. **Photo courtesy of Silicon Graphics, Inc.**

CISCO SYSTEMS, INC.

*T*he rise of Cisco Systems from home-based start-up in 1984 to the leading global player in its market in less than 10 years is the stuff of Silicon Valley legend.

Today Cisco is the worldwide leader in networking for the Internet. Its software and hardware products form the foundation of the electronically linked communication systems of many thousands of companies, universities, utilities, and government agencies worldwide.

With Cisco's products, geographically dispersed local-area and wide-area networks (LANs and WANs) are linked to form a single seamless information system, allowing organizations of all sizes to communicate more efficiently and effectively, regardless of differences in time, location, or type of computer system.

But in the early 1980s, these products didn't exist.

The Cisco story actually begins as a love story. Leonard Bosack and Sandra Lerner, who eventually married, worked in separate departments of Stanford University. They wanted to communicate with each other via computer, but couldn't because each Stanford department had its own computer network. The networks themselves were not connected because the only available solutions at the time required expensive mainframe computer hardware. As a result, it was hard for people in different departments to communicate and share data.

During the past two years as President and CEO, John Chambers has grown Cisco from $1.2 billion to its current run-rate of more than $4.5 billion by establishing Cisco as the leader in global internetworking solutions.

In frustration, Bosack and Lerner recruited some graduate students to help them solve the problem. Working together, this team developed a tool that connected the different networks for a fraction of the cost of existing technology. In the process, they created a niche in the networking market called "internetworking"–literally, networks of networks.

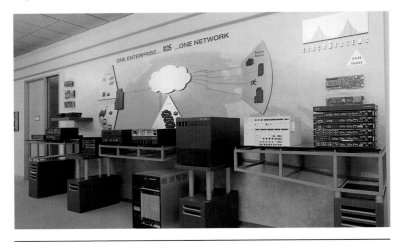

Cisco hardware products have become the backbone of most corporate Intranets and of the Internet itself. "Our software...is becoming a de facto standard." Chambers said. **Photo by Tom Tracy.**

The crucial innovation the team devised was a high-speed, relatively inexpensive device (a router) that forwards data packets from one computer to another. Equally important, the software the team developed allowed the data packets to be read by any kind of computer on the network.

Before long, they realized the significance of what they had created. So in December 1984, the team left Stanford, founded Cisco Systems, Inc., and set up operations in the Bosacks' Atherton home. Today, internetworking has become a multi-billion-dollar market, and Cisco Systems a multi-billion-dollar business. Cisco holds the number one or number two position in most segments of the industry, and its Cisco IOS software is a defacto standard for delivering network services.

And Cisco is one of the driving forces behind the exploding global Internet. More than 80 percent of the backbone routers used in the Internet come from Cisco, and the company offers a wide range of products for customers who want to connect to the Internet.

Cisco plans to do more than lead the networking equipment market. "We intend to provide an end-to-end solution for our customers," says Selby Wellman, senior vice president of business units at Cisco.

Put simply, that means Cisco now competes in every major market segment in the industry–not just the routers, on which its reputation and fortune were built, but also high-speed switches, remote access products, and Internet operating software, too.

Cisco's participation in multiple market segments is a response to the desire by many corporate customers who want a strategic supplier of networking equipment. Many companies find integrated networking solutions essential because timely information and high-speed communications are crucial to their operations. They need to be globally interconnected in order to remain competitive.

Internet access, customer support, product development, and networked commerce are only a few of the applications supported on enterprise networks. Benefits to firms whose operations are so interconnected include increased productivity, reduced expenses, improved client service, and faster product time to market.

Cisco's performance record has been impressive. "No technology company has lived up to Wall Street's high expectations better than Cisco Systems," boasts a recent article in *Financial World* magazine. "Not Intel, not even Microsoft." With an average annual growth rate approaching 90 percent and earnings at nearly 70 percent a year—consistently higher than management projections—it's no surprise that Cisco's stock has risen more than 8,000 percent since the company went public in 1990. Anyone lucky enough—or smart enough—to get in on Cisco's initial public offering has been a part of "one of the greatest gold rushes of the decade." Ten thousand dollars invested in Cisco in February 1990 was worth $750,000 by 1995!

Cisco's Silicon Valley beginnings spawned a corporate culture that is still ingrained at the company—and that still dazzles investors.

Wall Street loves firms that don't waste money, for instance, and Cisco takes pride in 'an almost ostentatious frugality.' Likewise, this eye-popping-performer company is known for its absolute commitment to giving customers what they want.

"We have no religion when it comes to technology," observes John Chambers, Cisco's president and CEO. "We remain committed to our customers and their changing needs as we continue to focus on expanding the frontiers of networking technology—and with it, extending our leadership position to take advantage of a world of opportunities."

Cisco employs 10,250 people world-wide with 7,000 in the Bay Area. Currently, Cisco occupies 15 buildings and plans are underway for 15 more (4.5 million square feet total) on recently purchased land (center background open space).

"Cisco's purpose is to shape the future of the network industry the way IBM shaped the mainframe and Microsoft did the desktop," said John Chambers, Cisco's President and CEO. "There is no doubt that Internetworking is the next major paradigm in our industry."

Cisco's commitment to responsiveness isn't limited to its customers and employees, but also to the needs of the communities in which it has a corporate presence. Reflecting the company's roots in education, Cisco emphasizes education in its corporate giving programs, but its support of the community extends well beyond education. Each year Cisco donates hundreds of thousands of dollars to such vital programs as Second Harvest Food Bank, InnVision (homeless shelter), Children's Discovery Museum, Child Advocates of Santa Clara County, and more.

Cisco has products, customers, and facilities all over the world—a world that is becoming smaller and more closely connected every day. And Cisco plays a key role in enabling those connections. "One planet. One internetwork. The best is yet to come," says Chambers, "And Cisco is leading the way." ✦

HALL KINION

Technology is transforming the world, blurring the distinctions between "here" and "there" with the instantaneous movement of thoughts and ideas to and from just about anyplace on the planet.

And these days, technology changes at such a dizzying pace that high-tech companies are increasingly relying on contractors—especially engineers—to enhance their staffing flexibility and keep their technical knowledge on the leading edge.

Contract engineers constitute as much as 20 percent of the engineering workforce of some technology companies who also use temporary employees to augment their regular technical staff. And the trend continues up.

A Hall Kinion Staffing Specialist interviewing a prospective applicant for a position. Photo by Pat Kirk.

All this spells opportunity in a big way to Brenda Hall, founder and chief executive of Hall Kinion, the biggest full-service high-tech staffing firm in Silicon Valley, and one of the fastest growing companies in one of the fastest growing industries in the country, if not the world.

Hall Kinion's 1995 revenues of $29 million earned it the No. 44 spot on *Inc.* magazine's 1995 list of America's 500 fastest growing private companies. And the company's 1996 revenue levels are twice as high. "Eventually, we intend to become a $1 billion company," says Hall.

The rising demand for highly trained information workers has generated vigorous growth—about 25 percent a year—for the entire staffing industry. What sets Hall Kinion apart is that it provides the entire range of services to its clients and concentrates exclusively on information technology companies like Sun Microsystems, Inc. and Oracle Systems Corp. This kind of specialization allows Hall Kinion to fill job requests faster than its competitors.

Another Hall Kinion advantage is its own investment in communications technologies. Client-accessible databases and sophisticated videoconferencing equipment that links its complex of offices make it easier for its corporate clients to interview and hire workers regardless of where they live.

Videoconferencing is also an important internal management tool, helping Hall manage the company's own network of offices. "We use our equipment to conduct weekly meetings with managers at each office," she said. "It's also great for orchestrating training sessions and helping us to resolve those unavoidable crises that occasionally materialize."

Hall is a dynamic visionary, who sees Silicon Valley not as a single place, but as a phenomenon that is spreading, "like little fires." The original Silicon Valley will always be the "heart and brain of high tech," she says, but the industry is creating less complex clones of itself all over the world.

Hall Kinion planned to capitalize on this technology spread from the get-go. It grew from one to five offices in Silicon Valley in its first few years of operation. In 1993 its first out-of-state office opened in Provo, Utah. Other branches followed in quick succession—in Denver, Seattle, Portland, Austin, Phoenix, and Raleigh. And the firm's first international office opened in London in fall 1996.

Underscoring Hall Kinion's dramatic growth is its base of satisfied clients, who confirm that the company usually outperforms its competitors in the speed with which it fills its orders for staff. David Borhk, a quality engineering manager at Lotus Development Corp.'s Cc:Mail division in Mountain View, says that it usually takes Hall Kinion less than two days to give him an ample list of qualified candidates. Hall Kinion's more generalized competitors typically take as long as a week to do the same thing, he says, and often try to place over-qualified—and therefore needlessly expensive—people.

"I like Hall Kinion best because it typically provides me with exactly the kind of people I'm looking for," Borhk said.

"We take the time up front to learn about our clients, their needs and their work environment," Hall says. "So that when they call us with an urgent request, we already know their preferences."

A Hall Kinion contract employee hard at work on an assignment at a high-tech company. Photo by Pat Kirk.

The speed and accuracy by which Hall Kinion can offer staffing solutions can be attributed to the company's unique internal structure of three distinct, individual divisions. Each of these divisions has its own scope, focusing on a client's specific staffing needs. Qualified contractors can be found through the Technical Contracting Services division; temporary staffing with the Technology Support Services division; and full-time professionals through the Technical Recruiting division.

The expertise of these three divisions is how Hall Kinion can fill the entire complement of staffing needs of high tech companies. It finds people by taking a multiple-track approach: networking, postings on Internet bulletin boards, and newspaper advertisements. And even though it uses videoconferencing technology to bring applicants and employers together quickly, Hall Kinion does its own candidate, in-depth candidate screen first.

"Matching skills to tasks is only the first step in the way we match people and companies," Hall says. "Are they quick learners? Self-starters? Team players? Are they creatively or organizationally minded? It takes a lot more than a database to make a good match."

Hall Kinion would rather leave an order unfilled than force a fit. "We won't put square pegs in round holes just to complete a transaction," Hall says. "Our goal is long-term relationships and referrals, not short-term, patchwork solutions."

To succeed in the kaleidoscopic world of high technology, it takes a firm that moves with lightning speed. "In the high-tech marketplace, the ability to adapt quickly to business opportunities can be a decisive advantage," Hall acknowledges. "And that has been our performance goal from the start."

Hall Kinion's explosive growth to the Silicon Valley lead spot in its field in less than 5 years is proof of the extent to which it has achieved its goal. With the continuing shortage of engineers and other technical professionals trained in the latest technologies, more and more high-tech companies have learned to turn to Hall Kinion to solve their staffing problems. ✦

Hall Kinion uses the latest technology to communicate with field offices and applicants throughout the United States and abroad. Photo by Pat Kirk.

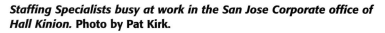

Staffing Specialists busy at work in the San Jose Corporate office of Hall Kinion. Photo by Pat Kirk.

INTEL CORPORATION

"D on't be encumbered by history," said Intel co-founder Robert Noyce in 1970. "Go off and do something wonderful." That's exactly what Intel's handful of founding employees did. In the process they inspired thousands of people—inside Intel, elsewhere in Silicon Valley, and throughout the world—to go and do likewise.

According to Gordon Moore, Intel's chairman emeritus and another of its visionary co-founders, the number of transistors unleashed on the planet since 1971 roughly equals the world's population of ants! That's when Intel put a transistor into a calculator and created the microprocessor that has been called "one of the most revolutionary products in the history of mankind."

"This is a phenomenal industry in which the only rule is change," Moore said.

When Intel was started in July 1968, Moore, Noyce, and within a few months, Andy Grove (now CEO and chairman), all dreamed of building a successful company. But the reality far outstripped the dreams. By the end of 1996, Intel employed nearly 50,000 people and had become only the second company in Silicon Valley to report annual revenues of more than $20 billion.

As the explosion of interest in global e-mail and the Internet's colorful World Wide Web continues, analysts predict that both consumers and businesses will be clamoring for ever-better, ever-faster computers. And Intel—which sells over 80 percent of the world's microprocessors, the calculating "brains" inside most personal computers—will be right there satisfying that demand. Predicted by San Jose-based Dataquest to increase to $33 billion in the year 2000—more than double its 1995 size of $14.2 billion—the global market is booming.

Intel's culture is at the core of its phenomenal success. Rejecting the status-oriented bureaucracy of traditional corporations, Noyce, who is internationally acclaimed as one of Silicon Valley's visionary pioneers, laid the groundwork for a more egalitarian, merit-oriented company. Noyce personified the open, accessible management, the no-frills attitude, and the high value on employees that have come to characterize Intel's behavioral norms and corporate values.

A regular on the list of "100 Best Companies to Work for in America," Intel was, for example, the first Silicon Valley company to offer its employees sabbaticals—eight weeks of paid leave every seven years in addition to their regular vacations. Profit-sharing payout for Intel's employees in 1996 was $820 million, including three bonuses and Intel's retirement contributions. That's more than Intel's total revenue in 1981 and about equal to its net income for 1991. And, in early 1997, Intel announced that all of its employees worldwide would be eligible for stock options—making it unique among large manufacturing companies.

Chip making in the 1970s—an early Intel manufacturing line.

Intel's history is one of continuing innovation. The integrated circuit, co-invented by Noyce in the mid-1960s, enabled the miniaturization of electronic circuitry on a single silicon chip, starting a trend that continues to this day.

Intel's founders set out to make semiconductor memory practical, and in 1970, two years after the company's founding, Intel introduced the 1103 dynamic random access memory (DRAM)—the world's first merchant market large-scale integrated DRAM, which is smaller, more powerful and more energy efficient than magnetic core memory.

In 1971, Intel introduced an alterable storage medium—erasable programmable read-only memory (EPROM)—that gave computer manufacturers a flexible, low-cost way to store microprocessor programs.

That same year, Intel introduced the world's first commercial microprocessor, the 4004. Smaller than a thumbnail and packed with 2,300 transistors, Intel's new chip executed 60,000 operations in one second. That's as much computing power as Eniac, the first electronic computer, which required 18,000 vacuum tubes packed into a room-sized 3,000 cubic feet.

Over the years, Intel has continued to announce dramatic increases in chip performance and speed at a record-breaking pace. In 1982 Intel introduced the revolutionary 80286, the chip used in the IBM Personal Computer and PC clones. Eleven years later, when Intel introduced the Pentium® processor, it contained 3.2 million transistors and ran at 100 million instructions per second (MIPS), better than 1,500 times the speed of the 4004. The first Pentium Pro processor was introduced in 1995; the chip contained 5.5 million transistors and ran at over 320 MIPS. And as they say...the beat goes on... .

Microcontrollers based on Intel technology can also be found in thousands of applications ranging from personal computers and automobiles to automated machine tools, home appliances, and medical instrumentation.

Thousands of Intel employees volunteer each year in the community. Shown here is an Intel volunteer at Earth Day '96. **Photo by David Reese.**

Chip making in the 1990s—bunny-suited manufacturing technicians in a fab clean room.

Intel invests for the future—not only in its products, but also in United States industry. In 1974, when Noyce turned over the actual running of the company to Gordon Moore and Andy Grove, his major role became that of spokesman for the Silicon Valley and the electronic frontier itself. He became chairman of the Semiconductor Industry Association and later went on to head Sematech, a consortium of companies dedicated to advancing the technological capabilities of U.S. industry.

In addition, Intel is dedicated to being a good neighbor and a good corporate citizen. The company invests thousands of volunteer hours in its local communities through its "Intel Involved" program, and a variety of education, learning, and technology literacy programs benefit from Intel's cash grants and scholarships, training fellowships, and equipment donations.

Thirty years ago, Gordon Moore formulated what has come to be known as Moore's Law: The power and complexity of the silicon chip will double in 18 months, with proportionate decreases in cost. Although the computer revolution is by no means finished, Moore now believes the time frame will slow early in the next century. In other words, his basic law of getting more electronics at a cheaper cost won't be reversed; it's just that the rate of technology change won't be as fast.

But by that time, says writer Robert Lenzner in a September 11, 1995, *Forbes* magazine article, "chips will be performing tricks that are only dreamed about today, the world will be a far more interconnected place, and there will be unpredictable changes, mostly for the better, in business and government."

Since its introduction of the world's first commercial microprocessor, Intel and its awe-inspiring founders have been at the start—and the heart—of it all. ◆

Intel's 106 employees in front of the Mountain View plant in 1969. Included here are Robert Noyce and Gordon Moore (front row, left to right) and Andy Grove (second row, far right). Next to Mr. Grove is Marcian E. "Ted" Hoff (with glasses), one of the inventors of the microprocessor.

BAY NETWORKS, INC.

Throughout history, barriers of time and distance have separated people from their aspirations and from each other. Breakthrough technology, going back to the printing press, has helped people dissolve these barriers and gain power by expanding their access to the ideas and resources of others.

Today, the power of the Internet, the global network of networks, is bringing people together in an electronic community unimaginable just decades ago. At the same time, these Internet technologies have enabled the creation of intranets, private Web sites built and maintained by organizations for their own use. Bay Networks, Inc., long a leader in the internetworking marketplace, is helping organizations answer the call for "anytime, anywhere" networking–connecting people and information together, wherever each may be located–smoothly, easily, flexibly.

Using Bay Networks technology, organizations can redefine the boundaries of their enterprise network and reshape the way that they conduct their business–sharing information without concern for time and geographic constraints.

The pace of business is accelerating and to remain competitive, organizations must move more quickly than ever before. For example, timely access to engineering drawings hastens new product development and helps beat the competition to market. Rapid credit card verification speeds point-of-sale transactions and keeps valuable customers happy. Information gained a few seconds sooner makes a bond trader millions of dollars. In every case, the enterprise internetwork is critical to improving business performance and bringing what's needed to the desktop.

Emerging applications such as image processing, videoconferencing at the desktop, date mining, information modeling, and multimedia are dramatically changing network service requirements and driving the need for greater network performance, availability, and scalabiltity. Yet these applications must share the network with already existing strategic business applications.

The global internetworking market, currently pegged at more that $15 billion, is expected to hit the $35 billion mark by 1999. "With an installed base of 3.1 million connections–one of every four user connections worldwide–we are a key player in this vibrant, exploding market," says Dave House, Bay Networks chairman, president, and CEO.

Based in Santa Clara, Bay Networks, Inc., is a global leader in the internetworking marketplace, providing a complete line of Internet and intranet products and solutions from 145 offices in 90 countries around the world. **Photo by John Sutton.**

With its strong portfolio of products–LAN and ATM switches, hubs, routers, remote and Internet access solutions, and network management applications–and an in-depth understanding of those industries that are using networking to help them gain a competitive edge–healthcare, financial services, government, education, telecommunications, Internet service providers, and cable operators–Bay Networks provide customers with the appropriate migration path for their unique needs.

Reinforcing its position as a technology leader in the internetworking market are the numerous accolades and awards that Bay Networks continues to earn. Highest Throughput Performance: The Backbone Concentrator Node router. Best Network Management Platform: Optivity application suite. The Editor's Choice Award and Editor Refuses to Give It Back Award: Instant Internet. Well-Connected Award and Winners Circle Standards Achievement Award: Best Enterprise Hub/Switch–System 5000 and Best Token Ring Switch–Centillion 100. Blue Ribbon Award: Branch Office router–BayStack Access Node. Remote Access Award: Remote Annex 4000. And many more.

But any company is more than the sum of its products. People are its lifeblood, "To be a leader in the internetworking industry takes more than superior technology, it takes strong connections with and among people," House observes. "That's why we're focused on finding new ways to meet customer needs, and on creating and atmosphere that values–and is valued by–everyone who works here."

With its installed base of more than 31 million desktop connections and over $2.1 billion in revenue, the environment at Bay Networks still seems more like a start-up than that of an established global leader. "We cultivate an atmosphere of creative freedom, where everyone contributes to the success of the team," points out House. "Where responsiveness and flexibility are held up as our most desirable qualities. And where the individual's ability to make independent, entrepreneurial decisions is praised and backed at every level of our company."

Cross-functional teams, widely used at Bay Networks, stimulate new

Using Bay Networks technology, organizations can redefine the boundaries of their enterprise network and reshape the way that they conduct their business–sharing information without concern for time and geographic constraints.

ideas and perspectives by bringing together people from various departments to help develop products from concept to completion.

For these reasons and more, Bay Networks has always attracted talented and energetic professionals who are ready to meet the challenges of this rapidly and constantly changing technology landscape. People who can overcome barriers and defy convention to answer customer needs and help them manage change with unprecedented ease. And beyond the challenge and the excitement, Bay Networks provides competitive salaries and an impressive array of generous and innovative benefits.

Only a handful of companies bring the experience and expertise needed to build the products and system-level services that will be required to succeed in the hectic pace of change. But only one company offers solutions that allow customers to evolve to the advanced networks of the future while protecting their existing investments. Only one company backs it philosophy with a clear vision of the future. Only one company stands at the forefront, providing customers with the solutions they need–when they need them, where they need them, and how they need them delivered. That company is Bay Networks.

"Over the next decade, we will see the power of networking technology change the face of the world," House contends. "We intend to remain part of this change by making products that increase the power of networking through the power of integration." ✦

NOVELL, INC.

"The Internet has become the center of innovation in the computer industry," says Joe Marengi, president of Novell, Inc. "It has given us a preview of a world in which the ability to obtain information from virtually any source will extend beyond the workplace, into our homes and daily lives. In that world, computing will become transparent and intuitive, just like electric power and the telephone."

At Novell, the world's leading provider of network software, this vision affects each of the market-leading products it develops for the business community. And it is a logical extension of the networking revolution which the company helped create more than a decade ago.

It all started with the personal computer (PC). When IBM introduced its PC, the IBM name generated such widespread business acceptance of PCs that it created a huge market in which PC applications that increased individual productivity flourished.

But as the PC became more essential to the

More than 1,000 engineers, programmers, executives, and other professionals work in nearly a dozen offices throughout the Silicon Valley, including this building in San Jose.

business world, people needed to share printers, files, databases, and other resources. Novell capitalized by introducing its flagship product: NetWare, the world's first network operating system (NOS).

NetWare has evolved into IntranetWare, anticipating the new needs of businesses in an Internet-centric world. IntranetWare creates a roadmap of the network as a single, enterprise-wide information system, guiding users through a complex electronic world. It brings a common framework and set of services to everyone on the network, regardless of where in the world they are or what type of computer platform they use.

The backbone of IntranetWare is Novell Directory Services (NDS), revolutionary technology that provides a database of all network users, applications, files, computers, and peripherals.

"Finding people and useful information on a global network without a directory," explains Marengi, "would be like trying to shop in a giant supermarket full of cans without labels."

By managing resources with NDS, companies can reduce the costs of owning and managing their networks because of greatly simplified administration. They can prevent unauthorized access to sensitive information. And they can take advantage of the powerful information-access capabilities for many other network software products, whether from Novell or third-party developers.

NetWare and IntranetWare have been such successes that Novell still controls better than half of the $6 billion global NOS software market. And through its two other major software applications, Novell aims to further simplify the way people work, learn, and govern.

Novell's GroupWise has become the industry's leading groupware application, allowing people to send E-mail, manage their schedules, and collaborate on projects across the network.

ManageWise by Novell helps companies stay in control of their networks. From one central location, administrators can monitor network traffic, diagnose and fix problems, and prevent potential outages.

Novell's education programs are equally renowned in the industry. Certification programs, such as the CNE, CNI, and Master CNE initiatives, ensure that administrators, consultants, and other Novell users have the knowledge and tools to provide maintenance, service, or training for their networks.

Today, nearly 60 million users in the LAN, Internet, intranet, and small-business markets, in some 90 countries, rely on Novell software to share resources, access information, and increase productivity via more than 4 million Novell networks–figures unmatched in the industry, and still rising. "We see the opportunity to double our servers installed by the year 2000 to 8 million," says Marengi.

A multibillion-dollar global giant, Novell is the fifth-largest software company in the world. It employs about 5,800 people who work at corporate subsidiaries throughout the world: in the Americas, Europe, the Middle East, Africa, and Asia-Pacific. In the United States, Novell operates major facilities in San Jose, California, and Orem and Provo, Utah. The company's sales channel spans the globe with more than 25,000 authorized resellers and distributors.

Novell has set its sights on providing the network software that connects every network, every file, and every resource. The evolution of the Internet is driving that mission.

Novell products make it easy for network administrators to manage an entire network from a single desktop.

"As organizations of every size and type establish their presence on the World Wide Web, PCs have changed from computing devices to communication hubs, and Web browsers and E-mail are becoming ubiquitous," says Marengi. "We envision an even greater convergence of the Internet with traditional corporate networks. The full-service intranet of tomorrow will connect to an enterprise's proprietary databases for instant but controlled access to critical information. And beyond an organization's border, non-proprietary information will be easily accessible to the company's universe of customers, partners, and suppliers. This seamless flow of information—securely managed yet easily accessed—will continue the Internet revolution, and Novell will be helping to lead the charge."

To achieve its ambitious goal, Novell has identified three requirements: First, to provide powerful new products and services that businesses can use to access information quickly and confidentially. Second, to embrace open computing standards that integrate a multitude of products and devices from many different vendors manufacturers. Third, to drive adoption of NDS as the industry's de facto standard for directories.

In pursuit of this mission, Novell has offered NDS to partners and competitors—a strategy Novell implemented to gain an important foothold in the booming market for creating and managing the private networks using Internet technology. And the strategy is paying off. Companies such as Oracle, Sun Microsystems, Hewlett-Packard, and The Santa Cruz Operation have already announced their plans to incorporate NDS into their applications and operating systems.

Ever since Novell created the first NOS more than a decade ago, one Novell product release after another has set the standard for the industry. Now the Internet and its related technologies have begun to transform the way people work, and Novell has responded with products and strategies that will help companies bring structure to the Internet and make it a serious business tool. Says Marengi, "Novell is giving businesses a rock-solid competitive advantage in this new world." ◆

The Novell Global Network Operations Center is a state-of-the-art facility that monitors traffic and proactively resolves problems across the company's worldwide network.

Novell's three flagship products have won countless awards and sold millions of copies throughout the world.

IBM & SAN JOSE UNIFIED SCHOOL DISTRICT

*I*BM—one of San Jose's largest private employers and one of its early "settlers"—has profoundly affected the development of Silicon Valley since opening its first laboratory facility here in 1952. In fact, the history of IBM San Jose is, essentially, the history of the computer information storage industry.

In 1952, most of IBM's 6,000 U.S. customers were storing information on as many as 16 billion punch cards, handsorting the relentless stacks of cards, and filing them in huge, space-wasting tubs. The system cried out for automation.

That year, under the guidance of gifted IBM inventor, Reynold Johnson, IBM opened a small laboratory in San Jose to focus on a way to store large quantities of information in such a form that any portion of it could be accessed in a matter of milliseconds. It was soon determined that a spinning magnetic disk had the most potential.

IBM in 1996 set an industry milestone of storing one billion bits of data in a square inch of disk space. This would allow you to save the text from more than 90 volumes of the *Encyclopaedia Britannica* on a disk this size.

Success came in 1956 when IBM San Jose introduced the first computer disk drive system—the 305 RAMAC (for Random Access Method of Accounting Control)—which automated data storage in a form that allowed sub-second access of stored data.

Today, disk storage is the preeminent method for storing data online for all computers—mainframes, desktops, and notebooks. IBM's Storage Systems Division, which is headquartered in San Jose, has created countless innovations in storage hardware systems, storage management software, and storage devices and components. IBM continues as a leader in this industry, and is also a leader in the San Jose community, especially with educational reform.

IBM's ability to attract, hire, and retain a highly educated workforce has been one key to its phenomenal success. Motivated by its belief in a sound K-12 education system that prepares students for the twenty-first century, IBM has worked closely with educators and other businesses on national school reform issues. The corporation also works directly with local schools through its partnership program, which was launched in 1985. That year IBM adopted Leland High School in the San Jose Unified School District (SJUSD).

Sharing a strong commitment to systemic educational reform, the partnership between SJUSD and IBM has deepened over the years. In 1995 this relationship resulted in a $2 million "Reinventing Education" grant by IBM to SJUSD to help implement the shared vision that education must incorporate the use of technology as a tool for teaching and learning. This begins with technology training for teachers.

San Jose Unified School District adopted technology in the classroom early, wiring all its schools and purchasing a computer for every classroom by 1990. Access to technology became an important method to remedy inequities identified in 1985 when the district was placed under Federal Court order to desegregate. Through the development of an extraordinary network of magnet programs in elementary, middle, and high schools, SJUSD met its goal of integration by attracting and busing students to schools of choice, drawn by the programmatic strengths of each school.

The challenge of "Reinventing Education" is one that SJUSD accepted gladly. The largest school district in the county and one of the largest in California, SJUSD serves more than 32,000 students in 44 schools that range from dense, multicultural, urban core schools in the north to more affluent, suburban neighborhood schools in the south. The student population throughout the district has been growing steadily with increasingly diverse needs. Developing high expectations and setting high standards while providing a meaningful education to children from such different backgrounds, SJUSD has become a nationally recognized model for education reform.

In this vital effort, there are many collaborators. The 1985 partnership between SJUSD and the IBM Corporation was a catalyst for the development of more than 100 business and industry partnerships that exist today. IBM, the Joint Venture/Silicon Valley Network, the San Jose Metropolitan Chamber of Commerce, and others have surrounded San Jose schools with a community that inspires students to be the best they can be, equipping them with world-class skills, a commitment to lifelong learning, active citizenship in a diverse society, and respect for themselves and others. ✦

Sharing a strong commitment to systemic educational reform, the partnership between SJUSD and IBM has resulted in a $2 million "Reinventing Education" grant by IBM to SJUSD to help implement the shared vision that education must incorporate the use of technology as a tool for teaching and learning.

As the semiconductor industry continues to mature, a new breed of capital equipment supplier is emerging. Sophisticated and global, these forward thinking companies provide the combination of advanced technology and support their customers demand. Lam Research Corporation is such a company.

Since its formation in 1980, Lam has provided front-end processing solutions for the global semiconductor industry. Lam's product offerings focus on wafer processing equipment for etch and deposition—two of the most vital steps in the device fabrication cycle, establishing Lam as one of the global leaders in the manufacturer of semiconductor processing equipment.

Founded in Silicon Valley, Fremont-based Lam Research has built its reputation on innovation, collaboration, and contributions to the evolution of technology. During the past decade, Lam has been gearing up for the new age of semiconductor dominance by creating leading edge technology solutions for its customers. Collaborative effort through partnerships with customers, research consortia, and the academic sector has been instrumental in accelerating the development of new technology. Lam has a commitment to continually evolve its products, software, and customer service. For nearly a decade, Lam has been distinguished as one of the Ten Best Worldwide Companies in customer satisfaction, based on an independent survey.

Founded in Silicon Valley, Fremont-based Lam Research has built its reputation on innovation, collaboration, and contributions to the evolution of technology.

A strong global presence fortifies resistance to the market fluctuations that have historically challenged the IC industry and its suppliers. With strategic diversification through a wide range of products, services, and technology, Lam has penetrated the semiconductor industry worldwide. Today, Lam operates its wholly owned subsidiary, Lam Research Co., Ltd. in Kanagawa, Japan. In the fall of 1995, it opened a 38,200 square foot manufacturing facility in Korea. These facilities, along with Lam's network of direct support centers, have given Lam a strong foothold in the critical Asia/Pacific region, including Taiwan, China, and Singapore.

Europe represents another major market for the company. Lam's office in Germany serves as its European headquarters, supported by sales and service centers across the continent, with offices in the United Kingdom, France, Italy, Ireland, the Netherlands, and Israel, to best meet the needs of this expanding market.

Strategic alliances form another key element in Lam's customer-oriented approach to business. Lam has joined with the United States Department of Commerce (USDC) in a $13.4 million research and development project for the growing flat panel display (FPD) industry, receiving the largest USDC contract awarded to date for developing an etch system for manufacture of FPDs.

In the same way Lam has been committed to our customers, Lam is also committed to supporting the communities in which it operates. Lam

LAM RESEARCH CORPORATION

has an ongoing commitment to support education through contributions of equipment, grants, scholarships, and cash donations to grades K-12, colleges, and universities. This past year; the Lam/Glenn T. Seaborg fellowship was established at UC Berkeley to recognize a top "College of Chemistry" student, along with, the launching of the Lam/Foothill Work Industry Program at Foothill Community College. In addition, a primary focus has been to develop outreach programs through collaborations with organizations like the Tech Museum of Innovation, San Jose Museum of Art, and Children's Discovery Museum to benefit Fremont schools. In 1995, Lam stepped forward as the founding sponsor of the TWIN (Tribute to Women and Industry) Academy for the YWCA Santa Clara Valley, providing TWIN honorees the opportunity to participate in programs that assist the community.

Lam is proud to be counted as a "good corporate citizen" through its contributions to nonprofit organizations that serve in areas of education, health, human services, and community development. ◆

During the past decade, Lam has been gearing up for the new age of semiconductor dominance by creating leading edge technology solutions for its customers.

DIONEX

Dionex is a leading developer and manufacturer of analytical systems and related products used to isolate and identify the individual components of complex chemical mixtures. The company's products are used extensively in environmental analysis and by the pharmaceutical, life sciences, biotechnology, chemical, petrochemical, power generation, food and beverage, and electronics industries. Within these areas, Dionex products are used to meet analytical needs ranging from basic research to in-process quality control. Its customers include many of the largest industrial companies worldwide, as well as government agencies, research institutions, and universities.

The broad Dionex product line offers analytical technologies to meet the needs of a growing number of customers. These technologies include ion chromatography (IC), high performance liquid chromatograph (HPLC), and accelerated solvent extraction (ASE). The company is also committed to designing powerful system accessories that maximize the effectiveness of Dionex products, including a premier laboratory data/automation system, as well as innovative columns, reagents, and standards that add versatility and performance.

Dionex is best known for pioneering ion chromatography, a powerful technique that separates ions, or charged molecules. Introduced in 1975, ion chromatography is now critically important in a variety of analytical areas including water quality, environmental contaminants in waste water, and on line monitoring of raw materials and production processes

in a variety of manufacturing facilities. Today, Dionex is the market leader in the $140 million ion analysis market.

Dionex has also been actively involved in expanding its HPLC capabilities for biological and environmental applications. For example, innovative HPLC capabilities developed by Dionex for analyzing carbohydrates have proven valuable in the development of therapeutic agents for heart disease, AIDS, arthritis, and other diseases.

In addition, Dionex is working together with regulatory agencies throughout the world like the United States' EPA in developing effective methods for extracting and analyzing organic contaminants in the environment. The company's Accelerated Solvent Extraction system (ASE 200) is used to extract organic compounds such as pesticides, herbicides, and polyaromatic hydrocarbons. This system, which is also used by consumer goods, pharmaceutical, food and beverage, and other related industries limits solvent usage and lowers extraction times, which in turn brings value to the customer by lowering the cost per extraction.

From its inception, Dionex has made customer satisfaction the cornerstone of its business—an emphasis that has clearly paid off. "Our continued growth is testimony to the strong foundation we have built with our customers around the world," says A. Blaine Bowman, Dionex's president and chief executive officer. "Virtually all aspects of our operations—from R&D to manufacturing to marketing and sales support—are in response to what customers tell us they need."

Based in Sunnyvale, California, Dionex employs more than 650 people worldwide and reported revenues of more than $133 million for its 1996 fiscal year. The company has regional offices throughout the United States, and subsidiaries in Austria, Belgium, Canada, France, Germany, Italy, Japan, the Netherlands, Switzerland, and the United Kingdom. Dionex shares are traded on the NASDAQ National Market system under the symbol DNEX. ✦

Dionex is a leading developer and manufacturer of analytical systems and related products used to isolate and identify the individual components of complex chemical mixtures.

ADOBE SYSTEMS INCORPORATED

As the third largest personal computer software company in the world, with 1995 fiscal revenue of $762 million, Adobe Systems Incorporated was the first of the Silicon Valley giants to recognize the economic and cultural advantages of locating its campus in the heart of downtown San Jose. The company established its corporate headquarters on Park Avenue in 1996.

Dr. John Warnock and Dr. Charles Geschke founded Adobe in 1982. Veterans of Xerox Corporation's Palo Alto Research Center, they

Adobe Systems founders Dr. Chuck Geschke and Dr. John Warnock.

believed that computers should allow people to express themselves and use information in imaginative and meaningful new ways. Out of their deep-seated conviction, the company grew—and grew dramatically. From the inclusion of its PostScript® software in the Apple® LaserWriter® printer to the release of the landmark design programs such as Adobe Illustrator® and Adobe® PageMaker®, concurrent with the explosive growth of its typeface library, Adobe Systems put desktop publishing on the map.

Since then, Adobe has continued to create tools that enhance the design, production, and distribution of business and personal communications. Its products and core technologies are taking computer publishing beyond the desktop, and beyond even paper itself. For example, Adobe's suite of authoring applications includes graphics and layout products, as well as multimedia and Internet publishing programs.

Its flagship authoring applications—Adobe Illustrator, Adobe PageMaker, Adobe PageMill™, Adobe Photoshop®, Adobe FrameMaker®, and Adobe Premiere®—each established a new category of software when launched. Since then, these products have continued to lead their respective markets by offering ever more useful and sophisticated features.

In addition to offering software powerful enough to author any message in any medium, Adobe wants users to be able to deliver their messages around the world and across different computer platforms with ease and flexibility. That was the idea, in 1984, behind Adobe's device-independent PostScript software, which now makes it possible every day for millions to print multiple typefaces and complex graphics on laser printers and other imaging devices, no matter what software or hardware created their files. It's the same independent thinking that was behind the release of Adobe Acrobat® software in 1993.

At the heart of Acrobat technology is the Adobe Portable Document Format (PDF), which allows fully formatted documents to be distributed, accessed, and reused—regardless of the computer software and hardware used to create the original. Better yet, recipients can search, navigate, print, and store PDF files easily on their own systems enabling organizations to simplify the distribution and repurposing of visually rich information.

But PDF isn't the only tool whisking messages of the global village on their way. Today there's hardly a visual communication that hasn't in

Adobe Systems' 18-story corporate tower complements adjacent Guadalupe River Park.

some way, been touched by Adobe's software technology. And, as the economics of distribution shift to favor electronic output, designers and business professionals can depend on one constant: Adobe's commitment to making the translation of bright ideas into reality as elegant and efficient as possible. Or, as its corporate slogan succinctly states, with Adobe software, "If you can dream it, you can do it™." ✦

EXAR CORPORATION

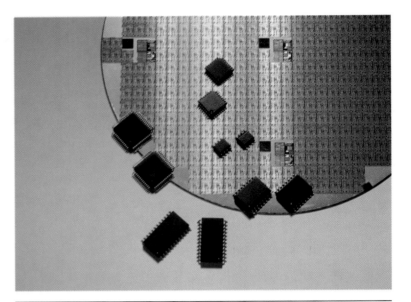

EXAR Corporation designs, develops, and markets innovative, high-quality, system-level analog and mixed-signal integrated circuits for the communications, consumer, and computer markets.

*I*f you have ever recorded a family event on an 8 mm camcorder, used a speakerphone, unlocked your car with a remote "clicker," scanned an image into a computer, or watched a Sony television set, chances are you've used EXAR technology. In fact, this technology is so pervasive in the many products that entertain us, ensure our security, and make our lives more convenient and pleasurable, we are hardly aware of its existence.

Founded in 1971, EXAR's pioneering efforts in analog semi-custom designs have made it a leading player in the billion dollar global analog and mixed-signal integrated circuit market. Based in Fremont, California, EXAR's facilities are international, with Exar Japan Corporation in Kawasaki, Japan, and EXAR, Ltd. in East Sussex, United Kingdom. EXAR's regional sales offices are spread worldwide.

Almost 90 percent of EXAR's multi-million dollar revenues comes from three market areas: communications, consumer electronics, and personal computers. In addition, with its versatile processes and design expertise, EXAR also develops custom products for industrial, automotive, and medical uses.

Now 450 employees strong, EXAR was the first Japanese subsidiary to locate in Silicon Valley; however, in 1985 the firm went public and ultimately became wholly American owned.

EXAR's strategic relationships with other global companies (Sony, AIWA, JVC, Sharp, Matsushita, Alcatel, Northern Telecom, Siemens,

Founded in 1971 and based in Fremont, California, EXAR's pioneering efforts in analog semi-custom designs have made it a leading player in the billion dollar global analog and mixed-signal integrated circuit market.

and others) have helped its technology and products achieve worldwide acceptance—even dominance in some markets. Because the ability to introduce technologically advanced products in a cost-effective manner remains critical to EXAR's continuing success, in recent years EXAR has aggressively acquired companies whose technology and products strengthen and complement its own: June 1994—Micro Power Systems, a firm with leading-edge, analog-to-digital and digital-to-analog converter products and technology; March 1995—Startech Semiconductor, a leading supplier of UARTS (a computer component that handles electronic communication), clock generator technology, and I/O circuits in the PC industry; June 1995—Silicon Microstructures, a firm that produces "smart" sensors, which are especially important in automotive and industrial applications.

With EXAR's leading-edge testing facilities and capabilities, quality is a vital consideration for the company. EXAR provides quality training not only in terms of its products, but also in terms of the human effectiveness of its staff. Its stringent quality program meets the most demanding customer requirements and is both ISO 9001 and QS 9000 registered. ✦

CADENCE DESIGN SYSTEMS, INC.

"A lot of people are afraid of change," says Joe Costello, president and CEO of Cadence Design Systems, Inc., "but my view is that change equals opportunity." The dizzying array of mergers and acquisitions Cadence has made since its founding is proof positive that change is a way of life at this dynamic public company. Factor in the fact that Cadence's business revolves around the ultra fast-paced world of electronics, and it's clear that change is a way of life at Cadence.

Formed in 1988 through the merger of ECAD, Inc., and SDA Systems, two pioneers in the electronic design automation (EDA) software industry, Cadence has grown under Costello's visionary leadership

Joe Costello has instilled a culture of fun and creativity at Cadence, where he has served as the company's only president and CEO since its inception. **Photo by Court Mast Photography.**

to become the world's leading supplier of EDA software tools and services used in the design and development of products for such industries as semiconductor, computer, networking equipment, telecommunications, consumer electronics, and a variety of others.

In 1995, the firm's sales shot past the half-billion-dollar mark—a first for an EDA company—and followed that with a $700 million-plus year in 1996.

Because Cadence serves the exploding electronics market—estimated by industry experts to grow to the size of $1 trillion worldwide by 2005—this high-flying outfit is well positioned for continued future success. Already Cadence has more than 3,000 employees who work at its sales offices and research facilities around the world, including its corporate headquarters in San Jose. It is one of the few companies experiencing strong business growth on an international basis, with approximately 50 percent of its sales in North American markets and 50 percent in the rest of the world.

The Cadence success story starts with its sophisticated software tools developed to help the engineers who design the products people use every day. The fact is, if you use merchandise manufactured by such companies as Intel, Motorola,

Sharp, Philips, and Sega—products like cellular phones and pagers, computers and automobiles, even dishwashers and refrigerators—you're probably using the results of Cadence technology.

The EDA industry was built on selling software products, not service. And Cadence started the same way. In its early days, customers simply bought the software tools that Cadence developed, and then tweaked the tools themselves to meet their own product development needs. However as EDA systems became more and more complex, customers no longer understood how to use these chip-designing software tools. They just didn't have the specialized technical knowledge needed.

That's when Cadence changed its focus and decided to sell not just the "spreadsheets," but also the "accountants" to go along with them. Cadence broadened itself to become a full-service product design solutions company, and began offering not only cutting-edge software products and technology, but also the consulting help and engineering support to go with it.

In 1995 Cadence fully implemented its new approach, and set the stage for its evolution into a totally new type of company. "We really believe that the blueprint hasn't been written on how to build an organization like the one we are constructing," Costello says.

Although there were a few naysayers as there are any time something new is tried, the results are in—and they're spectacular. "We have core technology strength and a two-year head start on this new business model, which will help us continue to build and reinvigorate our company," he said. "We not only have the golden eggs—we've got the goose, too!" ✦

Cadence combines leading-edge technology with a full spectrum of professional services to enable its customers to develop sophisticated electronic products.

CONDOR SYSTEMS

C ondor Systems is a private company whose high-tech expertise meets the needs of the rapidly evolving defense market. Founded in 1980, the firm is the 10th largest defense contractor in Silicon Valley. It designs and manufactures RF and microwave digitally controlled electronic products for sale to the reconnaissance and Electronic Support Measure (ESM) segments of the Electronic Warfare (EW) market.

Condor employs about 400 scientific, engineering, and other personnel at its San Jose headquarters office, plus its engineering support center and business development office in Sterling, Virginia, a suburb of Washington, D.C.

With the ESM market as its primary focus, Condor provides a full range of products that include antennas, receivers, signal processors, digitizers, and analysis equipment. Condor configures these into subsystems designed to address specific operational requirements of Condor's customers.

A highly trained technical staff ensures that Condor equipment meets customer needs.

Condor's state-of-the-art anechoic chamber is a key resource for the design and testing of its Electronic Warfare Systems.

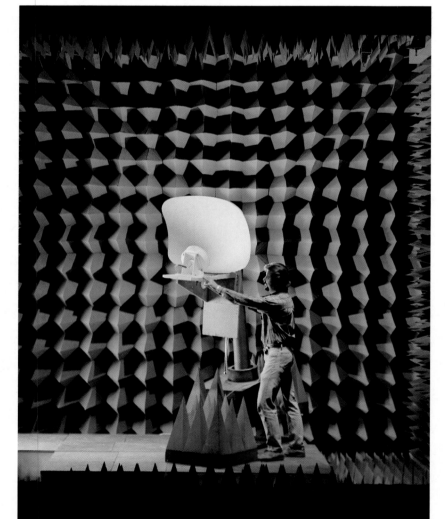

For example, Condor's diverse complement of high-performance antennas, millimeter-wave downconverters and receivers can be used on a wide variety of platforms–airborne, shipborne, and mobile; as well as land-based (portable or fixed). Its antennas span a frequency range between 100 MHz and 110 GHz, and the downconverters transform signals in the 18 to 40 GHz frequency range. The firm's fully-synthesized receivers are capable of performing signal intercept, spectral survey, and analysis from 20 MHz to 40 GHz.

Condor's products are based upon current technology, and are used for both tactical and strategic purposes. Using "open architectures" allows Condor to include current analog and digital technology in designs, while providing for the compatibility of future upgrades as technology advances.

Responding to the rapid consolidation of the defense electronic industry, Condor's strategy is to pursue acquisitions to enhance its technical and product resources.

In 1994, it acquired Electronic Support Systems, Inc. and certain assets of SCOPE, Incorporated, thus adding signal processing and analysis equipment, plus technical expertise, to its ESM/EW capabilities. In 1995, Condor acquired the Microwave Surveillance Systems unit of the Watkins-Johnson Company, to further strengthen its capabilities.

From its earliest days, Condor has sought to diversify its customer base. Current customers include national level intelligence agencies, all three U.S. Armed Services, major prime defense contractors–Raytheon/ E-Systems, Tracor-AEL and Flight Systems Division, GTE, Boeing/ ARGOSystems, TRW-ASG, Litton ATD, Mitsubishi Electric Company, several divisions of Lockheed Martin's Federal Systems Division, and others. Fortifying Condor's base of domestic business are its primary international customers: Japan, Norway, Taiwan, Canada, and Germany. In these countries, Condor has a continuing series of contracts.

Through a well-established network of foreign sales representatives and consultants covering Europe, Australia, South America, and the Middle East, Condor is working to build comparable relationships with other countries that offer similar market potential, such as the United Kingdom, India, Australia, Finland, Korea, and Turkey. ✦

*U*nited Defense, L.P., a joint venture between FMC (60 percent) and Harsco Corporation (40 percent), was established in January 1994. However, United Defense's roots in Santa Clara Valley go back to 1884 through FMC. That year, John Bean invented a crop-spraying pump to defeat a scale threatening his Los Gatos, California orchard. Soon others were clamoring for his sprayer.

By 1929, the growing Bean Spray Pump Company in San Jose changed its name to Food Machinery Corporation. During World War II, the company began manufacturing military armored vehicles and in

A Combat Simulation and Integration Lab in Santa Clara provides a virtual prototyping environment that includes hardware, software and man-in-the-loop simulation capabilities.

1960, officially adopted FMC Corporation as its name. As the company expanded its product lines across the country to include food machinery, combat vehicles, chemicals, agricultural products and energy and transportation equipment, FMC headquarters moved from San Jose to Chicago in 1972.

When the partnership was announced in 1994, United Defense formally became the defense arm of the FMC family. Today, United Defense, L.P. has five divisions: Ground Systems, International, Steel Products, Paladin Production and Armament Systems.

Ground Systems Division has sites in Santa Clara, California; York and Fayette, Pennsylvania and Aiken, South Carolina. It is responsible for tracked combat vehicles like the Bradley Fighting Vehicle, the M113 Armored Personnel Carrier and the Armored Gun System. The Bradley distinguished itself in the 1991 Persian Gulf War during Operation Desert Storm.

The Santa Clara site stands as a center of excellence for engineering, as well as technology and software development. Research and development continually enhance combat vehicle capabilities with state-of-the-art electronic systems that can be installed in current or new vehicles, as well as moved from one type of vehicle to another. Facilities in York, Fayette and Aiken produce or upgrade the vehicles.

UNITED DEFENSE, L.P.

A Combat Simulation and Integration Lab in Santa Clara provides a virtual prototyping environment that includes hardware, software and man-in-the-loop simulation capabilities. The Bradley Plus Simulator can be reconfigured to provide "virtual battlespace" for any vehicle in the Bradley family. These innovative environments provide a safe and cost-effective opportunity to explore concepts, integrate systems and analyze prototype operation in real time. They can also be used as personnel training tools.

The International Division headquartered in Santa Clara has offices in Malaysia, Korea, Taiwan, Saudi Arabia, Pakistan and Turkey. This division produces ground combat vehicles and systems and naval gun mounts and missile launching systems for these international markets.

The Steel Products Division in Anniston, Alabama makes military track and suspension forgings, alloy steel and specialty steel forgings and castings for armored vehicles. The Paladin Production Operation in Chambersburg, Pennsylvania produces M1096A6 Howitzers. The Armament Systems Division in Minneapolis, Minnesota develops military ordnance including naval gun mounts, automated shipboard guided missile handling/launching systems, land-based launching systems and autoloading systems.

United Defense's 6,000 employees count the U.S. Army, U.S. Marine Corps, U.S. Navy and the government among their customers. However, their most important customer focus remains the sailor or soldier on the front line.

"Our products are meant to make soldiers better fighters and assure them a high degree of survivability, " said Peter Woglom, vice president and general manager, Ground Systems Division. ✦

United Defense's 5,600 employees count the U.S. Army, U.S. Marine Corps, U.S. Navy and the government among their customers.

CALIFORNIA EASTERN LABORATORIES

Ah, Silicon Valley–a wild roller coaster ride of fortunes and flops, hiring anyone with a heartbeat one minute and laying off everyone in sight the next. An unstable, kaleidoscopic land where annual employee turnover rates of 30 percent, 40 percent, 50 percent, and higher are the norm. Right?

Wrong–that is, if you're thinking of California Eastern Laboratories. CEL's annual turnover is 10 percent.

Founded in 1959, CEL is the exclusive North American sales, marketing, and product development organization for more than 900 RF, microwave, and optoelectronic semiconductor products manufactured by NEC of Japan–one of the world's largest semiconductor manufacturers. Headquartered in Santa Clara, CEL maintains 17 field sales offices through the country and in 1996, approximately 93 million devices were shipped through its Santa Clara warehouse.

"The components we provide are used in cellular telephones, pagers, satellites, direct broadcast TV, wireless security systems, and literally hundreds of other products used by consumers and businesses," says Tina Banfill, CEL's director of human resources.

This firm is one of the oldest technology companies in Silicon Valley; yet, it has never once had to lay-off employees and has never had an unprofitable year. "That impresses job candidates," Banfill says. "If an engineer still has nightmares about a recent episode of unemployment, our stability is reassuring."

With its employee count rapidly approaching 200, this $80 million (and growing fast) company is exceptional in other ways, too.

Besides its extraordinary history of employment stability and profitability, CEL is 60 percent owned by its employees through an Employee Stock Ownership Plan (ESOP) established in 1983. That makes it one of largest private, employee-owned companies in California.

And, although the ESOP is a valuable tool in attracting and retaining talent, the company still supplements its ESOP plan with an impressively broad range of other benefits. "We need to increase our workforce by about 20 percent a year to keep up with the demand for our products," Banfill said. "And we expect to maintain this pace of growth into the 21st century."

With 90 percent of the world without telephone service, and less developed countries scrambling to build their wireless infrastructure, the telecommunications business has skyrocketed, creating a global shortage of wireless communication design and other engineers. These days, competition for technical talent in the microwave industry is so heated that firms have been known to fly banners from airplanes and offer huge signing bonuses to engineers and technicians. "The window of market opportunity is wide open for us," Banfill said, "but we need people!"

One of the few "swords to ploughshares" success stories, CEL transitioned from selling primarily to the military to selling to companies that produce cutting-edge consumer electronic products. And, unlike most others who have made that shift, they did it with nary a hiccup in performance or profits.

Running a business in which your employees are also your owners, requires much more open communication about financial details than is the norm at most companies. "We post graphs of financial performance on hallway walls, and report other news through an e-mail ESOP bulletin board," says Jerry Arden, CEL's chairman and CEO. "At quarterly all-employee meetings, I never know what pointed questions may be asked…employees take their ownership role to heart."

And not being publicly-traded allows management to take the long view in its business decisions. "You're not constantly looking over your shoulder–or worrying about a blip in quarterly numbers," Arden said. "This same ability to focus also applies to employees, who aren't bouncing off the walls every time the market takes a dip–morale and productivity are much steadier in our environment than in a public company." ✦

Founded in 1959, California Eastern Laboratories is the exclusive North American sales, marketing, and product development organization for more than 900 RF, microwave, and optoelectronic semiconductor products manufactured by NEC of Japan–one of the world's largest semiconductor manufacturers.

SMART PRODUCTS, INC.

D oris Patterson, CEO of Smart Products, Inc., is often asked how she got into the valve and pump business. After all, she was a California real estate broker and spent years marketing million dollar homes. Here's how it happened.

One day a client of hers called and said, "I've had it, Doris. I'm selling everything–including my business." Demonstrating that famous Silicon Valley entrepreneurial spirit, Patterson replied, "OK, your business is sold–I'm buying it. Now, let's talk about your houses."

A few days later, the business owner walked into his offices and said, "Good morning, employees. I've sold the business. Here is your new boss." "He walked out that morning, and we never saw or heard from him again," Patterson says.

That was in August 1985. Patterson's plan to actively manage the company for only six months was quickly abandoned when she realized the true potential of the product line. She quickly focused on sales and marketing. New applications were identified, advertising programs launched, and trade shows aggressively pursued.

"It was a challenge stepping into the traditionally male-dominated industrial arena. There were many obstacles to overcome, but once I made the decision to remain actively involved in the business beyond the initial six months, I was committed to building a successful, thriving business."

And thrive it has. Smart Products has steadily grown from a near bankrupt start-up when she bought the company, with still many new marketing opportunities open to them. "We are constantly discovering new markets and applications. We are currently working on new product development which will give us an even broader market appeal. And with the recent acquisition of our new building we have more than twice the capacity that we previously had. This will allow us to continue our plans for expansion."

Smart Products designs, develops, manufactures and markets pumps, check valves and fittings for a broad range of industries and uses. The company's patented design gives it a superior position in the low-pressure, low-flow niche market. "We are fortunate in that our market is horizontal," Patterson commented. "It crosses industry lines."

Among the industries served by Smart's product line are medical, environmental, food and beverage, water treatment, instrumentation and many, many more. "We serve everyone from mom-and-pop businesses to multinational corporations," she says. "And we ship all over the world."

Doris H. Patterson, President and CEO of Smart Products, Inc. Photo by Pat Kirk.

Smart Products designs, develops, manufactures and markets pumps, check valves and fittings for a broad range of industries and uses. Photo by Pat Kirk.

Asked for the secret of the company's success, Patterson glosses over the 12 to 14 hour days she and her staff often put in and focuses instead on personal character and ethics.

"To me, this business needs to be a win-win situation–for our customers, for our employees, and for me," she says. "This means that our employees work together to produce a total quality product in an upbeat environment. Quality has always been our highest priority, and we continue to add capabilities to allow us to keep pace with the changing demands of our customers in this regard. It is important for us to always stand for the very best." ✦

Photo by Dana L. Grover.

Chapter Fourteen

The Market Place

◆

STEVENS CREEK DODGE

Early in his career in the auto industry, President Dwight Goad was influenced by two dealers in the midwest where he was raised. From one, he says he learned the importance of continuous selling and maintaining a high profile. Goad's sales slogan, "I'll bet a dollar we can make a deal," is borrowed from that dealer's popular motto of two decades ago.

From the other dealer, Goad learned the "people" side of the business. "Every year, that Midwest dealer would turn his facility over to the church for bingo games for one week every May, which was an important part of Clinton, Indiana's Little Italy Festival," Goad said. "He treated his employees and customers like they were family. He bought a lodge for his employees and had regular potluck suppers for all the staff. He really took care of his people—and his business was a great success."

Those lessons helped shape Goad's management style. Now, 25 years later, they form the basis for his approach to dealing with people—employees, customers, friends, family…in fact, everyone—to the point where "family" is a word mentioned often at Stevens Creek Dodge.

"Working for Dwight has been a different experience for me because he looks at customers as friends, almost family," says Dan Wiseman, sales manager and a 21-year veteran of the car business, eight years of which he has spent on Goad's dealership team. "Dwight is very caring and respectful of people, and it translates into the way we treat our customers." Wiseman tells of selling a car to a driver for a large restaurant chain. "The driver was so pleased, he introduced us to the owner," Wiseman says. "And now the owner has bought about 15 cars from us over the years—both for his business, and for himself and his family. Plus, he's very vocal about referring us to others."

Wiseman says he has never before worked for a manager who cared about the welfare of his employees' families. But Goad does just that. "Dwight's always asking me about my wife, or about the activities of my kids," he says. "Dwight is interested, not only in me, but also in my family. He remembers what's going on in my personal life, and that means a lot to me."

Dwight Goad, president of Stevens Creek Dodge. Photo by Pat Kirk.

Goad's personal approach to people has paid off in award after award for his dealerships. When he ran Expressway Jeep/Eagle on Capitol Expressway's "Auto Row" in San Jose, it was Number One in Jeep-Eagle sales in Northern California for three years in a row, and consistently

---

The employees of Stevens Creek Dodge; **front row, left to right:** *Jesus Flores, Tom Denton, Silverio Perez, Jim Schwantz, Joe Mendoza, Jacob Salas, Bruce Craft, Ray Barghi, Dan Rey, Bob Alexander.* **Middle row, left to right:** *Rocque Portillo, David Super, Ben Phillips, Joe Mara, Amanda Hamilton, Dawn Cooper, Mary Murtey, Bernadette Erba, Milancy O'Brien-Roy, Gloria Zapien, Adria Goad, Paulette Walton, Terrie Markee, Kevin Jones, James Garcia, Bill Tiernan, Tommy Southerland, Robert Zimmerman.* **Back row, left to right:** *Dwight Goad, Ed Santos, Jay Shepard, Bill Brendle, Ken Siebert, Greg Minard, Scott Smith, Juan Gonzalez, Dan Wiseman, Phillip Murtey, Ron Schuster, Robert Silveira, Greg Burkett, Gilbert Datan, Art Boseman, Joe Spears, Craig Dunn, James Riddle, Roberto Villarreal, Conway Haley.* **Photo by Pat Kirk.**

ranked in the top 50 in Jeep/Eagle sales in the country. Also, for two years running Expressway Jeep/Eagle won the Chrysler 'Award for Excellence'–Chrysler's highest dealer award. Not an easy achievement, because this award measures all aspects of a dealer's performance: sales, service satisfaction, profitability, community service, and more.

Chrysler's standard of excellence (and Goad's) is ingrained in the employees at Stevens Creek Dodge. "We have a group whose main desire is to make our dealership successful, not only financially, but in terms of customer satisfaction," says Joy Solomon, the corporation's general manager

![The Management Team of Stevens Creek Dodge]

The Management Team of Stevens Creek Dodge; **front row, left to right:** *Sharon Mamola, customer relations manager; Joycelyn Solomon, general manager; Dan Rey, sales manager.* **Back row, left to right:** *James Garcia, service manager; Dwight Goad, president; Dan Wiseman, sales manager; Bill Tiernan, body shop manager; Phillip Murtey, parts manager.* **Photo by Pat Kirk.**

who has been a member of the Goad team since 1988. "We take a lot of pride in doing our best for our customers."

Solomon has worked in the automobile business for 30 years and says that, although other dealerships talk about excellence in customer service, they don't seem interested in practicing what they preach. But at Stevens Creek Dodge, making sure customers receive extraordinary service is a way of life. "We put a great deal of effort at all levels of our organization into making sure our customers get the very best," she said. "At Stevens Creek Dodge, we really do 'walk the talk'."

Sharon Mamola, customer relations manager, spent 15 years working for a large chain bank before entering the automobile business. Her job at Stevens Creek Dodge is to help solve customer problems and coordinate efforts between the different departments–sales, service, parts, body shop, administration, and customer relations–to better serve the customer.

Mamola has noted a real difference between the service philosophy she experienced in banking and the service philosophy practiced at Stevens Creek Dodge. "Here, we're concerned about the customer's coming back. We want our customers to be satisfied and happy, and we all work as a team with that end in mind–serving the customer on a personal level," she said. "I think banking has gotten very impersonal. And,

frankly, I did not observe that the banking industry had the same depth of concern–either for their customers or their employees–that we have here at Stevens Creek Dodge."

From their customers, the message is the same. James and Maria Estrada bought a vehicle from Stevens Creek Dodge. In the process, they spoke with a number of staff members in sales, financing, and service. "We left your dealership with the truck we wanted, informed and without the uncomfortable feeling of being strong-armed or pressured in regards to price or down payment," Ms. Estrada wrote. "On the contrary, we feel your employees showed a great deal of professionalism and empathy."

She noted that she and her husband have bought many vehicles from other dealers over the years. "But this is the first time we left with a warm feeling about the whole transaction," Ms. Estrada said in her letter. "This has changed our mind concerning automobile manufacturers…you truly have employees who go above and beyond their duties to make customers feel at ease."

Goad says his business philosophy involves trusting his people, not micro-managing, and emphasizing quality service with a focus on customer satisfaction. "Our employees have the credit authority of up to $100 to make the customer happy, on their own say-so. They don't have to ask their manager or anyone else. If it's needed and appropriate in their judgment, they can authorize the adjustment themselves."

Goad's trust in his staff is well appreciated and returned. "My faith in Mr. Goad is very high," says Phil Murtey, parts manager, who has been with Goad since 1989, and in the auto industry for more than 25 years. His wife also works for Stevens Creek Dodge. "The way Mr. Goad treats his employees…his concern for people…the way he values good staff…it makes you want to do your best and help him attain his goals for the dealership," Murtey said. "Plus his great sense of humor makes it fun to come to work."

James Garcia, service manager, and Sharon Mamola, customer relations manager, discuss the service requirement of the new Dodge Ram. **Photo by Pat Kirk.**

It's clear that the Stevens Creek Dodge employees really care about the organization's success. "You feel like you belong here because Dwight really listens to you," says Jim Garcia, service manager and body shop director. Garcia has been in the auto business for nearly 30 years, and with Goad for more than three. His second cousin also works there.

"I feel like it's my business, too. And I try to pass that on to our technicians—all of whom take pride in their work," he said. Of the dealer's 20 technicians, 12 have been with Garcia for more than six years. The firm invests a great deal in their training, Garcia says. The technicians appreciate that and reciprocate by giving outstanding service. "We try to do things right for the customer the first time," he says, "and in a timely manner."

Bill Tiernan, body shop manager, has worked in the car business for almost 20 years, the last two on the Stevens Creek Dodge team. "Dwight Goad is very caring and honest," he said. "He cares about your input and shares everything with his employees—asking for and considering your opinion before he makes his decision."

Craig Dunn, assistant sales manager, reviews the features of the Grand Caravan with Amanda Hamilton and her three daughters, Carina, Julia, and Alyssa. **Photo by Pat Kirk.**

Five of the original 45 employees from Expressway Jeep/Eagle that are still employed at Stevens Creek Dodge; **front row, left to right: Mary Murtey, Jacob Salas, Joycelyn Solomon. Back row, left to right: Dwight Goad and Daniel Wiseman. Stevens Creek Dodge currently has 125 employees. Photo by Pat Kirk.**

The Stevens Creek Dodge body shop is busier than most, giving exceptional service at a competitive price. "We try to treat each customer as an individual, rather than giving them an assembly-line approach," he said. "And we do the same with their cars. We not only fix their cars, we improve them. In fact, many cars leave us in better shape than when they came in. We take a lot of pride in that."

Business Manager Mary Murtey, Phil's wife, has worked with Goad for seven years out of the nearly 25 she has been in the automobile business. One of the aspects of Stevens Creek Dodge that excites her is its focus on the future. "We're a very forward-moving dealership," she said.

"Chrysler is coming up with innovative designs, and we're doing more with technology to meet our customers' needs." The dealership has an online presence, for example, and sells cars via its interactive World Wide Web site on the Internet—at a rapidly growing pace.

"We treat people the way they should be treated," says Dan Rey, sales manager. Dan is another veteran of the auto industry, with 12 years in the business, and six on Goad's team. "We don't want to be just another dealer with an average record of performance—we want to be the best. With our customers, we're in it for the long haul, because we want them to return and buy their second and third car from us, too." Rey, whose son Brent also works for the dealership, says that Stevens Creek Dodge is more caring than other car dealers he has worked with.

"A team attitude is important," Goad says. To help nurture warm, collaborative relationships among his staff, he sponsors dealer lunches every other month or so. In the beginning, the employees did the cooking—now the events are catered under a huge, outdoor tent.

Goad has invested as heavily in his facility as he has in his people. "I want ours to be a showcase dealership," he says. "The kind that, when you walk in the door, you can't help but say, 'Wow'!" Toward that end, he has doubled the capitalization, and massively upgraded the facility since he took over the Dodge dealership in 1993.

It's a continuing effort, but so far, the entire facility has been meticulously repainted and carpeted, with great attention to detail. The lifts have been upgraded. There are 35 rental cars at the dealership, available for customer use. Artwork, selected and framed by his wife Diana, adorns the walls of the attractive, terra-cotta tile-roofed facility. Painted yellow ground lines and an abundance of signage throughout guide customers smoothly through the three buildings on the dealership's 5.6 acres. Goad has even bought a state-of-the-art computerized paint mixing system for the Body Shop.

"When you care about people, you invest in them; you invest in your relationships with them," Goad says, "and you invest in the facilities and tools they use." His investments—both personal and professional—are yielding impressive dividends. Goad and his wife, his high school sweetheart, have been married nearly 30 years. They have two daughters, Dena and Adria. Adria works summers in the dealership while attending college. Many of his 120-employee team have been with him almost a decade. And sales, since he took over the dealership, are growing at a blistering pace—up nearly 46 percent from 1995 to 1996.

The employees of Stevens Creek Dodge; front row, left to right: James Beene, Danny Huerta, Jack Mayberry, Juan Lopez, Jose Fernandez, Robert Mora, Benjamin Francia, Ted May, Joe Bersick, Rodney Fuller. Middle row, left to right: Ismael Ortega, Alex Diaz, Glenn Shawcross, James Garcia, David Estrada, Joycelyn Solomon, Lori Gutierrez, Sheryl Ault, Maree Zapien, Marianne Enders, Sharon Mamola, Monica Gaeta, Yolanda Gascon, Cherie Rudolph, Phillip Murtey, David Halper, Erick Smith, Jesse Rodriguez. Back row, left to right: Jeff Wells, Dy Larson, Bob Tomasello, Adam Neipp, Michael Noble, Jim Collishaw, Albert Almadova, Paul Edwards, Chris Miller, Michael Brinkman, Michael Spolini, Bob Gohman, Bob Fernandez, Bill Tiernan, Dwight Goad. Photo by Pat Kirk.

As a history major at University of Missouri in St. Louis, Goad had planned on becoming a college professor. By the age of 23, Goad had gained several years of experience in the automobile industry and knew he wanted his own dealership one day. At 41, after spending 18 years with Chrysler Corporation, he achieved that goal with his first dealership—Expressway Jeep/Eagle.

Now Goad looks to the future. He has plans to increase the versatility and skills of his employees through cross-functional team training, and to increase the skills and service capabilities of his dealership through expanded use of technology.

Nonetheless, Goad holds on to the lessons he's learned in the past—the lessons about the importance of people, caring, and trust. "I want Stevens Creek Dodge to always be the kind of place where a handshake still means something," he says, "where customers and employees come to think of us as part of their extended family." ✦

Stevens Creek Dodge is located on Stevens Creek Boulevard, the premier Auto Row in Northern California. Photo by Pat Kirk.

HYATT SAINTE CLAIRE HOTEL

*K*nown in the 1920s as San Jose's "Million-Dollar Hotel", the historic Sainte Claire is San Jose's grande dame of luxury hotels. Ever since this elegant lady first opened its doors on October 16, 1926, its rare charms have drawn admirers from far and wide.

Built by San Jose real estate pioneer, T.S. Montgomery, on the former site of the Eagle Brewery at the corner of Market and San Carlos Streets, the Sainte Claire was designed by the renowned Weeks and Day, architects of the internationally famous Mark Hopkins in San Francisco and the Beverly Wilshire in Los Angeles.

Originally, the Sainte Claire featured an outdoor patio with a Spanish fountain, and the hotel's huge arched glass doors opened up to the biggest ballroom between Los Angeles and San Francisco.

Building with exuberant flamboyance, Montgomery supplied the hotel with the largest kitchen in Northern California, featuring five walk-in freezers, a meat-curing section, and its own bakery.

One hundred twenty attendants were hired to serve guests of the 200 luxuriously appointed rooms.

Now a City Historic Landmark, the Sainte Claire has also earned its place on the National Register of Historic Places.

Such a magnificent legacy of style and panache inspires the hotel's staff to create an unforgettable experience for its visitors and guests.

Its look is equally unforgettable. The Saint Claire's renovated Spanish-Italian Renaissance Revival architecture combines the best of historic grace and modern amenities—teaming gleaming marble floors, sparkling crystal chandeliers, and majestic wood doors, with state-of-the-art technology and contemporary conveniences.

Now part of the international Hyatt chain, the six-story Hotel Sainte Claire offers 170 guest rooms in superior, deluxe, and executive styles. Among them are 17 suites, including a Honeymoon Suite, two Executive Business Suites, and a Grand Suite with separate kitchen.

Popular with visiting celebrities and dignitaries, the Hyatt Sainte Claire was recently the choice of international movie star John Travolta, who stayed at the hotel during the filming of the movie "Mad City" in downtown San Jose. And you never know

Painstakingly restored to their original celebrated grandeur, each guest room at the Hyatt Sainte Claire Hotel has many amenities.

which celebrity you might bump into in the sumptuous, soaring lobby. For example, Dustin Hoffman, who also starred in "Mad City," often surprised delighted hotel guests while he was in town by playing piano in the Sainte Claire's luxurious lobby lounge and enjoying the hotel's elegance, richly reminiscent of bygone eras.

"We like to prepare the staff before some of our well-known guests arrive," said Curt Moore, hotel manager. "You can tell the newer staff by their excitement at meeting some of the stars."

Painstakingly restored to their original celebrated grandeur, guest room amenities at the Hyatt Sainte Claire include: European feather

Now a City Historic Landmark, the Hyatt Sainte Claire Hotel has also earned its place on the National Register of Historic Places. The six-story hotel offers 170 guest rooms in superior, deluxe, and executive styles. Photo by Maxine Cass.

The Saint Claire's renovated Spanish-Italian Renaissance Revival architecture combines the best of historic grace and modern amenities.

"The Sainte Claire has always attracted guests who value its elegant aesthetics and ambiance, and it continues to do so," says Roy Truitt, general manager. "This lovely lady reflects a time when hotels were crafted as unique monuments to their cities and regions, in contrast to the anonymity of so many chain hotels nowadays."

At the Sainte Claire, guests enjoy the very latest in design, comfort, and service. As they leave, they seldom fail to give compliments on their extraordinary experience during their stay—new-world convenience and technology on a foundation of old-world warmth and beauty.

In building the Hotel Sainte Claire, founder Montgomery wanted no expense spared in "fitting out a house which should be a byword for the most luxurious and at the same time the most homelike of hotels." Seven decades later, that standard still fits San Jose's grande dame—the Hyatt Sainte Claire Hotel. ✦

down mattresses in all rooms, 24-hour room service by the Il Fornaio Restaurant and Bakery, famous for its award-winning Cucina Italiana; three telephones in each guest room, featuring two lines, data line hook-up, voice mail, and speaker phone; inroom electronic personal safe, minibars, cable television, VCR, and nightly turndown service.

The hotel is conveniently located just seven minutes from the San Jose International Airport, across the street from the San Jose McEnery Convention Center, and right in the heart of San Jose's business, museum, and entertainment district. Featuring shuttle services to and from the San Jose Airport, laundry and valet same-day service, and concierge, the Hyatt Sainte Claire also offers guests the use of a private dining room, a well-equipped fitness center, and so much more.

Its 10,000-square-foot conference center provides the technological resources and amenities normally associated with only the largest hotels. The second floor conference wing—focus of the Sainte Claire's conference services—offers the most advanced satellite teleconference, audio-visual, and lighting systems.

Designed with special attention to detail, subtle elements such as comfortable furniture, access to natural light, and easy transition from large meeting rooms to smaller, more intimate spaces have been incorporated to make this center one of the country's most dynamic and welcoming business meeting environments.

Each breakout room has its own specially designed bathrooms, wetbar, and closet.

The executive business suite contains the same services, and can serve as a command center for the on-site person responsible for planning and executing the conference. Banquet and catering is provided by Il Fornaio, known for its incomparable Northern Italian cuisine and professional service.

The Hyatt Sainte Claire Hotel reflects a time when hotels were crafted as unique monuments to their cities and regions.

THE FLEA MARKET, INC.

Smack-dab in the heart of Silicon Valley, the global center of technological innovation, sits a bustling 120-acre bastion of "no-tech" business that hosts more than 80,000 visitors a week, more than 4 million people a year.

Largest open-air market in the country—some say in the world—the popular San Jose Flea Market flourishes in apparent contradiction to Silicon Valley's high-tech image. And yet, as the product of one man's entrepreneurial drive and passionate commitment to an innovative concept, the Flea Market represents the very essence of Silicon Valley.

In 1959, George Bumb had the germ of an idea. "He was in the solid waste disposal/landfill business," says John DeTar, marketing director for

The Flea Market's quarter mile long produce row is the busiest outdoor produce market in California and features produce from local farms and around the world.

The Flea Market. "He kept seeing all these wonderful things getting thrown away and felt there had to be a profitable way to sell them to people who would want them."

Hearing of the success of swap meets, which were just getting started in Los Angeles, Bumb traveled to Southern California and saw how the meets were organized and held at drive-in theater lots. Bumb took the swap meet approach and expanded it to encompass individual merchant

stalls, with on-site product storage. "That way the merchants could keep their product at the market during the week, even though our flea market sales were conducted on weekends only at first," DeTar said.

This granddaddy of U.S. flea markets opened its gates in March of 1960, with 20 sellers and about 100 curious customers on what was once an abandoned cattle feedlot. With $7,000 in cash, Bumb started The Flea Market farmland on Berryessa Road— then a narrow country lane surrounded by orchards.

It was a cautious beginning. The first office, staffed part-time by family members, housed the only restrooms and snack bar on the original 35 acres. The spartan menu offered homemade sandwiches, basic beverages, and some candy—that was it.

Today, The Flea Market averages more than 6,000 sellers each

Looking South over The San Jose Flea Market. Berryessa Road divides the 40 acre shopping area from the 80 acre parking lot. The Flea Market has over four million visitors per year.

week and is home to 30 snack bars, street vendors, and sit-down restaurants offering a delectable variety of international and American classic foods—plus more than 60 roving snack and beverage carts specially designed by the Bumb family.

From its initial handful of family members and part-time employees, The Flea Market has grown to encompass 500 service employees carefully trained and supervised by Ogden Entertainment Services, along with a direct Flea Market staff of 150 people who work in management, construction, food service, and maintenance.

The Flea Market property encompasses about 1,000 small buildings, 1,000 open-air stalls, and all sorts of amenities. "One thing we're especially fanatical about is having an adequate number of restrooms that are extremely clean and well attended," DeTar said.

"We're completely self-sufficient, too," he says. "We build everything here ourselves; we have generators, water pumps, sewage holding tanks—everything we need to sustain the market through a weekend if there's a failure of power, water, or sewer services."

And what draws the hordes of visitors Wednesday through Sunday, all year long, from dawn to dusk? A better question might be, "What doesn't draw them?"

At this flea market, you can find anything—from used treasures to brand-new items, from antiques to designer clothing, jewelry, and fur coats; from furnishings to food, and from toys to tires.

Tired of paying top dollar? This is the place to come for rock-bottom prices, even on new merchandise. "It used to be that all the dealers seemed to have just finished raiding their grandmothers' attics," says George Bumb, founder. "But since the 1980s, those sellers of Americana have been increasingly surrounded by entrepreneurs hawking closeouts, overruns, and factory-direct merchandise."

Why pay $12 for a T-shirt at a department store when you can get four for $9.99 at The Flea Market. Admission is free and all-day parking costs only $3 on weekends, $1 during the week.

Breeze through the gates and you're overwhelmed with a teeming universe of bargain-basement buys: sunglasses at 99 cents a pair, videos as low as $2, and similar deals on silk flowers, baby clothes, watches, baggy pants, laundry baskets and other household basics, sofas and chairs, baby strollers and high chairs, ceramics and artwork, skateboards, car seat covers, athletic and walking shoes, wrenches and other tools, luggage, dresses, dried-flower arrangements, knickknacks, collectibles, handcrafts, consumer electronics, military surplus, plants and decorator items, and more, much more.

Apartment managers buy their light bulbs and cleaning supplies in quantity here. People plan their purchases and arrive with detailed lists in hand. And bargain hunters are convinced they've died and gone to heaven.

"One of our biggest attractions is our famous produce row," DeTar says. Over a quarter of a mile long, it's the biggest, busiest outdoor food and vegetable market in California. Overflowing with produce of all kinds, buyers can pay just pennies on the dollar if they buy in the right quantities.

The ethnic and exotic food items, especially, are a gourmet's delight. According to TVs Fresh Grocer, Tony Tantillo, "The Flea Market has fruits and vegetables coming in from Mexico, for example–various kinds of peppers and mangos and other produce–that you can't find anywhere but at The Flea Market."

The benefits of this colossal bazaar flow to the entire community. "People who gain the most from The Flea Market are often those in greatest need," DeTar says. "We provide a vehicle for people to pull themselves up by their bootstraps, a way for them to test the waters, to experiment in business, to learn and prove themselves, and grow their ventures from there. It's probably the only place in the country where you can start your own business for less than $25."

Many merchants who began as Flea Market concessionaires have gone on to found flourishing corporations: Warren Gummow, founder of Royal Foods, for example; and Bob Fills, founder and owner of Stereo Habitat, a successful retail store chain.

Charities benefit, too. Each year The Flea Market conducts special events with proceeds earmarked to help organizations like CityTeam Ministries, Fund for the Homeless, the Police Activities League, the G.I. Forum, and others. Booth rental fees are waived, too, for organizations that want to "set-up shop" at The Flea Market for their charitable and community service causes.

What began in 1960 as a small family business has become a thriving California institution, providing products, entertainment, business opportunities, on-the-job training, cash savings, and income to millions of people every year. They come not just for the bargains and opportunities, but for the sheer spectacle of it all. The San Jose Flea Market is a carnival, a festival, a foreign bazaar, and a World's Fair, all rolled into one–an amazing outdoor emporium that people have to see to believe. ✦

The Flea Market in 1963. Berryessa Road is a country lane with orchards on both sides. In the 1950s this site was used as a cattle yard.

A westward view of The Flea Market in 1970 of the Berryessa district from above the intersection of Capitol Avenue and Penitencia Creek Road. The San Jose International Airport is at the top right of the photograph.

RADISSON PLAZA HOTEL SAN JOSE AIRPORT

Built to accommodate Silicon Valley's burgeoning need for deluxe business/leisure travel accommodations and for premier meeting facilities, the Radisson Plaza Hotel San Jose Airport opened in 1985. This elegant, 185-room facility is located less than two miles from San Jose International Airport and offers complimentary transportation to and from the airport. Close to all business areas, San Jose's vibrant downtown, nearby shopping centers and tourist attractions, the hotel is adjacent to major freeways, making picturesque Carmel and Monterey only a short drive away.

The Radisson Plaza is part of Minneapolis-based Radisson Hospitality Worldwide, one of the fastest growing international hotel chains featuring upscale inns, suite and plaza hotels, and resorts throughout the world.

A full-service hotel, the Radisson Plaza offers a welcoming blend of old-world elegance and service at a competitive rate. Plush carpeting, rich tapestries, exquisite antiques, classic furnishings, soft colors, and sparkling chandeliers, all surrounded by an abundance of leaded crystal and rich, oak woodwork—all are hallmarks of this lovely European-style facility.

Each of the Radisson Plaza's rooms is well-lit, luxurious, and tastefully appointed, including such special amenities as coffeemakers, hairdryers, and full-size irons and boards. Eight executive suites offer an upgraded

This elegant, 185-room facility is located less than two miles from San Jose International Airport and offers complimentary transportation to and from the airport.

A full-service hotel, the Radisson Plaza offers a welcoming blend of old-world elegance and service at a competitive rate. Photo by Miller's Professional Imagaing.

level of luxury, including entertainment and reception areas, in-room Jacuzzis, and dual bathroom sinks. The hotel's Plaza Level gives the privacy of an executive-level floor, with personalized concierge service and newspapers, plus a complimentary continental breakfast, cocktails, and hors d'oeuvres. For the physically active, there is an outdoor swimming pool heated year-round, a quarter-mile jogging course, and an exercise center with private indoor Jacuzzi.

Dining in the Radisson's Gallé Restaurant, with its French atmosphere, gourmet menu and European-trained chef is a special pleasure, whether one's taste runs to California, American, or international cuisine. Adjacent, Jacque's Lounge is just the place to savor fine wines, sip cocktails, and enjoy relaxing conversation.

The Radisson's singular commitment to quality service is evident at every turn. Staff have driven guests to meetings, loaned them personal articles, even literally given guests the shirt off their backs to meet those occasional "Lost luggage…need a business shirt—NOW!" emergencies. They are masters at the art of planning the perfect event—whether it's a small, intimate reception or a business meeting of hundreds. The hotel's 12 meeting facilities accommodate groups with as many as 300 guests. Its Versailles Ballroom is an exquisite setting for the most elegant function. And the lovely courtyard and patio areas make for delightful outdoor catered events.

"Guests are often pleasantly surprised at the exceptional values they discover in our service, comfort, and ambience," says Steven Goldman, general manager of the Radisson Plaza. "Whatever our guests need, we're here to provide it. That's what our 'Yes I can' philosophy is all about." ✦

Photo by Pat Kirk.

Chapter Fifteen

Building San Jose & Silicon Valley

RUDOLPH AND SLETTEN, INC.

"I had $800 in my pocket, if I remember right, and that was a lot of money at that time," says Onslow H. Rudolph, Jr. (known to his colleagues as "Rudy"), founder and chairman of Rudolph and Sletten, Inc. "I put $200 down on a brand-new pickup truck and started working." That was in 1959, and construction was what Rudy Rudolph knew.

A fourth-generation builder with family roots in Germany and the Old World traditions of craftsmanship, he had worked for various construction firms in his hometown Pittsburgh and served as a construction battalion company officer in the Army Corps of Engineers during World War II.

Rudolph's Army experience drew him to California, where he earned a B.S. in civil engineering at San Jose State University in 1950–the first person in his family ever to graduate from college.

"I liked living on the West Coast and decided to remain in the area," he says. "So after college, I spent the next nine years working for Bay Area contractors on construction and civil engineering projects, and traveling all the time." By the time the youngest of his three children was born, he decided he'd had enough of moving around. "I started my own small business with the idea of being able to stay put in one place."

He had others ideas, too–like the idea of quality construction and a target market of high-tech companies.

The world's largest viewing window, measuring 14' x 60', is at the Monterey Bay Aquarium. **Photo by Marvin Wax.**

Even though only a handful of electronics firms existed in the valley at the start of the 1960s, defense-related high-tech industry had begun to escalate in the late 1950s with the establishment of NASA's Ames Research Center in Mountain View and the opening of the first Lockheed Missiles and Space facility in Sunnyvale. Confident that more high-tech firms would move into the area, O.H. Rudolph, general contractor, decided to bet on the trend and worked hard to establish a reputation for quality construction.

His hard work paid off. The company's first big job–a $50,000 contract to construct a laboratory facility– was awarded to the firm because of its reputation for

The Monterey Bay Aquarium is a $40 million world-class aquarium, constructed on Monterey's Cannery Row, and is one of the Central Coast's leading attractions, drawing thousands of visitors every year. **Photo by Marvin Wax.**

doing quality work. "It doesn't cost any more to build it right the first time," has been the firm's motto from the start.

After a few years, with the company taking on increasingly larger projects, Rudolph began to feel he was spreading himself too thin. He decided he needed a partner, and the one he wanted was Ken Sletten, a 32-year-old project manager he'd worked with before going out on his own.

Sletten, a U.S. Marine veteran of the Korean War whose interest in construction dates back to his teens, had added a Stanford University MBA to his undergraduate degree in civil engineering from the University of Colorado in order to prepare himself for one day running his own company.

He was still working at the construction firm Rudolph had left when a telephone call from Rudy in 1962 initiated what turned out to be a lifelong relationship. "We had the same kind of goals from the very beginning," Sletten says. "Of course we wanted to make a profit, but mostly we wanted to have a really good reputation for doing the work right."

From the start, they hired only the best people and provided the best training available. Training, to them, was a long-term investment crucial to the development of the quality organization they had in mind. "Other companies seemed to just want to train somebody to get the job done today. They didn't care how many problems they got into afterwards," Rudolph says. "We cared because of our field experience and the technical training we both got in school."

In order to maintain their standards for delivering the best possible product, with the highest quality workmanship—on budget and on time—the founders realized that they would have to manage their own work. And that set the stage for the type of firm Rudolph & Sletten is today—a general construction company that manages and controls each project it takes on, from the ground up.

Silicon Valley's developed landscape is dotted with evidence of the success of this approach to the construction business. Among the firm's landmark buildings are Vallco Fashion Park, Stanford Shopping Center, Xerox Corporation's research center, Alza, Hewlett Packard's world headquarters, Syntex/Roche Corporation headquarters, Apple Corporate Headquarters Campus, Intel, 3 Com Corporate Campus, Sun Microsystems Corporate Campus, Digital, Rolm River Oaks Park, McCandless Towers, the Regency Plaza, the Doubletree Hotel, the Lucile Packard Children's Hospital at Stanford, Governor's Corner Student Housing, Gates Computer Sciences Building at Stanford, and more—many, many more.

The company's experience includes virtually all types of buildings, with an emphasis on electronics, high-tech research and manufacturing, healthcare, biotech/pharmaceutical, office building, hotel, entertainment, retail, and unique special-purpose projects. Its expertise runs to projects costing well over $200 million.

Probably Rudolph and Sletten's best-known project is the Monterey Bay Aquarium, that was built for David and Julie Packard. The $70 million world-class aquarium, constructed on Monterey's Cannery Row, is one of the Central Coast's leading attractions, drawing thousands of visitors every year. For its work on this project, the company, one of 135 entries, received an award of national excellence from the American Concrete Institute. It has also been featured in *Architectural Record, Sunset, California Builder and Engineer*, and *Concrete International* magazines. Rudolph and Sletten have just completed the second phase for the Outer Bay Wing addition.

Less well known to the general public but considered by the firm to be one of its most interesting projects, is the Skywalker Ranch Technical Building in Marin County. The $30 million two-story movie studio for George Lucas' (of *Star Wars* fame) Lucas Films, was designed and built to resemble a turn-of-the-century winery building.

Another conspicuous project, the Metro Center in Foster City, is home to Rudolph and Sletten's 30,000 square feet of corporate offices. A 100-acre, master-planned corporate community, Metro Center includes 1.4 million square feet of office/research and development facilities, housing, shopping, dining, and entertainment complexes. Besides constructing two of the development's 4-story office buildings, Rudolph and Sletten built the 22-story Metro Tower—centerpiece of the project and the tallest building between Los Angeles and San Francisco.

Noted for its expertise in the construction of special-design high-technology facilities, the company built the $42 million Center for Molecular and Genetic Medicine at Stanford University, and the Advanced Micro Devices Sub-Micron Facility in Sunnyvale—not to mention a host of laboratories and "clean rooms" throughout Silicon Valley.

As impressive as Rudolph and Sletten's list of completed projects, is its roster of clients—some of the valley's most important companies: 3 Com

The Sun Microsystems Corporate Campus in Menlo Park. Photo by Marvin Wax.

An overall view of Sun Microsystems Corporate Campus in Menlo Park. Photo by Marvin Wax.

Corporation, Alza, Amdahl Corp., Apple Computer, Inc.; ESL, Digital Equipment Corp., Genencor International, GTE Government Systems Corp., Hewlett Packard Co., IBM Corp., Kaiser Permanente, Lockheed Martin Missiles & Space, Measurex Corp., Raychem Corp., Siliconix, Inc.; Sun Microsystems, Inc.; Intel, Syntex Corp., Tandem Computers, Inc.; Varian Associates, Inc., and others. Its work isn't limited to Silicon Valley, either. San Francisco, Sacramento, Glendale, Irvine, and San Diego–regions where the firm maintains divisional offices–all have major projects underway and completed by Rudolph and Sletten. Besides California, the 600-employee company is licensed and qualified to provide construction services in Arizona, Nevada, Washington, Colorado, Idaho, and Oregon.

Just how do you build this kind of a quality company? How do you get the commitment from every employee, not just those at the top? The Rudolph and Sletten formula is easy to describe, but a lot harder to implement. Step One is to hire the best people. To ensure its growth in the years ahead, the company needs well educated, flexible, and responsible employees who think for themselves, act independently, exercise sound judgment, and solve problems.

That's why Rudolph and Sletten maintains an aggressive recruiting program, combing college campuses around the country every year for the best graduates in civil engineering, construction management, construction engineering, and related fields. Out of some 300 interviews, approximately 50 students are flown to corporate headquarters for in-person interviews. Of these, only 10 are offered positions with the firm.

The company's recruitment efforts are equally aggressive at trade programs, searching out the most promising young craftspeople to staff its field crews.

Step Two requires an ongoing investment in the best training available. Remembering how their own development efforts were thwarted at companies they worked for early in their careers, the founders made a point of establishing a work environment that fosters individual growth and recognizes and rewards personal achievement.

Rudolph and Sletten's training programs are unique in the construction industry. Nationally recognized, it has provided formal on-site and off-site training for employees since 1981. Even its most qualified staff members are required to attend regular, ongoing training.

For example, at least monthly (and often more frequently), classes are offered in technical areas, crafts, accounting, estimating, management/leadership skills, and health and wellness. Certain in-house programs are

Rudolph and Sletten is one of the foremost construction companies on the West Coast and is one of the largest general building contracting firms in America. Shown standing is John Rudolph, and seated to his left is Ken Sletten. **Photo by Jack Hutcheson.**

required for specific employees–such as first aid/CPR for field personnel, estimating and scheduling for project engineers, and accounting for employees who work in finance.

Most in-house education is provided at the company's training center. With comfortable seating for 35 people, this facility is equipped with visual aids, plus adjacent dining and breakout conference rooms.

Step Three means fostering a strong sense of teamwork, with an emphasis on good communication. "One method we used early-on was to have superintendents and foremen get together every other week to discuss safety over breakfast," Sletten says. "This was way back before Cal-OSHA even existed." At Rudolph and Sletten, it's not only important to have the smartest people, it's equally important to keep them safe and healthy. An in-depth focus on safety has become an integral part of the company's culture.

With many more participants and now a monthly schedule, these meetings and the safety exchanges they provide have made Rudolph and Sletten recognized as one of the most progressive contractors around. In addition, the firm, having worked over 1.3 million man hours in 1996 without a lost time injury, has been honored by the Associated General Contractors of California with the "Safest in the State" award.

Rudolph and Sletten's concern for people extends to its clients, too–present and former. The day following the 1989 Loma Prieta earthquake, which shook the Bay Area to its very foundations, the company's staff offered their on-site assistance at projects that might have been

A view of the original wing from the new Outer Bay waters wing at the Monterey Bay Aquarium. **Photo by Marvin Wax.**

The entrance to Apple Corporate Research and Development Campus in Sunnyvale. **Photo by Marvin Wax.**

affected by the quake. These were projects they'd worked on as far back as 10 years earlier! By making these resources immediately available during this disaster, Rudolph and Sletten helped many companies stay in business.

From that small investment of $800, Rudy Rudolph, and soon afterward Ken Sletten, created what has become one of the foremost construction companies on the West Coast. With several hundred million dollars in projects underway at any given time, it is one of the largest general building contracting firms in America.

Carrying on the family tradition, Rudy's son, John, joined the company in 1976 and is now president. A graduate of the University of Oregon, with an advance degree from University of Santa Clara, John is committed to carrying on in the tradition of the founders, while helping the company continue to evolve to meet the challenges of the future. Like his father and Ken Sletten, John believes that the strength of the company rests in the strength of its people.

"Our people are the ones who have earned our reputation for us," he says. "And that's the best thing Rudolph and Sletten has built in its 35-plus-year history." ✦

The 3 Com Corporate Headquarters Campus in San Jose is one of the firm's landmark buildings.

CORNISH & CAREY

Firsts are a way of life in Silicon Valley—just as they are for Cornish & Carey, its residential real estate services leader.

Founded in 1935, Cornish & Carey is Silicon Valley's number one firm in residential real estate market share, with 900 sales executives (agents), 24 offices, and billions of dollars in sales each year; and number one in sheer dollar volume of real estate sold. Cornish & Carey was the first real estate firm with over 100 listings and they placed 1,100 at that time on the net to establish its presence on the World Wide Web; and the first to create a Retirement Living Division focused on meeting the housing and residential care needs of seniors.

Headquartered in San Mateo, Cornish & Carey, over more than six decades of operations, has become the largest independently owned brokerage firm in the San Francisco Bay Area. Equally remarkable is the fact that it is the ninth largest residential real estate services company in America—despite operating in the region of Silicon Valley and not having the obvious size advantage of membership in a large, national chain.

"We are the high-end leader and the

Cornish & Carey Residential Update, *is their monthly newsletter that keeps the local area aware of the most current issues in real estate such as this inviting home available in Rancho San Antonio.*

marketplace leader in one of the leading markets in the country," says Roger Rickard, Cornish & Carey's chairman of the board and CEO.

How do they do it? Well, for one thing, theirs is a tradition of excellence, driven by a strong entrepreneurial spirit, a philosophy of leadership and innovation, and an unmatched commitment to professionalism and community service.

Cornish & Carey opened its doors in Palo Alto on April Fool's Day 1935. Its two young founders and friends—H.J. (Herb) Cornish and G.E. (Pat) Carey—began their company with a sales team of six and an investment of $2,000, the sum total of their pooled savings.

During the depression years, this small, dedicated team of talented professionals worked long and hard to build the business foundation and reputation for quality service that started Cornish & Carey on its steady march to industry leadership.

In 1953, the company opened its first branch office in Atherton. Herb Cornish's son, Jim, joined the firm in 1955, after graduating from Stanford University, and became Cornish & Carey's first sales executive under 30 years of age. In 1960, Jim became a partner and sales manager; and today, he is chairman of the board emeritus. It was his vision of a multi-office company that set the tone for Cornish & Carey's enviable record of growth.

The late 1950s heralded the widely publicized real estate boom that drove Bay Area prices skyward and triggered a tidal wave of new development that lasted for nearly 30 years. Cornish & Carey grew like wildfire, as did all of Silicon Valley.

The firm's commercial division was formed in the early 1970s. And by the mid 1980s, through internal growth and the company's purchase of the multi-office firm of Van Vleck Realty, Cornish & Carey had 14 offices and nearly 800 sales executives by the mid 1980s.

When the commercial and residential arms of Cornish & Carey decided to split and become independent companies in 1987, a door opened, creating the opportunity for new ownership in Cornish & Carey Residential. Roger Rickard stepped through that door.

Having joined the firm in 1977 as a sales executive, Rickard progressed to CEO in fairly short order, becoming manager of the Cupertino office in 1980, manager of the Palo Alto office in 1984, and South Bay Area regional manager in 1985, before moving on to his present position.

A Stanford University Ph.D., Rickard's early background as a high school and athletic coach has served both him and Cornish & Carey, well. "We're the most unique real estate company in the United States," he says. "And our success is due to our outstanding sales executives. They work as a team, with a dedication to serving their clients that is truly extraordinary."

Cornish & Carey is Silicon Valley's number-one firm in residential real estate market share. Shown is a dining room in one of their enchanting homes for sale.

Known for its unparalleled service and widespread visibility, Cornish & Carey offers clients a superb array of resources. "We do an incredible amount of advertising," Rickard notes.

More than 1,200 Cornish & Carey listings are available to home buyers throughout the world at the firm's home page on the World Wide Web, which draws over 30,000 hits a day. In the Bay Area alone, more than 500,000 professionals regularly use the Internet. Rickard says. "Through our site on 'The Web,' our clients' properties are exposed to these computer-literate professionals, who are some of the highest earning people in the world."

In addition, the firm's extensive billboard advertising at key locations throughout Silicon Valley, and targeted commercial spots during prime listening periods on highly rated radio stations, engenders high-level visibility that benefits each property Cornish & Carey represents.

"Our multi-media advertising approach, which is unique to our firm, gives us an enormous ability to attract buyers and market client properties," says Dennis Moreno, president. "And, unlike national and franchise firms, 100 percent of our marketing budget is used to market our local properties, giving our clients the greatest marketing punch for the sale of their home or property."

These mass-media marketing strategies are reinforced by an intensive program of direct mail, brochures, multiple listing services and tours, as well as an international marketing program, and a strong referral system throughout the Cornish & Carey office network.

"Our computerized, direct-marketing program targets specific households and communities, notifying them of our open houses, listings, and

Cornish & Carey's Chairman of the Board Jim Cornish (standing left) with President and CEO Rodger Rickard (right).

home sales," Moreno says. "And *Cornish & Carey Residential Update*, our monthly newsletter, keeps the local area aware of the most current issues in real estate."

Through its Relocation Division—which also handles the needs of corporate and industry clients—Cornish & Carey participates in "Realty Alliance Relocation Network," a national cooperative group of independent Realtors with nearly 4,000 offices and more than 50,000 salespeople across the country. These offices have generated more than $50 billion in real estate sales, and encompass 13,000 communities in all major markets.

What's even more impressive is the firm's international marketing program. Providing an exceptional and highly valuable special service to Cornish & Carey clients, this program gives extensive, comprehensive marketing exposure of the firm's listings to residents of more than 40 countries, and includes visibility in the International Multiple Listing Service and high-profile overseas publications.

Since its inception, Cornish & Carey has been the clear leader in marking prestigious properties. That tradition continues today through its Executive Properties group.

As the local exclusive affiliate of the internationally renowned *Christie's Great Estates* magazine, Cornish & Carey helps its clients capitalize on this powerful international showcase for distinctive

More than 1,200 Cornish & Carey listings are available to home buyers throughout the world at the firm's home page on the World Wide Web, like this beautiful home listed in Woodside Estate.

properties, by promoting and displaying their properties to a worldwide audience. Such exposure is complemented through Cornish & Carey's own quarterly publication, *Cornish & Carey's Showcase of Homes*, which is mailed to top Silicon Valley area business executives.

In keeping with the international scope of Silicon Valley and with diverse nature of its own clients, Cornish & Carey has an unexcelled capability for multi-lingual communication. Everything from Arabic and Armenian to the primary Chinese dialects, from the major languages of the European Common Market countries to languages of the Far East and Pacific Rim, and more–40 different languages, in total, are represented on the Cornish & Carey team.

Corporate services are another important component of this market leader's capabilities. Its innovative Marketing Group offers corporate clients a wide range of specialty materials and services–including advice from the firm's House Counsel on increasingly complex legal matters.

Cornish & Carey's services for seniors, provided through its Retirement Living Division, are unusual for their depth and scope. Valuable information on housing, continuing care facilities, and other living choices are available, along with a special Cornish & Carey publication: *Where To Live, A Guide For Senior Adults*, an in-depth, highly praised resource.

Carrying its commitment to services all the way through to financing, Cornish & Carey is in the mortgage lending business, too.

"By streamlining the home buying process, our C&C Capital division offers our customers significant advantages over other loan institutions," Rickard says. "With lower loan origination fees, sophisticated loan tracking computer software, and video-teleconferencing capabilities, our one-stop

Bryant McOmber, general counsel with Zoe Theodoros, legal secretary of Cornish & Carey.

system gives our clients better service, more control, and improved flexibility throughout the entire home buying process."

No matter how extensive the facilities and equipment, the funding, and the services of an organization, it's always the people who make the real difference. That's especially true at Cornish & Carey because of its selectivity at "the front end," and its continuing investment in intensive training and support once the sales executives are on board.

"Our sales executives average nearly 15 years of experience," Moreno noted. "Most live in the areas where they work, and many have done so for most of their lives. We're particularly proud that they all actively involve themselves in public service activities and volunteer their time for the benefit of the community."

Carefully chosen, Cornish & Carey sales executives are recognized throughout the country for their integrity, their professionalism, and their outstanding levels of achievement–both professionally and as contributing members of their communities.

Carol Burnett is typical of the caliber of sales executive at Cornish & Carey. Senior vice president and managing executive of the firm's Saratoga office, she serves as a director of the Saratoga Chamber of Commerce and on the KTEH (public television channel) board of directors. In addition, she is active in the Junior League of San Jose, Saratoga Rotary, Saratoga/Los Gatos Board of Realtors, and more.

With all that community activity, it's hard to believe she has also won a string of professional awards–but she has. "The word 'no' just isn't in her vocabulary," said Pat Richard, owner of Pat Richard Insurance Agency in Saratoga, in a recent profile of Burnett. "This is a dynamic lady who gets things done."

Community service is a long-standing tradition at Cornish & Carey, an important

Cornish & Carey's own quarterly publication, Cornish & Carey's Showcase of Homes, is mailed to top Silicon Valley area business executives informing them of homes available like this one in Rancho San Antonio.

part of its commitment to integrity and to community. "We live in our community; it's where we earn our living," says Rickard. "And it is our pleasure to give back to the community, primarily by investing in our community's most important resource—its youth."

Cornish & Carey has given hundreds of thousands of dollars in its educational scholarship program that recognizes outstanding graduating high school seniors in the communities it serves. The firm has also supported for many years such other important community causes as Junior Achievement, San Jose Museum of Art, Child Advocates, San Jose Police Activities League, New Children's Shelter Fund, and many more.

"Christmas in April" is among our favorite charities," Rickard says. This non-denominational, community-based project helps low-income, elderly, and people with disabilities live in warmth, safety, and independence through a program of volunteer repair and renovation of owner-occupied homes and not-for-profit living centers.

With Cornish & Carey's strong, active presence on the Internet's World Wide Web, its multi-million-dollar computer network, its state-of-the-art technology that allows clients to take comprehensive video tours of properties and tap into an electronic property listings database that is not only local and regional, but also national and international; and its video-teleconferencing capabilities that help make the homebuying process a one-stop shopping experience—this dynamic company's position as the leader in high-tech real estate services is well deserved.

It's characterized by a passion for quality and integrity that runs strong and deep in every single person on the Cornish & Carey team. And it all starts at the top.

"We're number one because we have the best agents in the business, and because we're committed to giving them the tools they need to do their jobs—the most advanced technology in the industry, the best training, the strongest management team, the finest facilities, and the most aggressive marketing program around," Rickard says. "It has been, is, and always will be a thrilling ride to the peaks of success at Cornish & Carey." ✦

Cornish & Carey's computerized, direct-marketing program targets specific households and communities, notifying them of open houses, listings, and home sales like this elegant home shown.

One of Cornish & Carey's newer office buildings in Redwood City that opened in 1995.

COLLIERS PARRISH INTERNATIONAL, INC.

In the world of Silicon Valley Commercial Real Estate, J.R. is first associated with J.R. Parrish, founder, chairman, and CEO of Colliers Parrish—not the television character of "Dallas" fame.

For a company that is part of Colliers International, Inc.—the world's most comprehensive provider of commercial real estate services, operating throughout North America, Europe, and the Pacific Rim through a network of 195 offices on 6 continents in 40 countries—Colliers Parrish is astonishingly low key in its approach to business.

"It's not up to us to blow our own horn," Parrish says, "If you do your job right then others will do that for you."

And others do. "When you are working with Colliers, you are comfortable in the knowledge that you are represented by honest, hardworking professionals who understand the client's requirements," says a testimonial letter from Chrysler Corporation, "Colliers' high standards show in the finished product," says another from General Foods.

This firm has been exceptional from the start. When Parrish needed financial help to start his own commercial real estate business in San Jose in 1974, he turned to David Cooper, a local executive who gave him office space and staked him from the start. "Jim Parrish could sell coals to Newcastle. Whatever I staked him to, I was paid back tenfold," Cooper said in a *Business Journal* article profiling J.R., "Why did I know he was good? You could simply see the spark, the enthusiasm, and the drive to succeed."

Those qualities have become part of the culture that defines Colliers Parrish—a culture based on dealing honestly and effectively with people, on trusting and sharing with others, on putting others' interests ahead of one's own, on seeking first to understand before seeking to be understood.

"I can't point to any one thing," Parrish says, "It's just your total way of living and working."

Treating one another with integrity and respect is one reason why Colliers Parrish draws the top experienced brokers to its team—and keeps them. "We've never lost a broker to a major competitor—ever," says Corporate Director Jeff Fredericks.

Colliers Parrish International applies to its clients that same code of honesty and integrity—and backs it with impeccable performance and exceptional innovation. That's an important reason why clients such as Seagate Technologies, Adobe Systems, Hewlett Packard, Oracle Corporation, Microsoft, Equitable Life Insurance, and countless others use Colliers Parrish International as their real estate service provider.

"We rely heavily on our reputation of consistent, full-service excellence," comments President Dave Schmidt, "emphasizing our local and regional expertise plus our worldwide capabilities and services."

Those services are broad indeed. They encompass R&D, office, industrial, and retail leasing and sales; investment analysis, disposition, and acquisition; land disposition; construction management; build to suit brokerage, consulting; tenant and landlord representation; feasibility and market studies; site acquisition; property valuation and appraisal; financial services and corporate services.

Colliers Parrish offers its clients the benefits of local knowledge and worldwide expertise whether transacting business here in the Silicon Valley, negotiating an institutional sale on the east coast, or consulting a tenant on its lease alternatives in Singapore.

Seated is Dave Schmidt, president, and standing is J.R. Parrish, chairman of the board and CEO of Colliers Parrish International, Inc.

Colliers Parrish International, Inc., San Jose headquarters.

Clients benefit from the firm's global coverage. They can expand their facilities or relocate them with the confidence that they've been briefed on all the alternatives, that they have all the information they need to make the best decisions.

They gain the benefits of experience. The Colliers Parrish team is made up of seasoned professionals who average 15 years in the profession.

Clients gain the benefits of technology as well. "To ensure that we provide the best, most timely answers, opportunities, and solutions available, we document our collective skills, experiences and contacts in a proprietary database," Schmidt says, "and we put the database on-line because the answer to a client's specific problem may be half a world away." Colliers Parrish has harnessed state-of-the-art software to make certain that distance presents no obstacle to client satisfaction.

Whether the client's need is in the Americas, Europe or the Asia Pacific region, this firm virtually dissolves geographic boundaries and language barriers. "We can offer a single point of contact in our client's market supported by English-speaking project managers in each trading bloc", Schmidt says.

Clients also gain the benefits of long-term relationships. This is a company that invests the time to understand the issues and objectives of its clients, whose needs dictate Colliers Parrish's design and implementation of new innovative services.

Colliers Parrish's commitment to the importance of people extends beyond staff, clients and prospects to encompass community. It isn't mentioned much outside the company, but this firm has adopted a local elementary school, where brokers donate their time reading to the children, securing new equipment for the students, helping to upgrade the school's facilities, and more.

These brokers contribute to the community in other ways, too—serving on the volunteer boards of community service organizations, for instance. And, unlike many who donate their services the folks at Colliers Parrish do this all without fanfare.

"Colliers is poised to become the number-one real estate provider in the world," Parrish says, "That's my dream. It's very clear; I see it as plain as day—the Colliers name and colors recognized in every city in the world, Colliers as the preeminent firm in each of its markets, providing every needed service; the best, safest choice for corporate clients; the technological leader in our industry."

Based on the Colliers Parrish style of doing business—with a powerful sense of quality, character, consistency and community—it's a good bet that Parrish's dream will come true. ✦

J.R. Parrish, chairman of the board and CEO of Colliers Parrish International, Inc.

Dave Schmidt, president of Colliers Parrish International, Inc.

SOBRATO
DEVELOPMENT COMPANIES

A family operation since its early beginnings in 1955 when grand-mother Ann Sobrato developed one of the first "tilt-up" style buildings in the valley, Sobrato Development Companies remains a close knit family business to this day. It has also become one of the most successful real estate organizations in the nation, topping the *Silicon Valley Business Journal*'s annual list of largest commercial developers year after year.

"You might say that my mother had a real nose for dirt," says company founder John A. Sobrato. "She started investing in local real estate when I was still in grammar school. I worked a couple of summers as an apprentice carpenter and eventually followed her into the business."

Two decades later, John brought his son, John Michael Sobrato, into the business in much the same way that his mother did—as a youth, working on construction sites and learning from the bottom up. Now co-principal, John Michael handles day-to-day operations of the firm while his father oversees the more complex long-range planning.

Apple Computer campus headquarters in Cupertino, California.

Sobrato Development Companies has developed and owns over nine million square feet of office, R&D and apartment buildings in the Bay Area, from San Mateo in the north to San Jose in the south. Its organization is unique among the Valley's development companies; it holds its properties entirely within the family, without the joint-venture arrangements typical of most developers.

The list of Sobrato tenants reads like a "Who's Who" of Silicon Valley. From Hewlett Packard's campus in Cupertino to the Kodak Center in San Jose; from Amdahl's headquarters in Sunnyvale to Knight Ridder's headquarters in Mountain View; from the sprawling campuses of Bay Networks in Santa Clara to Apple Computer in Cupertino, Sobrato Development Companies has left an indelible mark on the real estate landscape of the Valley. The next generation of high-technology giants are also prominent in Sobrato's portfolio: Netscape Communications, S-3 Corporation and Komag combined occupy over 1.2 million square feet of the Sobrato family's buildings.

Sobrato Development Companies' success in Silicon Valley is the result of industry focus. It has long since established itself as the specialist in large scale real estate development for high-technology companies, most of which require sophisticated interiors including energy efficient

office, clean rooms, fabrication and manufacturing areas, and biological and medical labs. In all, Sobrato has developed and built facilities for more than 250 technology companies. Many of these projects involved historic "firsts" for the Valley: Sobrato was the first to develop mid-rise office buildings in a suburban setting; was the first to incorporate parking structures into its R&D developments as a means of increasing density; and was the first to plan and construct a major campus facility on a build-to-suit basis for a single tenant (Amdahl corporation in 1973), considered at the time to be extremely risky. The functionality and attractiveness of the campus today, still leased to Amdahl Corporation after 24 years, is a testament to the foresight of its developer. Ever striving to keep pace with improvements in construction techniques, Sobrato was also the first developer to raze its own buildings in favor of new state-of-the-art development.

Sobrato Development Companies has survived several downturns in the Valley's economy including a commercial real estate recession in the early 1990s that spelled financial Armageddon for the majority of local real estate developers. Sobrato not only retained all of its buildings during this period foreclosures and defaults—it enjoyed a record development year.

How could one developer survive the tumultuous ups and downs of Silicon Valley? And not only survive, but emerge on top, innovating all along the way? Sobrato credits the firms longevity and phenomenal success to hard work and the family's willingness to take a risk. "My mother 'bet the farm' over and over in the 1950s," he says. "And I did, too. The last time we were at that level of risk was in 1973 with the Amdahl project. Now we just bet a piece of it." In other words, the Sobratos have

Interior lobby of Sobrato Development Companies' headquarters in Cupertino, California.

emulated the entrepreneurial style of the technology leaders for whom they build. "Entrepreneurship is a way of life around here," John says. "But we didn't have venture capital when we got started. We had risk, and cooperative banks."

With a management staff of only 16 people, Sobrato is proud of his lean organization. He says it allows the company to be more responsive to client needs. "We've built our reputation on our responsiveness," he says. "If someone comes into our office and wants a building, he talks to me or my son. Either John or I am involved all the way through every deal."

Ever the pioneer, Sobrato Development has positioned itself to be even more responsive to major users as it enters the 21st century. For example, the company has employed a strategy of pre-planning campus sites so that plans can be drawn with permits in place long before a client decides to build. This strategy enabled Sobrato to deliver a 280,000-square-foot, multi-building campus in North San Jose to Pyramid Technology in six months–instead of the usual 12-18 months.

Most recently, the company has begun work on a two building, 300,000-square-foot mid-rise campus for S-3 Corporation in the heart of Silicon Valley at Great America Parkway and Highway 101. It is also underway on the first of two 140,000-square-foot office buildings for Verifone. This year has already proven to be another record year for Sobrato Development, with over one million square feet of new development and additional pending developments of over 500,000 square feet.

At the end of the day, good old-fashioned entrepreneurial virtues underlie the success of most Silicon Valley companies– including Sobrato Development–but there is no mistaking the overriding principle at this family business. "Work for your clients' best interests with a view toward building long term relationships," says Sobrato, "and remember– whatever money or service you put into the community will come back and benefit your business tenfold." ✦

Knight Ridder Information Services headquarters in Mountain View, California.

Netscape Communications corporate headquarters in Mountain View, California.

THE REDEVELOPMENT AGENCY OF THE CITY OF SAN JOSE

*T*oday's modern Downtown is striking in its similarity to San Jose's Downtown of the 1930s–the business, social, and cultural center of the entire Santa Clara Valley. Civic pride in the rebirth of Downtown San Jose–encompassing the impressive McEnery Convention Center, the innovative, purple-walled Children's Discovery Museum, the five-Star Fairmont Hotel, the historic Plaza Park, the magnificently restored De Anza Hotel and Hyatt Sainte Claire Hotel, the Museum of Art, the dazzling San Jose Arena, the European-style San Antonio Plaza, the scenic Guadalupe River Park, a granite-paved Transit Mall shaded with sycamores, abundant public

art, History Walk markers, ample plazas and seating areas scattered throughout, and more–is luring many thousands of longtime residents back to the Downtown area for the first time in decades.

The bridge connects the Center for Performing Arts to the River Park Towers office and retail complex on the banks of the river in the heart of Downtown San Jose.

Downtown San Jose began a steady decline in the 1950s, as business fled to the suburbs and major government

buildings moved to large new facilities north of Downtown. At the same time, San Jose's population began growing at breakneck speed, more than doubling from 1950 to 1960. The epidemic of home building to serve the city's mushrooming population led to an unhealthy urban sprawl that lacked a vigorous Downtown, active job centers, and effective transportation systems.

By 1960, block after block of boarded storefronts and vacant office buildings served as stark testament that San Jose's once vibrant Downtown suffered from rampant urban blight.

Enter The Redevelopment Agency of the City of San Jose. Created in 1956, its mission was to strengthen the community's industrial and commercial tax base and bring economic and employment growth to the city.

One of its early developments, the Rincon de Los Esteros project area, was planned and established in 1974. Initial improvements funded by the Agency included streets, flood control infrastructure, and sewers. Today Rincon is one of the nation's most prosperous and productive technology parks, with more than 2,000 employers providing over 66,000 jobs, and more than 35 million square feet of R & D, manufacturing, and office space.

In the late 1970s, the Agency created a new Downtown plan. The new plan–modeled on the "walking" cities of Verona and Barcelona, both cities with climate and cultural

influences similar to San Jose's–sought to revitalize the Downtown in a way that would draw people for everything from "family outings to lovers' strolls."

With financing and investment of over $500 million–in partnership with over $1 billion in private investment–the Redevelopment Agency creatively subsidized nearly two decades of construction activity not seen Downtown in over 50 years.

Park Center Plaza, one of the first new Downtown office developments, created 412,000 square feet of office and retail space, plus public amenities such as public art, landscaped seating areas, and more than 1,200 public parking spaces.

Increasingly, valleyites want to live in the elegant, exciting, culture-rich, and convenient Downtown San Jose center. New condominiums and apartments, plus rehabilitated masonry buildings, offer a range of housing choices–from high-end condominiums to moderate and low-income apartments. The new Repertory Theatre, opening in fall 1997, the new Tech Museum of Innovation, set to open in 1998, and the planned Mexican Cultural Heritage Gardens, along with the San Jose's Neighborhood Business District revitalization program and the comprehensive transportation network partially funded with $75.2 million from the Redevelopment Agency–assure that San Jose will enter the new century in splendid form, function, and style.

Thanks to the Redevelopment Agency and the foresight of city leaders that created it, San Jose has been able to reclaim its former status as the valley's center for business and government. And, with the Redevelopment Agency's help, San Jose is fast becoming a world-class leader in the arts, in culture, and in quality of life.

Still, San Jose will never forget its rural roots and the neighborly warmth that characterizes its past. As long-time residents and first-time visitors regularly observe in surprised delight, San Jose really is a big city that feels like everyone's idea of Hometown. ◆

The Redevelopment Agency built the Downtown San Jose Arena, home to the NHL Sharks hockey team and host to the 1997 NHL All-Star Game. The San Jose Arena attracts well over one million people to sports and cultural events and family entertainment each year.

Chapter Sixteen

Business & Finance

◆

COMERICA BANK-CALIFORNIA

*I*n a region known throughout the world as much for its nonconformist attitude and entrepreneurial fervor as for its innovation and technological leadership, it is fitting that its largest, fastest growing bank should reflect the same attributes.

Based in San Jose, the capital of Silicon Valley, Comerica Bank-California is a bank like no other. Like the legions of entrepreneurs who dominate its customer ranks, this bank knows how to deliver cutting edge, world-class performance–and have fun doing it.

Not long ago, Comerica Bank-California's top executives fought in a sumo wrestling contest. A group of its corporate banking officers–all made up, wigged, and costumed as characters from the "Wizard of Oz"–performed to the obvious delight of employees in the bank's main office lobby.

"We're not the norm," observed Mike Fulton, president and CEO. No kidding!

This is a bank whose employees celebrate their business achievements by running and jumping through a Velcro obstacle course...that accompanies customer deposit receipts with free dog biscuits at its drive-up windows...that distributes more than 40,000 pounds of world-famed Walla Walla onions each summer...and whose confidential on-site review team checks out potential bank acquisitions by disguising themselves as the weekend rug cleaning crew.

And when it comes to competing for new customers, this is a bank that doesn't fool around. From its founding in 1991, Comerica Bank-California took only 5 years to build its assets up to $4 billion, making it the 8th largest of the state's 350 banks–and still climbing.

"Our success rests with our employees and their ability to execute a plan focused on the essentials of our three core values," Fulton says, "which are: being the preferred bank for business, delivering the highest level of customer service possible, and ensuring that employees enjoy themselves in the process."

As a "Super Community Bank," Comerica Bank-California is able to offer its customers and employees the best of both worlds–big-bank resources with small-bank responsiveness and flexibility.

Visit our home page on the World Wide Web!

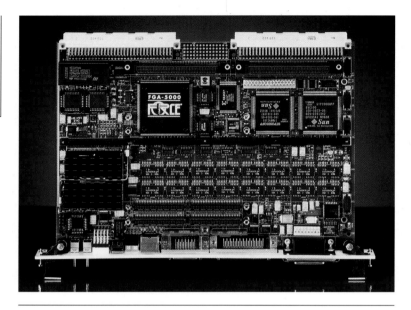

FORCE Computers, founded in 1981, is a leading supplier of open, scalable system and board-level computer platforms for communication and control applications in the embedded market. FORCE is a processor-independent company and delivers products based on SPARC, PowerPC, 68K, and Intel technologies. End-user equipment using FORCE products include switch control systems, Telecom network management systems, industrial control systems, radar and simulation systems, and medical scanners.

A subsidiary of Solectron Corporation, FORCE is an ISO 9001 certified company with its corporate headquarters in San Jose, California. European headquarters are located in Munich, Germany, and Japanese headquarters or located in Tokyo, Japan.

Its big-bank capabilities come from its affiliation with Detroit-based Comerica Incorporated. Formed in 1849, this super-regional bank holding company is the 25th largest in the United States and operates commercial banking subsidiaries in Michigan, Florida, and Texas, as well as California. It is the nation's 14th largest commercial business lender, and the 16th largest small business lender.

With nearly 12,000 employees, $34 billion in total assets, $2 billion-plus in equity, impressive institutional ratings, and a record of financial performance that consistently lands it in the first quartile of America's top 50 banks, Comerica Incorporated has the resources–the people, technology, connections, facilities, and equipment–to provide a full range of banking services, up through the most sophisticated, both domestic and international.

Global banking, corporate banking and institutional trust, consumer banking and lending, mortgage finance, small business banking, private banking, and the full scope of cash management and investment services, including insurance, are all part of Comerica's comprehensive portfolio of "big-bank" capabilities.

Its California affiliate's race to the number one spot in Silicon Valley's banking community–nothing short of spectacular in anybody's book–has been fueled by internal growth as well as by mergers. "We're the fastest-growing entry in the banking business," Fulton says, "and a top player in the state."

During Comerica Bank-California's first five years of existence, this banking dynamo acquired three valley financial institutions–Plaza Bank of Commerce in 1991, Pacific Western Bank in 1994, and University Bank & Trust in 1995–plus the $1.3 billion Los Angeles-based Metrobank in 1996. What's more, it shot to prominence as the valley's largest bank while still one of the youngest.

The Comerica Bank-California headquarters, San Jose, California.

When the merger dust had settled, Comerica Bank-California had more than 800 employees working in branch offices in Northern California–virtually all in Silicon Valley communities–and throughout Southern California.

Its market focus is strongly business oriented, with an emphasis on serving a range of companies from start-ups to those with revenues of $250 million and more. "Businesses very seldom outgrow us," Fulton says. "We can meet their needs through every stage of their development."

This bank has established its expertise in a number of specialized business areas–small business, commercial real estate, mortgage banking, trust and private banking, treasury management, and international banking. But high-tech commerce is one of its strongest area of emphasis, because the leadership at Comerica Bank-California has such an intimate understanding of the unique characteristics and banking issues of that market.

Comerica Bank-California is so committed to the high-tech market that it maintains two specialized high-tech banking units–one in each half of the state.

"We've experienced the same kind of explosive growth that technology companies typically do, so we have firsthand insight into their special problems and needs," Fulton observed. "That's an extraordinarily valuable resource that few other banks–if any–can offer."

Comerica Bank-California was the presenting sponsor for the tennis championship Sybase Open at the San Jose Arena.

San Jose State University's Central Plaza fountain in front of the Event Center, sponsored by Comerica Bank-California through the Heritage Gateway Campaign. The first privately funded university-wide capital improvement campaign in more than 125 years. **Photo by E. Chris Wisner.**

Headed by David Stearns, senior vice president, Comerica Bank-California's High-Tech Lending Group is a team of skilled experts that really knows how to meet the banking demands of fast-track technology companies.

"We make a point of staying close to the latest developments in semi-conductors, telecommunications, computers, peripherals, networking tools, medical instruments, and the software industry," he says. "Not only are we a leader in Silicon Valley high-tech banking, we are also members of the broader technology community through our active participation in trade conferences and associations."

Comerica Bank-California's high-tech team is well experienced at working with emerging growth companies at every stage of their development–from startup to established public companies.

"We stay close to our customers," Stearns says. "We listen and ask questions. We assess and then review the full scope of their needs with our team of internal experts in the right disciplines for each business. And then we create customized solutions for every customer."

Those solutions are drawn from the bank's full range of financial services.

During the early stages of fast-growing companies, when cash to fund that growth is under intense pressure, Comerica Bank-California's fast response with working capital lines of credit, along with equipment loans, can make all the difference.

"Comerica Bank-California understands what we're doing and what high-tech and high-growth companies are all about," says Bryan Stolle, president of San Jose-based Agile Software Corporation, a venture capital funded, start-up corporation. "When we needed a major letter of credit to do an office space lease, they came through very quickly, and with a minimum of hassle. Same thing with our line of credit."

In 1996, this firm had begun shipping products and generating revenues, but was not yet profitable. "Most banks wouldn't know how to even structure a credit line for a company in our stage of development," he said. "But Comerica recognized the potential value of what we could become and gave us a level of banking services that a company our size normally wouldn't get."

As firms go global, importing raw materials, parts, and sub-assemblies; and exporting finished products and goods, Comerica's international trade finance products and services help reduce a company's financial risk by providing hedges against swings in foreign currency values. With its strong program of export financing, Comerica helps underwrite increases in international sales. And the bank's letter-of-credit capabilities can streamline the import/export process by helping to smooth out problems and keep activities on schedule.

According to *International Business Magazine*, Comerica's international capabilities rank it among the top trade finance banks to middle market firms in the U.S.

"The relationships we maintain with more than 1,400 correspondent banks worldwide allows us to expand on these capabilities, offering diversified products with local execution and state-of-the-art automated systems," Stearns said. "As a result, our high-tech clients receive expert solutions that are quickly implemented to keep them 'worlds ahead' of their competitors."

John Finegan, chief financial officer of Cornerstone Imaging, Inc., a software imaging company based in San Jose, gives high marks to the international support his firm receives from Comerica Bank-California. "Comerica has done a great job of supporting our international needs–both before and after they had established our line of credit," he says.

"They've been competitive at setting up letters of credit, and prompt and flexible in amending them as required."

Cornerstone Imaging, now a $100 million public company, became a Comerica customer when it was privately owned and one-tenth its present size. "We've grown with the

Comerica Bank-California colleagues celebrating their traditional Halloween Costume competition.

Agile Software Corporation, San Jose, California provides a product data system that enables your company to produce products faster, more economically, and with higher quality than ever before.

bank and they've met our growth needs very well," Finegan says. "It's the front-line people that make or break a banking relationship, and Comerica's staff are very attentive and proactive in meeting our needs."

As these dynamic companies become more established, the treasury function assumes critical importance for them. That's where Comerica Bank-California's cash management expertise comes to the fore, freeing cash to fund additional expansion by helping to speed up the inflow of cash into the firm's accounts and to slow down the outflow. Its investment management capabilities assist businesses achieve the top return on their investment funds, while maintaining risk at an acceptable level.

High-tech companies know better than most that their technology advantage is a function of the talent and commitment of their people. That's why they are especially concerned with providing for the security and well-being of their employees through such tools as 401(k), pension, and profit-sharing plans. With its extensive range of institutional trust services, Comerica can relieve a company of the administrative burden of managing these important employee benefit programs, freeing it to concentrate on its core business.

And when the company goes public, creating wealth for its shareholders, Comerica Bank-California's private banking services are there to even out the financial details for key executives, saving them time and frustration and making their personal banking and investment transactions easy and convenient. "We know how demanding and stressful the high-tech life can be," Stearns says. "That's why we created our private banking unit to help simplify and 'de-stress' personal finances."

"Bottom line," Stearns says, "we do whatever it takes to make it easier for high-tech companies to grow and succeed in their industries, and for their key executives to do the same." Unlike many other financial institutions, Comerica Bank-California can do what it takes–because it knows what it takes. "We really understand the high-tech banking business," adds Stearns.

Comerica Bank-California really understands relationship banking, too. As all business people know, finding the right bank can be a tricky proposition. The friendly small bank down the street usually can't help when something big happens–and big-bank customers get bogged down in impersonal bureaucracy, losing the benefits and flexibility of a close working relationship.

"We became a Comerica Bank-California customer because of their credentials and their high-technology focus." Agile Software's Stolle says. "We had been at a huge chain bank where we were a nobody–just an account number. But at Comerica, whenever we need them they're right there. We couldn't be more pleased. In fact, their level of service is better than I would ever have expected or hoped."

Even though Comerica Bank-California has all the technology and expertise of a $34 billion bank–including its own presence on the World Wide Web–it is staffed and managed by people who know the territory. Decisions are made locally...and fast.

"We're the local bank for the San Jose Sharks," Fulton says, "and frequently a key sponsor for local community events, like the Stanford/San Jose State University football game. In addition, serving as long term sponsors to community projects and program like City Year."

Comerica Bank-California's management team lives and works right here. They are active members of the Silicon Valley professional and social community. And they give back in the form of extensive charitable and public service through donations and volunteer efforts in support of vital community organizations in the arts, in public education, in athletics,–and in services to children, to people with disabilities, and other special needs like the frail elderly and the homeless.

With its awesome record of success, you'd think that Comerica Bank-California would take a breather–but no. Like the fast-track entrepreneurial company it keeps, Comerica Bank-California has its eyes on the heavens.

"We're headed to the moon," Fulton declares.

And if history is any guide, they'll get there. ✦

J. Michael Fulton, president and CEO and Mary Beth Suhr, vice president, High Technology Banking Division, and the co-sponsored Comerica-Hewlett-Packard City Year Team, the country's national community service version of the Peace Corps. Photo by E. Chris Wisner.

SAN JOSE METROPOLITAN CHAMBER OF COMMERCE

Since 1874, the San Jose Metropolitan Chamber of Commerce has championed the interests of business to assure that Silicon Valley's famed quality of life continues to flourish.

The Chamber's broad mission–to improve the success of the business community in general, and of its members in particular–has made it a leader in virtually all matters affecting Silicon Valley. "The Chamber of Commerce plays a vital role in the civic life of San Jose," says Mayor Susan Hammer. "It is one more reason why San Jose is a very special place to live and do business."

Issues of business and the economy, education, the environment, health care, regulations, taxes, technology, transportation, and more are all fuel for the Chamber's advocacy engine. And not just on its home track, either.

"The San Jose Chamber is an extraordinarily dynamic organization," affirms Kirk West, president of the California Chamber of Commerce. "It's an outstanding advocate at all government levels–local, regional, state, and national–consistently and effectively promoting the interests of employers and business." He characterizes the San Jose Metropolitan Chamber as one of the most active and forward-looking in all of California, a state known for its leadership in responding to challenges of commerce and community.

Advocating expansion of San Jose International Airport is one example of the Chamber's proactive role in efforts to build infrastructure to support business growth.

A not-for-profit membership organization fully funded by business community support, the San Jose Metropolitan Chamber represents a broad-based coalition of commerce and industry throughout Silicon Valley. Firms of all sizes, locations, and sectors belong–from Fortune 500 multinational corporations to home-based solo operations. Collectively, the Chamber's members employ nearly 200,000 people; yet 61 percent of its 2,500 business members have 10 or fewer employees.

Organizing and harnessing the power of business, the Chamber lobbies government to cut red tape and lower the costs of doing business. It fights for and helps maintain a business-friendly setting by advocating improvements in the physical infrastructure needed to accommodate economic growth–supporting major commute rail and road projects, for example, and promoting needed expansion of San Jose International Airport for air cargo and passengers alike.

Helping the Chamber achieve clout in its advocacy efforts is the Commerce Political Action Committee, known as COMPAC. As the Chamber's political endorsement and funding arm, COMPAC supports candidates and campaigns that promise to maintain the Silicon Valley's legendary economy and pro-business climate. COMPAC has carefully built credibility and impact over the years so that candidates eagerly seek the committee's endorsement in local elections.

On environmental issues, the Chamber has helped carry the banner of regional cooperation–co-founding, among other initiatives, a coalition of independent groups to identify causes and efficient, effective ways to reduce the flow of copper and nickel into San Francisco Bay.

"This is as effective a local trade association as I have ever seen," says John Kennett, past chairman of the Chamber board of directors and co-president of Pizazz Printing.

Part of the Chamber's reputation for stellar accomplishment comes from its ability to negotiate and "hammer out" solutions to complex problems by drawing from a variety of perspectives. "Some issues are black and white, but most things need compromise," says Steve Tedesco, the Chamber's president and chief executive officer. "To make the best decisions you can make from the options available to you is my definition of progress–it's constant motion."

Constant motion describes the Chamber's continually expanding array of member services, too. From the Chamber's annual trade show and monthly "business-after-hours" membership mixers, to its regular luncheons featuring top-ranked business speakers…from its extensive network for business referrals to its wealth of workshops, seminars, publications, and one-on-one consulting help…from its thriving system for international trade connections and resources to its special offerings of group health care coverage and credit union benefits–the San Jose Metropolitan Chamber marshals the talents of its diverse membership and skilled staff to make great things happen.

"This is an exceptional organization," says Armon Mills, 1996 chairman of the Chamber's board of directors and publisher of *The Business Journal.* "You make a simple suggestion about addressing a member need–and a short time later, it just happens. I'm constantly amazed at the outstanding quality of the Chamber's services and products."

The Chamber's role as a resource center for business information is a good example. A series of business directories covering the entire Bay Area are available to assist businesses in expanding their customer bases. Start up kits offer a well-organized "one-stop" bundle of information and forms to help the prospective business owner get off on the right foot. Economic and demographic data enable firms to define their local marketplace. Community information helps newcomers learn more about their new home.

In the 1980s, America's free-spending decade, the Chamber fought excessive business taxes and business-damaging government controls. In the 1990s, America's decade of cutbacks, consolidations, and collaborations, the Chamber is forging partnerships between business and government aimed at developing efficient solutions to crucial business and community needs.

And now, as it prepares for the new millennium, the Chamber is intent on the next generation of entrepreneurs and employees. To help

The Chamber's education efforts have one goal—to forge links between business leaders and educators to strengthen the area's public schools.

ensure that the valley's youth have access to the best K-12 education possible, the Chamber has established a business-supported Education Foundation, which funds innovative educational initiatives. The Chamber has also fostered partnerships between business and education through such creative programs as "Principal For a Day" and "Adopt a School." It helps sponsor Future Connections, a creative program that arms teams of teachers with firsthand knowledge of industry trends and leading-edge technology advances to take back to the classroom. And it lobbies for legislation to improve the quality of education throughout the state.

Once these students find jobs with area firms, the Chamber's role continues. A program called Fast Forward 2000 offers businesses a series of management training opportunities for up and coming employees. Geared to the next generation of business leadership, the program lets employers reach down and bring targeted staff members to the Chamber to help develop their potential.

The Chamber is developing leaders for the broader community as well. Community Leadership San Jose takes some 30 selected individuals each year and runs them through a comprehensive curriculum designed to offer insight into the workings of the Silicon Valley community as well as into their own leadership potential. Most of the candidates are sponsored by their business, nonprofit or government employers who see the value of developing skilled leaders to help the entire community prosper in the 21st century.

In the Silicon Valley, technology is vital—not only to the birth of the Valley, but also to its continued existence. And the Chamber is active in that arena, as well. Take Joint Venture Silicon Valley, for example. It was such a successful Chamber initiative that it is now a separate organization,

representing the region from San Mateo to Santa Clara counties and providing information and support to the region's high-tech industries and endeavors.

Set in the heart of the world's center of technology, entrepreneurship, and innovation, the San Jose Metropolitan Chamber of Commerce helps determine and decide issues of the present, while preparing to define and decipher issues of the future.

"We've survived from the 19th century through the 20th, achieving a solid record of success," says Tedesco. "And now as the 21st century approaches, we're gearing up to guarantee that we continue to deliver on our promise to maintain the Silicon's Valley's legendary economy while providing services and programs to insure the success of our individual members." ✦

The annual summer barbecue for COMPAC—the Chamber's influential political action committee—raises funds to back business-oriented candidates and participate in campaigns on issues affecting the Silicon Valley business climate.

INSTITUTIONAL VENTURE PARTNERS

Following a simple formula–"Make your first investment the most successful"–Reid Dennis sank his $15,000 savings into Ampex Corp. in the early 1950s, and watched his investment swell to $1 million in a few years, when the company introduced the first commercial VCR. He's been investing ever since.

Through the knowledge he gained from his Stanford University degrees in engineering and business, Dennis was able to recognize early-on the significance of the technology movement developing in Silicon Valley. He applied that insight and became one of the first to play a key role in providing seed money for young technology companies in the 1950s and 1960s, as a personal risk-taking adjunct to his 21-year career in investment management within the insurance and mutual fund industries.

He left American Express in 1973 to form Institutional Venture Associates with two other partners, and in 1980 formed Institutional Venture Partners as the sole general partner. The firm prospered and Dennis continued to play a key role in the venture capital community–not just in Silicon Valley, but on a national level. In 1974, for example, IVA raised a $19 million venture capital fund–nearly half the total venture capital raised in the entire country that year ($45 million).

IVP's Information Technology Group are pictured **(left to right)** *T. Peter Thomas, Geoffrey Y. Yang, and Ruthann A. Quindlen.*

Today, IVP has eight general partners and nearly $750 million under management. One of the largest venture capital firms in Silicon Valley, it has invested in more than 150 companies, of which more than 80 have gone public. These firms have combined annual sales in excess of $25 billion, a total market value of more than $60 billion–and they have created jobs, in the aggregate, for more than 125,000 people.

IVP is an active, lead investor in early-stage ventures that have major market potential. Although the firm will consider investments in any field, the partners prefer to invest in the semi-conductor, software, communications, and life science industries.

Traditional Wall-Street-types invest in companies with a record for strong performance, but the companies IVP invests in have little or no track record at all. Instead of investing based on the past, IVP bases its investments on the future. In essence, IVP bets on ideas, on people, on potential, and on markets–and it forms close, long-term relationships with their portfolio companies.

Recognized for its proven integrity, its depth of expertise, and its positive, partnering attitude, IVP has a well-earned reputation among entrepreneurs as one of the most supportive venture firms in the business–a savvy, committed investor who cares as much, and works almost as hard for the start-up's success as the founders do themselves.

It's easy to see that patience, tenacity, and confidence are important watchwords at IVP: The firm is known for continuing to work with conscientious management teams far beyond the industry norm.

"IVP has provided the kind of assistance and guidance that we needed–not only in the beginning, but also now that we're a public company with a billion dollars in market capitalization," says Dave Stamm, president and CEO of Clarify, Inc. "We're continuing to work to grow very

rapidly, so IVP's participation on our board and their guidance for our strategic decisions continues to be critical."

The IVP team has a depth of knowledge and a breadth of resources that allow it to contribute in crucial ways to its portfolio companies. With about 100 years of combined venture capital and business management experience, IVP's partners have been involved in virtually every activity needed to grow a successful company.

Who you know counts as much–maybe more–in Silicon Valley as anyplace else. And the number and type of networking contacts IVP brings to their portfolio companies it invests in are enormous.

Through close relationships with key managers in their portfolio companies, consultants, industry experts, other entrepreneurs, and key industry figures–not to mention their long-standing ties to a host of lawyers, accountants, search firms, and investment bankers–IVP can assist with recruiting, marketing strategy, corporate partnership, customer introductions, organizational development, strategic planning, and the coordination of future financing.

The Life Sciences Group of IVP are pictured (left to right) *L. James Strand, John K. Tillotson, and Samuel D. Colella.*

Take Geoffrey Yang as an example. An IVP general partner, he sits on the board of directors of MMC Networks, one of IVP's portfolio companies. According to P.K. Dubey, MMC's president and CEO, Yang is known in high-tech circles as "Mr. Networking"–a smart guy who invested in famous companies of today back when they were still in the 'garage stage.'

Dubey says that IVP has contributed immensely to MMC's success, helping the company determine the right strategy, helping attract potential employees who are "superstars," and lining up connections to key customers and markets.

"I find the participation and support of Geoff Yang and the IVP folks to be very positive and motivational–above and beyond the call of a normal board member," Dubey said. "It's a real pleasure to work with them."

Every member of the IVP team takes great pride in the role that venture capitalists have played in the phenomenal success of Silicon Valley.

"Venture capital has made an enormous contribution to what has gone on here, raising the money that allows companies to grow and hire thousands of people," Dennis said. "Venture capital is both a fuel and a lubricant, for without sufficient capital, it is difficult (if not impossible) for the enterprise to continue to operate efficiently."

IVP gets very personal with the people and companies it invests in. "We feel the entrepreneurs are working on something great," Yang says. At IVP there's a real sense of excitement in the magic of technology, in the romance of helping to create the future.

"Things are changing so quickly. Technology is becoming such an important part of the world economy. And Silicon Valley's role is becoming increasingly essential," Dennis says. "It's a great place to be–part of the seedlings, in the fastest growing segments, of the fastest growing industries in the world. Our nation's economy has evolved from agrarian, to industrial, to financial. Now we're becoming an information-based society. Silicon Valley is at the very heart of that transformation."

And IVP is at the very heart of Silicon Valley. ◆

IVP is an active, lead investor in early-stage ventures that have major market potential. Pictured are (left to right) *Norman A. Fogelsong, Mary Jane Elmore, and Reid W. Dennis of the Late Stage & Public Market Group.*

SAN JOSE CONVENTION & VISITORS BUREAU

"Do you know the way to San Jose?" asks the popular song of the 1960s. The answer is "If you don't, you don't know what you're missing," says Marian Holt-McLain, who has headed the San Jose Convention & Visitors Bureau (SJCVB) as president and CEO for nearly eight years.

"San Jose is the 11th largest city in the country, and the 'Capital of Silicon Valley.' It offers visitors big-city adventures and attractions, yet is safe, friendly, easy to get around, and an excellent value," she said. "As a destination city, we're becoming a force to be reckoned with on the national scene."

Since 1989 when the San Jose McEnery Convention Center opened, SJCVB-driven meetings, convention and trade show bookings, and resulting economic value to the community have steadily—sometimes dramatically—increased. In fiscal year 1995-96, for every $1 invested by the city, SJCVB returned $61.70 in current and future economic impact. For example, in the summer of 1996 when the National Junior Olympics

Events at the San Jose Arena–like games of the San Jose Sharks and the Golden State Warriors, plus concerts and other attractions–add to San Jose's image as a "city on the rise." "Our combined marketing efforts with our hotel and Convention Center partners to position San Jose as a convention, trade show, and business destination have made us a hot market for business and leisure travelers," Holt-McLain said.

Spurred by the increasing number of excellent visual and performing arts activities in San Jose, plus an eclectic array of events and festivals–sports, ethnic, cultural–the SJCVB has developed an innovative new program called "Destination: San Jose."

A joint venture between the city and local visitor-related businesses and organizations, Destination: San Jose is an integrated city-wide marketing and image development campaign. Its goal is to increase the number of San Jose visitors, ticket sales, weekend hotel occupancies, and more.

Interact San Jose (ISJ)–a sophisticated, city-wide and unique web presence in destination marketing–plays a big role in the Destination: San Jose campaign. It's the most interactive, comprehensive Web site covering things to do and see in San Jose. In addition to providing visitors general information about the city, ISJ includes links to the home pages of other San Jose area businesses, custom information searches, on-line reservations, and ticketing services.

"We're excited, not only about our achievements, but also about San Jose's phenomenal future," Holt-McLain says. "And that includes the expansion of the Convention Center; the opening of additional hotels; the move to expanded, new facilities for the Tech Museum of Innovation and the San Jose Repertory Theatre; the completion of the Guadalupe River Park; and perhaps, even the Sharks bringing home a Stanley Cup!"

With more than 550 members and extensive public-private collaboration, it's clear that the SJCVB enjoys widespread community and business support. Holt-McLain credits many people with forging these partnerships and helping to put the shine on San Jose's prospects. "Every day these dedicated, enthusiastic folks market San Jose's 'small-town heart and big-city soul,'" she said. "In the process, they contribute a little heart and soul of their own." ✦

The San Jose McEnery Convention Center. Photo by Sonya Bradley.

Volleyball Championships were held in San Jose, city businesses benefited to the tune of $8.8 million in direct spending. During fiscal 1996, convention business brought in direct spending of $83.2 million, up from $70.3 million the previous year. And San Jose's fast-growing tourism economy generated 11,100 full-time equivalent jobs.

LEASING SOLUTIONS, INC.

*L*easing Solutions, Inc. (LSI) has created a high-tech niche for itself in an industry populated with large national capital equipment leasing companies. There are many players in this industry, but only one is dedicated to being a full-service vendor leasing company that specializes in leasing information processing and communications equipment.

Its success is evident. A regular on the annual *Inc.* "100: America's Fastest Growing Small Public Companies in America" list, LSI has also been named the fastest growing independent leasing company in the U.S.

"How do you become one of the fastest growing computer equipment leasing companies in America when you're competing against all the big guns?" asks Hal Krauter, LSI president, CEO, and co-founder. "You do it," he says, "providing competitive pricing and by treating your customers with individual attention and a personal interest in their success, and by being timely, creative and flexible in meeting their needs."

LSI focuses on leasing local and Wide Area Networks, computers and other high-tech equipment to Fortune 1000-level companies, who benefit from the lower operating costs associated with leasing the equipment. Corporations have a variety of choice with LSI,–from database machines to character-based "dumb" terminals to "intelligent" personal computer terminals, and more.

A full-service lessor known for the exceptional quality it provides, LSI also inspects, repairs, and remarkets the equipment, leasing to firms who want the economic benefits of leasing used high-tech equipment. LSI also manages all administrative functions for its corporate clients–from the initial signing to lease expiration.

At the heart of LSI's quality service are its vendor programs. By forging strategic alliances with leading equipment vendors such as Dell Computer, Apple Computer, Cisco Systems, NCR and Sybase, LSI is able to offer very competitive rates on each lease agreement.

Leasing capital equipment is big business. According to Timothy Laehy, LSI's vice president of corporate finance, 32 percent of all productive assets in the country are leased each year. "It's a $130-billion-a year industry," he says, "and growing."

Founded in downtown San Jose in 1986, LSI began with a small staff, considerable experience in computer manufacturing and leasing, and high expectations. The founders wanted to provide corporate customers the best of both worlds: all the options (and more) typically offered by large leasing companies,–yet with the flexible, personalized service; exceptional quality of performance; and lack of red tape that small firms are noted for.

It's a formula that has served the company and its customers well, one that's reflected in LSI's history of long-term relationships with its customers. In fact, 90 percent of LSI's lessees are repeat customers.

Capitalizing on its impressive record of performance and profitability, LSI went public in 1993, and has expanded its field operations in the U.S. to include offices in Atlanta, Boston, Chicago, Dallas, Los Angeles, New York City, and San Jose metropolitan areas.

In 1996, LSI gained a toehold in the European market by acquiring a UK based leasing company along with its two UK operations. The acquisition was consolidated into a single entity, Leasing Solutions (UK), Ltd.,–under LSI's European holding company, Leasing Solutions International, Ltd. The Compaany also has offices in Germany, France, Belgium, and The Netherlands.

"LSI's exceptional growth rate continues because our corporate philosophy works," Krauter says. "Business is about customers, and at LSI, no one ever forgets that." ✦

Leasing Solutions, Inc., with corporate offices in downtown San Jose (the high-rise on the right), has been named the fastest growing independent full-service vendor leasing company in the U.S., specializing in leasing information processing and communications equipment. **Photo by Pat Kirk.**

SUTTER HILL VENTURES

People all over the world recognize that northern California's Silicon Valley isn't defined so much by its geographic boundaries, as by its driving entrepreneurial spirit and commitment to investing in the future.

Nowhere is that spirit and commitment more valued than at Sutter Hill Ventures, the oldest venture capital firm in Silicon Valley and fourth oldest in the country. A leader in financing technology-based companies since 1962, Sutter Hill is, in fact, one of the architects of Silicon Valley.

"There isn't a company today whose business hasn't been touched by the industries Sutter Hill funds," says Paul Wythes, one of the firm's general partners.

Sutter Hill invests primarily in high technology startups that pioneer products or services for worldwide growth markets. The list of companies whose growth this venerable firm has helped create over the past four decades reads like a "Who's Who" of high-tech success stories:

- Measurex Corp., one of the companies Sutter Hill started in the 1960s, develops, manufactures, and sells process control instrumentation, equipment, and software, primarily for the paper industry. A multimillion-dollar corporation today, its stock trades on the New York Stock Exchange.
- Dionex Corp., started by Sutter Hill in the 1970s and now publicly traded on the NASDAQ exchange, is the worldwide leader in isolating and identifying the components of chemical mixtures. The technology this multimillion-dollar company invented is used in environmental analysis, biotechnology, power plants, semiconductor manufacturing, and food processing throughout the world.
- Linear Technology Corp., one of the companies funded by Sutter Hill in the 1980s is another multimillion-dollar, NASDAQ-traded corporation which designs, manufactures, and markets a broad line of high-performance integrated circuits used in telecommunications, notebook and desktop computers, industrial, automotive, process control, and factory automation the world over.

Linear Technology's Corporate Campus.

- Forte Software, Inc., which Sutter Hill started in the 1990s, is one of the fastest growing companies in the San Francisco Bay Area. Forte designs, develops, markets, and supports software application development tools for high-end client/server applications. With stock traded on the NASDAQ exchange, its customers

include such global giants as AT&T, Bank of America, Hewlett Packard, Digital Equipment, Merrill Lynch, Philip Morris, EDS, and many others.

Since Sutter Hill's founding, it has invested in over 300 businesses, many of which have gone public, creating jobs in the hundreds of thousands, and market values totaling well into the multibillions of dollars.

Sutter Hill is one of the larger funds in the United States, but its investments mean more than just money. With operating and investment backgrounds that help the partners understand the challenges early-stage companies face, Sutter Hill's five general partners (David L. Anderson,

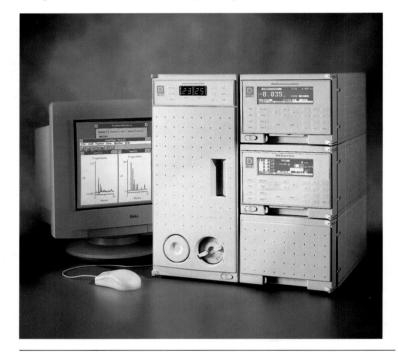

Dionex Chromatography System.

G. Leonard Baker, Jr., William H. Younger, Jr., Tench Coxe, and Paul M. Wythes) collaborate with the management of firms they invest in, helping to solve the financial, recruiting, and strategy problems that crop up daily in the life of young growth companies. In essence, the firm becomes a true partner with the managements of its portfolio companies by providing strong networking contacts with lawyers, CPAs, investment bankers, portfolio entrepreneurs, industry consultants, search firms and so on.

"Making money is important, but it's not everything," Wythes says. We're trying to build companies that are going to stand firm in a strong wind, like a tall oak tree—and that takes, on average, six to seven years." "Too many people in our business think 'you've got to accomplish it all in three years,'" he says. As a result, they sometimes make poor decisions and create companies that lack staying power. Collaboration is another key value at Sutter Hill—inside the organization as well as with the managements of its portfolio companies. "We tend to be collegial in our investment decision-making. We can move fast when we need to, but our decisions are made thoughtfully, with a lot of due diligence," Wythes comments. "At Sutter Hill, when you work with one partner, you really get the whole firm's expertise."

The ties Sutter Hill forms with the companies it helps incubate give it an enormous sense of contribution and pride. "We help fuel an engine that creates jobs, products, services, taxes, and wealth that benefit the entire world," says Wythes. "That puts us on the cutting edge of the future—a truly exciting place to be." ✦

Chapter Seventeen

Education & Quality of Life

◆

UNIVERSITY OF CALIFORNIA, SANTA CRUZ, AND UCSC EXTENSION

On the list of Silicon Valley's most vibrant industries and organizations, many may be surprised to find the University of California, Santa Cruz. They shouldn't be. One of the nine University of California campuses, UC Santa Cruz–in conjunction with UCSC Extension–is playing a key role in the education and training of the people who launch and make successful the numerous companies that form the backbone of the Silicon Valley economy.

Described by its Chancellor, M.R.C. Greenwood, as a "jewel in the finest research and teaching university system in the world," UC Santa Cruz exemplifies the decades-old symbiosis between California and the UC system. The state provides core support for the University's triple missions of teaching, research, and public service. In return, the University attracts billions of dollars in non-state funding and reinvests this money in California, primarily through research. This, in turn, helps generate new technologies, new products, and thousands and thousands of new jobs.

"Today, millions of people eat food produced with the help of UC researchers, travel on safer highways, drink California wines, explore the Internet, and depend on medical technologies–all developed by UC scientists," Chancellor Greenwood says. "And thousands of Californians work at jobs that were created as a result of UC innovation."

As a group, the University of California faculty is internationally acclaimed as the most talented and creative in the world, and faculty at UC Santa Cruz are among the most honored within the UC system.

Scholars who have been attracted to the campus of more than 10,000 students include 12 members of the National Academy of Sciences, 17 members of the American Academy of Arts and Sciences, and 1 member each of the National Academy of Sciences' Institute of Medicine and the National Academy of Engineering.

UCSC faculty are known for more than their cutting-edge research. In a survey conducted by *U.S. News and World Report* (1995), UCSC was ranked 13th among all U.S. universities for its commitment to undergraduate teaching. Undergraduates at UCSC are members–not outsiders–of the research community. "Papers are written by our faculty that cite the important contributions of undergraduates," Chancellor Greenwood says. "You see undergraduate involvement in research at a much higher level at UCSC."

UCSC is also an acknowledged leader in postgraduate education. The most recent survey by the National Research Council ranked two of UCSC's doctoral programs–astronomy and astrophysics, and linguistics–in the top 10 programs nationwide.

In fact, the campus is considered one of the emerging stars among this country's postwar research universities. In a comprehensive new analysis of more than 200 top universities, UC Santa Cruz ranks 15th in the nation in the quality of its research productivity. The study and rankings are detailed in a recent book that chronicles the rise of a new generation of research universities in the United States.

Undergraduate student Zoe Wood (left) and assistant professor Alex Pang of UC Santa Cruz examine meteorologic and oceanographic data from central California, using special computer graphics tools developed at UCSC. The screen displays ocean current data from Monterey Bay (central purple patch and inset at lower left), as well as a temperature profile recorded by a weather balloon over the San Francisco Peninsula. New graphics techniques are a key component of an ongoing $4.7 million computer engineering project at UCSC to create a "real-time" environmental monitoring network for the Monterey Bay region. Photo by R.R. Jones.

UCSC Extension's prominence in high-technology training has evolved to a great extent from relationships developed with Silicon Valley's businesses. Photo by Paul Bousquet.

under consideration for the engineering school are biotechnology engineering, environmental instrumentation, manufacturing engineering, applied mechanics, engineering management, and mechanical engineering.

Providing opportunities for life-long learning in these and other disciplines, University Extension is the foremost university-level program in the nation in size, scope, and quality of instruction, and serves about 500,000 students throughout California each year. America's largest provider of continuing education, it is also the largest provider of professional education in Silicon Valley and on California's Central Coast. With eight campuses around the state, University Extension programs have grown steadily and impressively over the decades.

The analysis and ranking are contained in the book *The Rise of American Research Universities: Elites and Challengers in the Postwar Era* (Johns Hopkins University Press, 1996). The authors, historians Hugh Davis Graham of Vanderbilt University and Nancy Diamond of the University of Maryland, assessed the postwar performance of 203 research universities. They measured per capita faculty research productivity—the creation of new knowledge—in everything from medical science to the classics.

It is this creation of new knowledge that makes the UC system as a whole such a driving force behind the economy of the entire state. Literally hundreds of California companies are UC spinoffs in that they were founded by UC scientists or graduates, established based on UC technology, or spun off from a UC-connected business.

The experience of UCSC alumnus and Silicon Valley entrepreneur Brent Constantz illustrates the linkage. In 1985, Constantz was in the South Pacific near Tahiti, working toward his Ph.D. on how corals make their skeletons. Today, he heads Norian Corporation, a Silicon Valley enterprise making headlines for a new product: a paste that dramatically speeds the healing of broken bones.

The already-initiated development of a School of Engineering at UCSC will only expand the campus' significant presence in the Silicon Valley—included in UCSC's "service area."

"We are the UC campus closest to the Silicon Valley, and we have a special opportunity to serve the Silicon Valley population," observes Professor Patrick Mantey, UCSC's associate dean for Engineering. "We have shown with our computer science and computer engineering programs that we can respond to the needs of the region."

Already, the campus has created new departments in electrical engineering and applied and engineering mathematics. Other programs

But in recent years, the growth at UCSC Extension in particular has been explosive—more like the pattern of a fast-track, high-tech corporate break-out than that of a mature educational agency. "Our outlook, experience, and culture very much mirror the dynamic community we serve," says Janice Corriden, dean of UCSC Extension. "We operate very much like a business, but with a strong public service and public education mission."

Organized as a self-supporting not-for-profit organization, UCSC Extension's enrollments have more than doubled, from 20,000 to nearly than 50,000, in just five years—and they continue to soar. Its classes have more than doubled, too (from 320 to 760 per quarter), as have its full-time equivalent staff (from 41 to 87) and its revenue (from $4.7 million to more than $17 million). With its course catalog on the Internet and its own site on the World Wide Web, UCSC Extension takes enrollments online in greater numbers every quarter.

"UCSC Extension is a major presence here in Silicon Valley," says Steven Tedesco, CEO of the San Jose Metropolitan Chamber of Commerce.

Professionals across all fields attend UCSC Extension courses to stay current and to self-manage their careers. Photo by Paul Bousquet.

Hands-on training using the most current hardware and software is requisite for Silicon Valley professionals. **Photo by Paul Bousquet.**

"Probably more than any other place in the world, we need convenient access to world-class, frequent, continuing education. And in the fast-paced, high-tech Silicon Valley economy, the presence and magnitude of a preeminent institution of higher learning like the University of California has been an essential ingredient in keeping our workforce literally on the cutting edge of global knowledge."

With four of its six sites in Santa Clara County—Cupertino, Milpitas, Santa Clara, and Sunnyvale—800 adjunct instructors, and 10 academic departments, the flexible and fast-moving UCSC Extension is eminently equipped to meet the learning needs of its nearly 50,000 students, drawn from the four-county area it serves—Santa Clara, San Benito, Santa Cruz, and Monterey. Sixty-four percent of the 2.25 million people in its service area live in Santa Clara County.

Just who are the UCSC Extension students? They come from industry and from the community at large. Eighty percent have one college degree, and half have earned two degrees or more. Approximately two-thirds are between 30 and 50 years old, with household incomes exceeding $50,000 a year. And 60 percent have their tuitions reimbursed by employers.

UCSC Extension began offering courses with the opening of the UC Santa Cruz campus in 1965, joining the well-established program of life-long learning that started with the very first UC Extension in 1891.

Through Extension, UC's scholars, research facilities, and resources link with California's people, businesses, and communities, meeting a wide range of educational, economic, and social needs. Its abundant top-quality course offerings help keep professionals and businesses updated on emerging business practices and technologies.

Among UCSC Extension's disciplines of instruction are: art and design, behavioral sciences, business and management, computer engineering, computer science, English language/multicultural, environmental sciences and management, health and healing, humanities, legal and public policy, spoken international languages, and teacher education.

Focused on keeping professionals abreast of the most current practices in their fields, UCSC Extension's Certificate Programs cover a broad, diverse range of fields. Everything from advanced environmental management and marketing to UNIX programming and VLSI design engineering, from business administration and human resource management, to video arts and human services counseling, from graphic production to interior design, from multimedia production to interior design, multimedia engineering, and network management, to object-oriented programming and software engineering and many, many more areas of concentration is represented in the UCSC certificate training curricula.

As a result of the talent and expertise of the instructors—all working professionals in the subject areas they teach—UC Extension programs help Californians run their businesses better, enhance the skills of workers at all levels, and sharpen student interest and attention through the sheer pleasure of learning.

From its inception, University Extension has responded to the changing needs of California, from helping men and women develop careers in the face of the Great Depression in the 1930s, to helping contemporary students adapt to the demands of the Age of Information in our ever-changing, multi-cultural, increasingly global society.

A common theme running through UCSC Extension is partnership—the willingness to cooperate and work with outside groups to understand and help solve major community issues and needs. A few examples: Extension works with Private Industry Councils (PICs) to retrain displaced professional workers under the federal Job Training and Partnership Act in such programs as "Mini and Microcomputer Local Area Network Support and Programming" and "Hazardous Materials Management."

UCSC Extension's Corporate Training department works directly with individual companies to create custom programs which can be delivered on site or in a nearby classroom facility. **Photo by Paul Bousquet.**

Northern California Business Environmental Assistance Center (BEAC) at UCSC Extension in Santa Clara helps small businesses comply with environmental regulations by providing information, services, and resources, including financial assistance. BEAC is the initiative of a consortium of organizations, including Extension units at several other UC, California State University, and college campuses, as well as the California Trade and Commerce Agency and the California Air Resources Board.

On the campus and through its Extension program, UC Santa Cruz has played a leading role in the reuse efforts at nearby Fort Ord. Under UCSC's supervision, UC is developing its Monterey Bay Education, Science, and Technology (MBEST) Center—a next-generation technology park at the former military base. Only 70 miles from the heart of Silicon Valley, adjacent to nearly 600 acres of natural habitat, and strategically located between the nation's largest marine sanctuary and the exceptionally rich agricultural land of the Salinas Valley, the MBEST Center is a perfect home for corporate and public organizations with research components. It offers

Geared for today's workforce, courses are taught by experienced industry professionals to provide skills that can be used immediately on the job. Photo by Paul Bousquet.

location, size, access, visibility, and University affiliation—undergirded by a foundation of advanced infrastructure and supporting research and training services specially designed to meet the needs of the industries that will shape the future of the Monterey Bay Region.

Another important component of UCSC Extension's partnering approach is its popular corporate training program. "We take our publicly offered programs into the workplace and schedule them at company sites for the convenience of working professionals," says Extension Dean Corriden. "We also tailor programs to meet the needs of specific companies, offering practical, hands-on training that employees can apply the next day at work."

Dr. Albert Lowe, manager of SunU-Workgroup Solutions at Sun Microsystems, is a real fan of UCSC Extension. "They provide us with academic credibility for training and educational programs in the generic areas of education so we don't have to 'reinvent the wheel,'" he says. "The quality of their instructors and training content is rock-solid. They give us a responsive, quality, broad-based technical and higher educational resource that augments Sun's own educational development programs."

Like the Silicon Valley entrepreneurs, employees, and residents it serves, UC Santa Cruz is characterized by its optimism, its youthful spirit, and its focus on the future. There's a passion that infuses this young, vital UC campus, born of the idea that education changes the world and makes it better. Its commitment to the communities it serves is to give UC quality with a difference that makes a difference—a precious gift, indeed. ◆

Providing opportunities for lifelong learning, University Extension is the foremost university-level program in the nation in size, scope, and quality of instruction, and serves about 500,000 students each year.

THE ROMAN CATHOLIC DIOCESE OF SAN JOSE

"San Jose is California's oldest city and newest metropolis. St. Joseph of San Jose is California's oldest parish and newest cathedral," wrote The Most Reverend Pierre DuMaine, Bishop of The Roman Catholic Diocese of San Jose, in his foreword to the 1990 book *San Jose and Its Cathedral*, by Marjorie Pierce.

"The origin of Catholic life in this valley is Mission Santa Clara de Asis, established in 1777," Bishop DuMaine says. "St. Joseph Cathedral was established in 1803 as a mission of Mission Santa Clara."

St. Joseph was formally made a parish by the first Archbishop of San Francisco in 1849 and thus became the "mother parish" from which were formed the 54 parishes, missions, pastoral centers, and campus ministries now serving Santa Clara County. In 1981, Pope John Paul II separated Santa Clara County from the Archdiocese of San Francisco thus creating the Diocese of San Jose.

Today, the diocese covers an area of 1,300 square miles and has an estimated 400,000 Catholics out of the county's total population of about 1.6 million.

St. Joseph Cathedral has always been the focus, not only of the diocese, but of the entire community. "San Jose grew up around that site," Bishop DuMaine said.

Lovingly restored and reconstructed from 1986 to 1990 at a cost of about $17 million, the historic St. Joseph Cathedral today–in its inspirational beauty, its resplendently renewed paintings and murals, statuary and altars, and its gleaming copper-sheathed domes–is well worth its cost. According to Pulitzer Prize-winning architecture critic with the *San Francisco Chronicle*, Allan Temko, it is "something close to a miracle in downtown San Jose."

In 1996, St. Joseph Cathedral was designated by the Holy See as a Minor Basilica, a title awarded by the Vatican to churches for their special historic and artistic merit.

Accessing the Internet is a daily activity in schools in the San Jose Diocese.

St. Joseph is not only a center, but a vital source of community services through the Office of Social Ministry. There is St. Joseph the Worker House, a transitional housing program; Shelter Plus Care, a collaborative venture with other organizations providing case management services; the free Walk-in Medical Clinic; Morning Ministry, which provides Saturday breakfasts to people without homes or living in shelters; Family Self-Sufficiency to enable families to become free of government assistance; and the JobSearch Program, which has achieved an 80-percent success rate in its job placements.

These programs, staffed mostly by volunteers, help upwards of 20,000 people each year get food and shelter–both temporary and permanent–clothing, transportation, training and education, counseling, medical services, and jobs. Provided free to the participants, these services not only help with basics of survival, they also help people reclaim their dignity, their self-respect, their spirit, and their lives.

As Marjorie Pierce said of St. Joseph Cathedral in her book, "It is the heart and soul of the city, its stately presence a focus of faith and a monument to the city's past, present, and future."

Outreach to people in need, regardless of religion, marks not only the cathedral parish and other Catholic parishes of the Diocese, but is also the goal of Catholic Charities of Santa Clara County, the largest non-governmental provider of such services in the area. Its $10 million annual budget provides extensive professional programs for families and children, for the elderly, for refugees and immigrants and for affordable housing, among other activities. "Our role is to help people help themselves," says Dee Wischmann, chief executive officer of this United Way agency.

CTN provides individualized Internet and W.W.W. training sessions for Catholic school teachers and administrators.

"We see thousands of success stories every year," Wischmann notes, "people who are now holding full-time jobs, living in their own homes, raising their families, paying taxes. With the help of Catholic Charities they have been able to become productive members of society."

Developing productive, well-rounded members of society is an important part of the mission of the Diocesan Department of Education, headed by Sister Mary Claude Power, PBVM, Superintendent of Schools. "We have an educational mission," she says, "but we're really trying to form the whole person. We'd like the graduates of our educational system to be well-rounded spiritually, socially, and academically."

The Catholic school system in the Diocese of San Jose is one of the largest in Santa Clara County. The 6 secondary and 28 elementary schools enroll more than 16,000 students.

Catholic schools are renowned for the quality of their academic instruction. Ninety-nine percent of their students go on to college. "We have high academic expectations of all our students with a strong focus on higher-order thinking and problem-solving skills," Sister Mary Claude says. "And we give children the structure, discipline, guidance, and direction they need. Virtually every one of our schools has a waiting list."

Faculties are exceptionally qualified. Every teacher has a bachelor's degree and nearly every one has a teaching credential. A significant number have master's degrees. "Every one of our schools is accredited by the Western Association of Schools and Colleges," Sister Mary Claude noted.

That Catholic schools work with disadvantaged populations in their educational system is not nearly so well known. "We have a substantial number of students from low-income and minority families in our system," she says.

Although school tuition is paid by parents, the Diocese and individual parishes offer scholarship assistance to both elementary and secondary school families. And every elementary school in the system provides extended care services, accommodating families from 6:30 A.M. until 6:30-7:30 P.M. on school days.

St. Joseph Cathedral has always been the focus, not only of the diocese, but of the entire community. In 1996, it was designated by the Holy See as a Minor Basilica, a title awarded by the Vatican to churches on the basis of their special historic or artistic distinction or merit.

San Jose students participate in an interactive electronic field trip linking England, New Mexico, and California.

In trying to prepare children for the 21st century in Silicon Valley, the Diocesan Department of Education has a strong focus on technology. "Our system is on the cutting edge," Sister Mary Claude says. "All of our schools are electronically linked; most are networked; each has a home page on the Internet. We're not only teaching our students about technology, we're teaching them how to use it by incorporating technology into our entire curriculum."

Faith and values and the religious character of its schools are naturally paramount for the Church. "We're here to teach the gospel message and to inspire our students to service," Sister Mary Claude noted. "Our goal is to inspire our students to respond to the world they're going to have to live in based on a tradition of faith and moral values; and, we do this in an environment committed to academic excellence."

Mathematics instruction is provided via computer, for example, the same is true of the language arts. "We have a strong focus on higher-order thinking and problem-solving skills," she says. "And we do a lot with a global approach to learning—instruction in multi-culturalism, critical thinking, and cultural pluralism."

Catholic Telemedia Network (CTN) transmits educational and religious programming over four television channels from its main station in Menlo Park to more than 150 locations in the greater Bay Area. Through digital technology, CTN's capacity is expanding to eight or more channels, "to allow us to handle anything that can be done electronically," says Bishop DuMaine.

In operation since 1970, CTN serves schools, parishes, hospitals, retirement centers, and other groups. From its start in instructional education

nearly 30 years ago, CTN's services have expanded to encompass television programs for education and professional training from a library of more than 4,000 videotapes; satellite downlink services, and videoconference facilities—a means of "holding meetings over the air;" a full production studio where one can create their own programs under professional direction; technical and in-service support for using video and distance learning in the classroom, as well as interconnecting computer, video, and telecommunications technologies.

For parishes and diocesan agencies, religious communities, and retreat centers, there are programs that vary from adult and staff education in sacraments, scripture, family life, and liturgy, to seasonal specials for Christmas and Easter. CTN also offers programs designed for groups with special interests such as senior groups, people with disabilities, health care agencies, and students from various language and ethnic groups.

"With today's emphasis on lifelong learning, our programs and services go beyond helping classroom students benefit from computerized learning and access to the Internet," says Shirley Connolly, CTN's general manager. "They also assist adults who can benefit from updated learning, teachers who need continuing in-service training, and administrators who need to keep up with current practices."

CTN is building Local Area Networks (LANs) in the schools, that will allow students to electronically access the school library, public libraries, classrooms across town, fellow students around the Bay Area and, via the Internet, around the world. Connolly says, "We are trying to make our system as user-friendly as possible in order to help educate our communities and to help teachers communicate and share electronically."

CTN is also exploring collaborations with Corporate America to generate even more educational opportunities for young people. "Working with industry, we could build 24-hour computer resource centers in the inner cities to help level the playing field for children who have no access to computers at home or single mothers trying to learn a job skill and raise small children."

"CTN's focus is interconnecting–using multiple technologies for the benefit of students in Catholic school classrooms, parishes, and diocesan and community service agencies. Beyond that, CTN seeks to benefit of the greater human community." she said. "In essence, our hope is to provide appropriate and affordable technology to enhance and strengthen the global community to which we all belong and for which we share responsibility."

For over two centuries, the Catholic community has played an integral role in the health and well-being of Santa Clara Valley, its diverse communities, and residents.

Today, through an exemplary system of education, the Diocese of San Jose nurtures the minds, talents, and values of this valley's young. Through its comprehensive array of helping programs, the diocese ministers to the physical and emotional needs of all who can benefit. Through its state-of-the-art technology and skills, the diocese helps link the valley's residents and lead them into the world of tomorrow. And through its magnificent cathedral/basilica and the inspirational religious services of its parishes, the diocese helps sustain the spirits of all who pass through its portals.

Silicon Valley may dance to the tempting tune of technology, but thanks to the Diocese of San Jose, its soul is nourished by a strong sense of ethics, humanity, and community. ✦

The historic St. Joseph Cathedral today–in its inspirational beauty, its resplendently renewed paintings and murals, statuary and altars, and its gleaming copper-sheathed domes–was lovingly restored and reconstructed from 1986 to 1990.

SANTA CLARA COUNTY OFFICE OF EDUCATION

Santa Clara County has more distinguished schools (177 awards) than any other county in the state, "reflecting the commitment to excellence that characterizes so many of our schools," says Dr. Colleen Wilcox, county superintendent of schools.

Santa Clara County exceeds both the state and national averages in SAT scores and in percentages of students enrolled in advanced science and math classes, students qualifying for advanced college placement, and students going on to college.

What's more, these results were achieved at a time when equity and access issues, school choice initiatives, and language barriers have all changed the environment in which educators work. During this period of rapid social change, the county also has been faced with shortages of qualified teachers and drastic financial cutbacks. "So, you could say we're doing more with less," Dr. Wilcox observes.

In the face of the community reality, the staff of the Santa Clara County Office of Education (COE) serves an education community by creating innovative approaches to increase student learning even more.

Directly or indirectly, COE services benefit more than 240,000 students in Santa Clara County.

Targeted Direct Services

Its direct service programs are targeted to students—from preschoolers to adults—who have special interests or needs. These direct services are supported by more than half of the COE's annual budget of $110 million. More than three-fourths of its 1,300 staff members are involved in day-to-day activities of children in classrooms.

• The Head Start and State Preschool programs serve over 3,000 preschool and kindergarten children annually. More than 1,800 of

Helping children develop a love for learning is one way to increase their chances for success in the future. "We want to prepare the children of Santa Clara County to be leaders in the next century," says Dr. Colleen Wilcox, Santa Clara County superintendent of schools.

those children are enrolled in the COE's Head Start program, which has been praised by representatives of the federal government as one of the most outstanding in the nation.

• The Migrant Education program supplements a school's core curriculum with additional support from teachers, tutors, instructional aides, and counselors for the area's 17,000 eligible migrant students. The program includes parent and preschool education, and is coordinated with other support resources.

• Alternative Schools educate young people who are not attending regular school for a variety of reasons or who are under court supervision. Designed to meet the needs of some 8,000 students per year, this program helps students return to their home school district, receive their diplomas, and achieve success in the adult world.

• The Special Education Department serves more than 1,200 students, from birth through age 22, with physical, emotional, or mental disabilities in more than 138 classrooms throughout the county.

• Located in the Santa Cruz Mountains, the COE's 32-acre Walden West Center for Environmental Education has enriched the lives of more than 400,000 students over the past 50 years. Each year, nearly 10,000 fifth and sixth graders spend a week at Walden West, learning environmental and natural science concepts in its inspirational outdoor setting.

• Regional Occupational Programs provide high school students and adults the opportunity for skills training, which prepares them for a wide variety of increasingly technical occupations.

Indirect Services Support Education

In its role as an "arm of the California Department of Education," the COE is responsible for functions such as teacher credentialling, student attendance accounting, district budget monitoring, adjudicating expulsion and interdistrict attendance appeals, plus a wide range of other services.

The COE also provides opportunities for educators to continually hone their skills. This vital role affects teaching and learning in all of the county's schools, influencing the instructional techniques of some 13,000 classroom teachers countywide.

The Santa Clara COE Head Start preschool program serves 1,800 children in sites throughout Santa Clara County. Head Start bolsters its educational program with a strong emphasis on parent involvement, health and nutrition, and family support.

Through its teacher preparation programs, and the media and technology centers, the COE supports districts as they move from the present level of national excellence in education toward quality education on an international scale.

New Expectations

According to Dr. Wilcox, "When the valley's products were agricultural, we had one set of expectations for our children's education and we met those well. Now that we are 'Silicon Valley' and our products are the most advanced technology in the world, we have another set of expectations. We are moving toward an internationally competitive level of education in our public."

Thus, developing world-class skills in the county's young people and their teachers—especially in the areas of science, math, and technology—remains the theme that underlies the COE's policies, programs, and plans.

In the technology training lab, teachers gain hands-on experience at computers connected to the "information highway." Industry collaborates with the COE to electronically link all of the county's schools. Companies such as Sun Microsystems, Pacific Bell, and Silicon Graphics have donated computer equipment, training, and technical services in support of this ambitious initiative.

"We live and work in a very special part of the world," Dr. Wilcox says. "With our region's commitment to educational, social, and industrial excellence, its incredible ethnic and cultural diversity, and its global technology leadership, the children of Santa Clara County are growing up in a microcosm of the world of the future. We want them prepared to be leaders."

The Santa Clara County Office of Education is a partner with the county's 33 K-12 school districts in championing the educational needs of more than 240,000 students.

Elementary School Districts
- Alum Rock Union School District
- Berryessa Union School District

There's more than reading going on here. A high school student in a Santa Clara COE alternative school can learn as much from his buddy in special education as she can learn from him.

Fifth graders attending science camp at Walden West Outdoor School learn about more than bugs and leaves. This Santa Clara COE environmental education program teaches students about ecology and about their connection to the environment.

- Cambrian School District
- Campbell Union School District
- Cupertino Union School District
- Evergreen School District
- Franklin-McKinley School District
- Lakeside Joint School District
- Loma Prieta Joint Union School District
- Los Altos School District
- Los Gatos Union School District
- Luther Burbank School District
- Montebello School District
- Moreland School District
- Mount Pleasant School District
- Mountain View School District
- Oak Grove School District
- Orchard School District
- Saratoga Union School District
- Sunnyvale School District
- Union School District
- Whisman School District

High School Districts (HSD)
- Campbell Union High School District
- Central County Regional Occupational Agency
- East Side Union High School District
- Fremont Union High School District
- Los Gatos-Saratoga Joint Union HSD
- Mountain View-Los Altos Union HSD

Unified School Districts
- Gilroy Unified School District
- Milpitas Unified School District
- Morgan Hill Unified School District
- Palo Alto Unified School District
- San Jose Unified School District
- Santa Clara Unified School District ✦

THE TECH MUSEUM OF INNOVATION

In mid-1996 with the help of four robots and an audience of enthusiastic youngsters, teens, and adults, Silicon Valley luminary William Hewlett, co-founder of Hewlett Packard, shoveled a spade of dirt. With that bit of ceremonious labor, he broke ground for construction of the new home of The Tech Museum of Innovation in San Jose—a $59 million, 112,000-square-foot, world-class facility scheduled to open in 1998.

Firmly rooted in the center of downtown San Jose, "designed with sparkle and intelligence" and dressed in "dazzling neon-ochre walls," the new three-story building will include a 1,200 square foot, large-screen, 300-seat, IMAX®*Dome* theater that blends education and entertainment; four main galleries in 32,000 square feet of space housing 250 interactive exhibits and displays, and 3,500 square feet devoted to four student hands-on workshop/laboratories.

The product of a classic public-private partnership, this new facility is partially funded by the City of San Jose Redevelopment Agency and partially by private sources. Mr. and Mrs. Hewlett, along with nearly 50 Silicon Valley companies—including Cirrus Logic, IBM, Applied Materials, Silicon Graphics, Lam Research, Hewlett-Packard, Intel, Lockheed, and Adobe Systems—have contributed toward the multi-million-dollar project, indicating the strength of their commitment toward the future of technology.

Currently operating in 19,000 square feet of space, The Tech Museum of Innovation is a private, not-for-profit education resource—the premier science and technology museum serving Northern California with a specific focus on the advanced technologies emerging from Silicon Valley and beyond.

These days, the museum is known as "The Tech," but it was called "The Garage" when it first opened in 1990, in tribute to

A popular exhibit is this billiard table sized microchip that will calculate the day of the week for any date desired. It will calculate in real time or slow down to 90 seconds to show the processing of information. The Tech Museum of Innovation also has a Clean Room exhibit that shows how a chip is fabricated. Photo by R. Kalischmidt, PG&E; Courtesy of The Tech Museum of Innovation.

one of the most powerful of the Silicon Valley legends—the backyard start-up, initiated in 1938 by William Hewlett and David Packard, and duplicated by many valley entrepreneurs in the ensuing decades.

In 1996, The Tech hosted more than 130,000 visitors including 28,000 children who came to the museum on school field trips. By 1999, the museum estimates that 650,000 people will visit annually.

The Tech was ranked by travel experts as one of the top 10 new U.S. tourist attractions of 1990—just one month after its November opening. And still, operating in less than one-fifth of the space it will have, The Tech tops *Hemispheres* magazine's list of "High-Tech Attractions Around the World"—a list that includes The Science Museum in London, La Cite Des Sciences Et De L'Industrie in Paris, The Science Museum in Tokyo,

and the Singapore Science Centre.

"We focus on advanced technologies being developed in Silicon Valley," says president and CEO Peter Giles. "And we focus on the real-world uses of those technologies."

Unlike traditional museums, The Tech looks to the future, challenging visitors to learn how technology, computers, and sci-

Visitors to The Tech Museum of Innovation can custom design their own high-tech bicycle at a CAD (computer-aided design) workstation and take home a printout of their design. Photo by R. Kalischmidt, PG&E; Courtesy of The Tech Museum of Innovation.

ence fit into and change their lives—not just today, but into the next century. In its new home, The Tech will issue its challenge in the form of four main galleries presenting innovation and creativity in Silicon Valley (Innovation); explorations of the earth, sea, and space (Explorations); opportunities in the information age (Communications and Information); and technology and the body (Life Tech).

Experience it now in The Tech's current exhibits. Picture a 23-foot double helix made entirely of telephone books. Or a nine-foot-square "microchip" that calculates the day on which your birthday will fall in the year 2020. Or a robot that draws your portrait. With today's technology, anything is possible, and The Tech wants to make sure its visitors have an unforgettable experience with technology. "These aren't exhibits about technology," says P.B. Wall, Jr., the museum's building project executive director, "These are exhibits with technology."

Visit The Tech and you get a fun, user-friendly exploration of applied technology—lunch prepared by a voice-controlled industrial robot, for example. You can design your dream bicycle, join a Voyager mission over Mars, or investigate the effect of earthquakes on a skyscraper. Or, you can simply play with the computers. "The exhibits are first class, as you'd expect from a museum where the corporate sponsorship list reads like a who's who of the computer industry," noted a recent *Hemispheres* magazine article about interesting high-tech things to see and do around the world.

At the 1996 groundbreaking ceremonies, Giles unveiled the museum's latest innovation: HyperTech. A new interactive technology museum on the World Wide Web, HyperTech features on-line exhibits created by The Tech and its technology partners, among which are educational institutions, renowned scientists and technologists, local community groups, and corporations.

The Tech Museum of Innovation in San Jose, CA, features an Exhibit Hall displaying interactive, hands-on high-tech exhibits. **Photo by Richard Barnes; Courtesy of The Tech Museum of Innovation.**

Each on-line exhibit fits within one of the museum's four themed areas. HyperTech's first exhibit is "Get A Grip On Robotics," which explores robotics and the effects robots have on people's lives.

Adobe Systems, The Tech's first web development partner, collaborated with the museum to develop another HyperTech exhibit–"Make a Splash with Color." University of California at Santa Cruz, another partner, teamed with The Tech's staff to create four virtual on-line exhibits addressing earthquakes, the DNA/Human Genome Project, lasers, and privacy and security on the Internet.

"HyperTech will enable Web visitors to interact with museum guests and exhibits, whether it be controlling a robot or listening to a live lecture," Giles said. "It reflects our commitment to link institutions and organizations interested in helping us provide educational, non-commercial information to a global community."

By providing hands-on, engaging experiences, and informal learning, plus school field trips and labs, The Tech occupies a leading role in promoting scientific literacy and understanding about the technologies changing people's lives. Its goals are not just to educate and inform the public at large, but also to foster a love of technology in the next generation.

"Our bottom line is to inspire middle and high school students to seek careers in science and technology," Giles stresses. "We want to propel the natural curiosity that most people have as youngsters into more serious lifelong interests." Still, The Tech's public programs and interactive exhibits aren't just for young people. They're for everyone.

"Silicon Valley is where microprocessors, personal computers, and semiconductors were born," said Mary Anne Easley of Hewlett Packard. "The valley has a special story to tell, and the museum tells this story in a unique and dramatic way."

As columnist Alan Hess says, "Don't think of it as a museum. Think of it as The House of High Tech." ✦

A replica of the Hubble Space Telescope's primary mirror, with a cutaway section showing its honeycomb structure, helps visitors to The Tech Museum of Innovation better understand the construction and design technology of this high tech eye in space. **Photo by R. Kalischmidt, PG&E; Courtesy of The Tech Museum of Innovation.**

SAN JOSÉ STATE UNIVERSITY CONTINUING EDUCATION

So many professionals in this region are graduates of San José State University that it has been called the "engine that drives Silicon Valley." But this, California's oldest public institution of higher education, is no narrowly focused school of applied sciences, business, or the technical arts.

Founded in 1857, San José State University is a regional, comprehensive university that prepares its students for careers in a diverse array of professions, including engineering, business, teaching, nursing, journalism, and design, as well as in the sciences, the arts, and the humanities.

Excellence in classroom teaching has been San José State University's

hallmark since its earliest days. That same quality, breadth of perspective, and instruction characterize University Continuing Education (UCE). Dean of Continuing Education programs, Mark Novak, Ph.D., says UCE's focus is on students, and eliminating the barriers they face to achieving personal and professional educational goals. More than 40,000 enrollments each year are in UCE programs.

One of Dean Novak's inviting points of access

Comfortable, well-appointed classrooms provide an excellent environment for University Continuing Education classes, private meetings or special training at the off-campus Professional Development Center. Photo by Sharon Hall.

is the Open University program. The SJSU program, serving as many as 5,000 people in a typical academic year, is a model to other such programs throughout California.

"Open University meets an important community need by giving people a convenient way to experience the university, maintain or upgrade their skills, or sample university life for the first time," says Robert Donovan, director of the Open University and Studies in American Language (SAL) programs.

"SAL has taught approximately 4,000 students from more than 50 countries, many of whom have gone on to matriculate at San José State University or another American college or university," he says.

Helping Silicon Valley workers succeed in the knowledge-based economy of the 21st century is the mandate of SJSU's state-of-the-art Professional Development Center on Tisch Way, near the 280/880 interchange.

This center offers top-flight seminars, leadership lectures, professional business and technical training certificates, and a variety of training/retraining programs contracted by industry. "The Professional Development Center serves students at the off-campus location, at company sites, and via video-assisted learning programs," says James Beck, director.

UCE at San José State is becoming even more responsive and student-centered by offering courses via the Internet, the World Wide Web, television, e-mail, independent learning packages, CD-ROM, videotapes, and other media. And it's creating new partnerships with universities in other parts of the world, as well as with even more Silicon Valley organizations.

"Continuing education, lifelong learning, isn't even a choice anymore," Dean Novak says. "We all need it to survive. If we resist, we become obsolete."

Working toward the ultimate goal of fully flexible, learner-centered, barrier-free, education on demand, helping people keep pace with the dizzying rate of change in our technology-rich environment—these are crucial objectives. And they're what San José State University's Continuing Education programs are all about. ✦

San José State University, founded in 1857, is Silicon Valley's Metropolitan University today, a multicultural campus producing innovative leaders and experts for tomorrow. Photo by Sharon Hall.

THE HARKER SCHOOL

Now located on a modern 16-acre campus in San Jose, The Harker School has its origins in Palo Alto, where two schools–Manzanita Hall and Miss Harker's School–were established in 1893 to provide incoming Stanford University students with the finest college-preparatory education available.

Run today as a nonprofit organization, Harker is a coeducational elementary school for children in junior kindergarten through grade eight. In many ways, it has become a neighborhood school for its 775 young students. Professional families from throughout the Bay Area especially like the convenience of Harker's location at the intersection of I-280 and Saratoga Avenue. And the close-knit community of student parents actively volunteers for school fundraising projects that generate approximately $275,000 each year to enhance such programs as computer technology and fine arts.

Accredited by the Western Association of Schools and Colleges and a member of the California Association of Independent Schools, Harker offers a full-day schedule, with extensive recreation and sports programs included in tuition.

"We also have a junior boarding program that lends an international aspect to Harker," says school President Howard Nichols. "Some boarding students are enrolled in our English as a Second Language program, while others come from other parts of California and the U.S." The boarding program also serves the families of day students with meals and extended-care services. "It's another example of how we continue to adapt to changing lifestyles and needs of busy professionals," Nichols said.

Harker's reputation is one of excellence. For example, Harker students consistently score among the highest percentiles in nationally normed achievement tests. And each year, an impressive number of seventh-grade students qualify for academic recognition as Johns Hopkins University Scholars by scoring above 500 on the SAT I. In fact, virtually all Harker graduates are accepted to their choice of the nation's most prestigious secondary schools.

"We begin in kindergarten with a deeply held conviction that children want to learn; that, given the right circumstances, they want to be challenged," says Nichols. Harker's "right circumstances" include a talented faculty, small class sizes, and a strong academic curriculum enriched with art, music, dance, drama, writing, computer technology, and the foreign languages.

Kindergartners, for example, take lessons in one of the school's two computer labs; and first-graders are taught Spanish. French and Japanese are taught at the middle and junior-high level. "All the courses, including physical education, are taught by specialists," Nichols said. "Individualized instruction is an important part of Harker's educational philosophy."

Leading-edge computer technology programs, sparkling new buildings, and extensive academic offerings, augmented with fine arts and sports, ensure that every Harker student can meet the challenges of the future. "We look enthusiastically to the future. Still," Nichols says with a smile, "we have parents tell us that Harker is truly a school for the whole family–and that's one thing we never want to see change!" ✦

Leading-edge computer technology programs, sparkling new buildings, and extensive academic offerings, augmented with fine arts and sports, ensure that every Harker student can meet the challenges of the future.

Run today as a nonprofit organization, Harker is a coeducational elementary school for children in junior kindergarten through grade eight.

PARAMOUNT'S GREAT AMERICA

Paramount's Great America is Northern California's premier entertainment provider offering 100 acres of non-stop fun. For two decades, guests of all ages have enjoyed exhilarating roller-coasters, world-class thrill rides, breathtaking shows, and a variety of tempting restaurants and shops to delight every member of the family.

Consider free-falling 22 stories at 91 feet per second on the world's tallest and most intense free-fall ride, the DROP ZONE Stunt Tower™. Thrill-seekers barely have time to scream as they plummet 224 feet at 62 miles per hour delivering a thrilling rush known only to skydivers.

After braving the DROP ZONE Stunt Tower™, feed your need for speed on the TOP GUN® inverted coaster, inspired by Paramount's hit movie, *Top Gun*. The park's first movie-themed attraction, TOP GUN®,

Take a spin on the beautiful Carousel Columbia, the world's tallest double-decker carousel.

a suspended jetcoaster complete with wingovers, afterburn turns and zero gravity rolls, delivers an adventure similar to Maverick's aerial acrobatics in the popular Paramount movie.

Paramount's Great America offers a total of 45 pulse-pounding rides, including 3 exhilarating water rides that are sure to please and keep you cool. Take a spin on the beautiful Carousel Columbia, the world's tallest double-decker carousel. This is just the beginning... .

Little ones enjoy enchanting, interactive children's shows in the Forest of Fun and thrill at the sight of their favorite Hanna-Barbera characters like Yogi Bear and Scooby Doo. You'll hear shrieks of excitement at the sight of the extraterrestrial Star Trek aliens. Prepare to get messy in *Nickelodeon*® SPLAT CITY™, three acres of wet, slimy, mega-messy entertainment that brings to life the zany and messy antics of the popular TV network created just for kids.

If you'd rather have your feet on the ground, there are plenty of fun and exciting entertainment choices. Be sure to test your skills at thrilling games that reward you with great prizes, sing along with *Al Cappelli's Karaoke*, or escape to the *Pictorium Theater* where you will enjoy the current IMAX® feature on a magnificent seven-story screen enhanced by a superb specially-designed six-channel, multi-speaker sound system.

For your entertainment, Paramount's Great America plans special events throughout

The park's first movie-themed attraction, TOP GUN®, a suspended jetcoaster complete with wingovers, afterburn turns and zero gravity rolls, delivers an adventure similar to Maverick's aerial acrobatics in the popular Paramount movie.

the season. Locals come year after year to the number one spot in Silicon Valley to witness the most awesome firework shows in the South Bay. Paramount's Great America is the site for thousands of spectators to watch dramatic pyrotechnic laser and firework extravaganzas on Memorial Day, Fourth of July, and Labor Day weekends.

Towering above the San Jose skyline, the DROP ZONE™ and other roller coasters are a constant reminder of the presence of Paramount's Great America in the community. The park employs nearly 4,000 people and is the largest employer of youths in the San Francisco Bay area. But it doesn't stop there. The park is the site of many annual community sponsored events that benefit children and families in the Bay Area. These events support education, scholarships, and terminally ill children, just to name a few.

In an era when people in Silicon Valley are working harder than ever, Paramount's Great America is *the* place in northern California to spend an adventurous, fun-filled day with family or friends. Whether you visit once a year or buy a season pass, you'll enjoy an astounding array of ever-changing rides, shows, and attractions. Paramount's Great America is the ultimate entertainment experience for the entire family. ◆

Chapter Eighteen

Health Care

O'CONNOR AND SAINT LOUISE HOSPITALS

O'Connor Hospital in San Jose and Saint Louise Hospital in Morgan Hill have the distinction of being the oldest–and the newest–community hospitals in the Santa Clara Valley. Oldest because O'Connor Hospital, founded in 1889 by the Daughters of Charity of St. Vincent de Paul, was the first community hospital in the area. Newest because the third O'Connor facility, opened in 1983, and Saint Louise's facility, opened in 1989, are the newest hospital facilities in the area, boasting the most modern design and technology.

Both are part of Catholic Healthcare West (CHW), a not-for-profit system of acute hospitals, ancillary facilities, home-care agencies and physician organizations dedicated to providing services to improve the overall health of the communities it serves in California, Nevada, and Arizona.

The hospitals, licensed for a total of 420 beds, offer a full range of medical/surgical, outpatient, subacute, homecare, and community education services, including the Heart Center at O'Connor Hospital, the Cancer Center at O'Connor Hospital, Family Centers at both hospitals, transitional care centers at both hospitals, the Wound Care Center at O'Connor Hospital, Center for Life (obstetrics) at both hospitals, and home care services at both hospitals.

Meeting Special Community Needs

As Catholic hospitals, both hospitals are committed to serving the whole person–body, mind, and spirit–with dignity and respect and to extending their care beyond the hospital walls. With special attention to serving the needy, the hospitals have contributed nearly $67 million in

Saint Louise Hospital in Morgan Hill, opened in 1989, is among the newest hospital facilities in the Santa Clara Valley, boasting the most modern design and technology.

O'Connor Hospital in San Jose was founded in 1889 by the Daughters of Charity of St. Vincent de Paul, and was the first community hospital in the Santa Clara Valley.

charitable care for the poor, community benefit services, and educational programs since 1990.

Typical of the hospitals' efforts to build a healthier community are these projects:

- Both hospitals are working with Alexian Brothers Hospital in San Jose and Catholic Charities on the Asian Seniors Assistance Program (ASAP), which is addressing the problem of severe depression in the elderly Asian population. The initiative combines health and social services programs to reduce isolation and increase social support for Asian seniors.
- Both hospitals also participate with other local hospitals, community agencies, and public health providers in a program addressing the serious problem of diabetes in the Latino population. The project's goal is to reduce complications from diabetes through early detection and education.
- Saint Louise Hospital sponsors a primary care clinic offering services to the entire family without regard to ability to pay.
- Both hospitals offer the Center for Life, which provides prenatal and maternity care to women regardless of their ability to pay for services. O'Connor Hospital has extended this program to include pediatric services.
- Teens who have been unsuccessful in mainstream education study for high school diplomas and gain valuable work experience at O'Connor's on-campus Career Academy. These young men and women are mentored as they work in the hospital and attend academic classes in a unique–and very successful–collaboration between the city's school district and the hospital. ◆

COMMUNITY HOSPITAL OF LOS GATOS

Community Hospital of Los Gatos believes that prevention is the best medicine. As an acute care, full-service, 164-bed hospital, and the Official Medical Provider of the San Jose "Clash" professional soccer team, the importance of preventing sports injuries and illness, carries over to an emphasis on wellness that benefits all patients who receive the Hospital's care.

A member of Tenet HealthSystem, Community Hospital of Los Gatos offers many free preventive medicine seminars and support groups on a variety of issues, such as women's health, senior health, diabetes, stress management, smoking cessation, diet and nutrition, and much more.

The annual KidSafe health fair, one of several free community health fairs the Hospital sponsors each year, is an especially popular wellness event. In the past, KidSafe's offerings included free fingerprinting and health screenings, seminars taught by public safety and medical professionals, as well as healthy snacks, and a keepsake shirt.

The main entrance of Community Hospital Los Gatos where the 60-foot cedar tree still stands today. **Photo by Russ Lee Photography.**

KidSafe emphasizes that learning about wellness can be fun.

Fully accredited since its opening in 1962, Community Hospital of Los Gatos provides a wide range of health and medical services. The medical staff is made up of more than 600 physicians who represent almost every major specialty.

Since its founding, Community Hospital of Los Gatos' mission has been to serve the community by delivering the best in modern medical technology, equipment, and expertise—supported by an old-fashioned sense of caring and concern for individual needs.

Perhaps the premier example of Community Hospital of Los Gatos' "high-tech/high-touch" orientation is its award-winning Family Birth Place. A maternity nurse is provided for mom, and a nursery nurse for baby. The Family Birth Place provides accommodation in a beautifully appointed private suite—home for mother and child during labor, delivery, recovery, and postpartum. Each suite features a large bath with full-size shower and bidet. Mothers-to-be can choose to relax and labor in the Jacuzzi, and the father or support person may remain with the mother during her entire stay.

From the peace-of-mind provided by an infant and child security system, to the small personal touches like foot printing baby just after birth, and snapping their first photo, Community

Hospital of Los Gatos strives to make the whole family feel welcome and secure through the entire birth experience.

Among the Hospital's other specialties are, the new Women's Cancer Center of Northern California; the Arthritis Center; the Spine Center; the Joint Care program, which provides a multi-disciplinary team of specialists to address the needs of patients with joint pain; the acute Rehabilitation Services program, which provides therapeutic rehabilitation to patients recovering from strokes and other neurologic and orthopedic injuries and disorders; and the Western Kidney Stone Center, which uses lithotripsy to treat kidney stones.

Community Hospital of Los Gatos covers a wide continuum of hospital care. Acute care, diagnostic treatment, surgical care, transitional care, acute rehabilitation, home health care, outpatient services, and emergency services combine to meet patient and community needs.

Three decades ago, in appreciation of the quality of their care at Community Hospital of Los Gatos, a husband and wife planted a cedar tree in front of the Hospital. Today, that tree stands 60–feet tall. "The tree's enduring presence is a visible reminder of what we are privileged to stand for," says Truman Gates, chief executive officer, "help, compassion, and renewed health and vitality for those entrusted in our care." ✦

The Family Birth Place provides one-on-one nursing care for both mom and baby, to help make the birthing experience unique and personal. **Photo by Russ Lee Photography.**

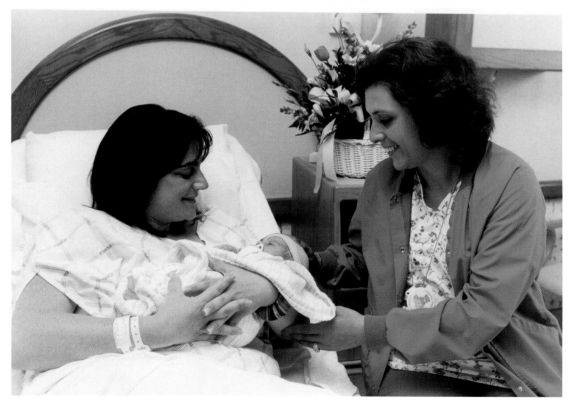

COLUMBIA BAY AREA HEALTHCARE NETWORK

What's in a name? A lot, when the name is "Columbia."

Largest provider of health care services in the country, Nashville, Tennessee-based Columbia/HCA Healthcare Corporation is the architect of major change in our national system of health care.

"In a relatively short amount of time, we have built a highly respected network of health care facilities staffed with thousands of dedicated health care professionals," says Thomas J. May, president and CEO of Columbia Bay Area Healthcare Network. "Our network of caregivers is a model for the entire industry."

Columbia San Jose Medical Center, located in downtown San Jose, is a designated trauma center. It has more than 1,100 employees and serves more than 84,000 patients a year.

Some very impressive facts back up his affirmation. For example:
- Columbia has 102 hospitals that have earned the highest evaluation given by the Joint Commission on Accreditation of Healthcare Organizations—"Accreditation with Commendation." That's a rate of excellence more than four times the industry average.
- According to an HCIA/Mercer study, 30 of the top 100 U.S. hospitals based on quality of service and financial viability are part of the Columbia system.
- In a recent customer satisfaction survey, 95 percent of patients were "satisfied" to "very satisfied" with the health care they received at Columbia hospitals.
- *Fortune* magazine rates Columbia one of the top 50 Most-Admired companies in America.
- Columbia's financial strength allows it to provide more than $1.2 billion annually to people who need care but lack the insurance and personal resources to pay for it.

Known throughout the country as a patient-sensitive innovator, Columbia brought its name, its reputation for health care excellence, and its wealth of resources to Silicon Valley in 1996 when it purchased the Good Samaritan Health System, which included among other facilities the 529-bed San Jose Medical Center, established in 1923, and the 533-bed Good Samaritan Hospital, established in 1965. Now known as

Columbia Good Samaritan, the hospital is known for its comprehensive women and children's services, its cardiovascular program and orthopedic surgery. Columbia San Jose Medical Center is the busiest of Santa Clara County's three trauma centers and offers a wide range of services, including physical, occupational and speech rehabilitation services, women and children's services and critical care.

As a matter of policy, Columbia is continuing the tradition of community service begun by the organizations with which it affiliates. In Santa Clara County, for instance, Columbia has:
- Significantly increased the amount of charity care provided.
- Continued important services in the community, such as trauma and neonatal intensive care.
- Invested significant capital to bring the facilities of newly affiliated hospitals current on maintenance they had previously deferred.
- Installed Meditech, a new clinical and financial information system, to improve the accuracy and efficiency of patient records, as well as the overall effectiveness of patient care.
- Enabled the creation of the largest health care charitable foundation in Santa Clara County—The Good Samaritan Charitable Trust.

"All of us here at Columbia are working day in and day out to bring patients better medical care. For example, we routinely survey our hospitals, surgery centers, and other facilities to find the best medical procedures; then we share them nationwide," May said. "In other words, when patients check into a Columbia health care center, they have more than 350,000 of the best medical people in the nation caring for them."

Columbia also has a well-earned reputation for scrutinizing administrative systems in order to eliminate the waste and inefficiencies that drive up costs. That kind of attention pays real dividends by creating the financial stability needed for continued quality health care service. Since Columbia came to Silicon Valley, four community hospitals, an outpatient surgicenter, and a home care and hospice service which had been threatened with closure in late 1995, have been restored to full capacity and now are thriving once again.

"We at Columbia believe hospitals and health care systems benefit from good business practices devoted to quality patient care and customer satisfaction," said May. "We're proud to be a part of the Silicon Valley community, and are dedicating our management, resources, and fiscal strength for its present and future benefit." ✦

Columbia Good Samaritan Hospital, in the West Valley area, has 1,750 employees and serves more than 78,000 patients a year. Its maternity program is one of the busiest and most comprehensive in the area.

LIFEGUARD, INC.

Mark Hyde, president and CEO of Lifeguard, Inc., freely admits that it took a "wake-up call" from a client company to induce Lifeguard to put a formal quality program in place. That was in 1993.

The program was surely a good one, because for the past two years San Jose-based Lifeguard, a not-for-profit independent regional health plan, has received high marks for customer satisfaction in a survey conducted by the Pacific Business Group on Health–a San Francisco-based coalition of large employers that provide benefits for more than 2.5 million people.

Founded in 1977 by a group of Santa Clara County physicians, Lifeguard has become the fastest-growing HMO in California, according to Department of Corporations statistics for fiscal year 1996.

With an employee count approaching 500, a headquarters and separate operations facilities, and five branch offices in Northern and Central California, Lifeguard serves over 200,000 members through its provider network of over 10,000 physicians and 100 contracting hospitals. Half of Lifeguard's members are in the Silicon Valley, working at companies such as Hewlett-Packard, Inc., IBM Corp., and National Semiconductor, Inc.

Lifeguard was recently honored with the 1996 Enterprise Award presented by Arthur Andersen, the Haas School of Business at U.C. Berkeley, and TEC. Each year, San Francisco Bay area companies are recognized for best business practices, making a single award in each of three categories. Lifeguard was recognized in the category of Customer Satisfaction.

To meet industry and customer demands, Lifeguard has become a diversified managed care corporation with a full range of products. And its geographic scope continues to expand. It now serves members in 25 Northern and Central California counties.

Besides its focus on quality and customer service, Lifeguard is known for its emphasis on prevention. Believing that traditional approaches to managed care, by themselves, are insufficient to cure America's health care ills, Lifeguard works hard to manage and promote good health through a strong program of preventive medicine. "Because we pay

Founded in 1977 by a group of Santa Clara County physicians, Lifeguard has become the fastest-growing HMO in California.

directly for medical services, we not only know what percentage of women had various tests or children received immunizations, we also know specifically which individuals have and have not," said S. Joseph Aita, MD, Lifeguard executive vice president and medical director. "Under our Preventive Health Outreach Program, every year, we directly contact members and their physicians if our reports indicate they haven't received important prevention services." Among Lifeguard's other wellness initiatives is "Lifestart," which encourages early and continuing prenatal care.

Each member of the Lifeguard, Inc., team is an experienced professional with a solid background in the health care and insurance industries. Together they manage what has become one of the leading health plans in the West, widely recognized for its expansive provider network; its independence and innovations; and its consistently high ratings in customer service. ◆

Lifeguard works hard to manage and promote good health through a strong program of preventive medicine.

"We've become successful by doing something mundane," says Lifeguard President Hyde "…pleasing the customer."

EL CAMINO HOSPITAL

"I knew I was going to be okay because I was coming to El Camino Hospital," one recent incoming patient told a hospital volunteer. In part, he was referring to the hospital's well earned reputation for medical technology, innovation, and expertise.

Silicon Valley's first laparoscopic laser cholecystectomy surgery (gallbladder removal) was performed there, for example. And El Camino was the first hospital in the world to install a state-of-the-art computer-aided Medical Information System, which significantly improves the speed and quality of patient care, plus the cost-effectiveness of the hospital's services.

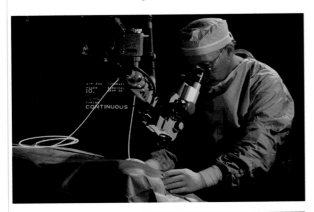

El Camino Hospital has a well earned reputation for medical technology, innovation, and expertise.

In part, the patient was also referring to El Camino Hospital's full range of medical capabilities. They encompass a new Maternal Child Health complex that reflects the latest advances in technology and patient care, including same-room labor and delivery, and a lactation center; and extensive acute care services including cardiac surgery and coronary care, an intensive care unit, cardiac catheterization, laboratories, a diagnostic imaging unit with two MRIs, a full range of interventional services, and much, much more.

That incoming patient was also referring to the hospital's human side—its emphasis on caring service, and the way it reaches out to the community. "Patient satisfaction surveys always rate us extraordinarily high," says the hospital's director of clinical effectiveness. "We have always had an incredible reputation in the community."

Established in 1961, this fully accredited and licensed, not-for-profit, community hospital has 468 beds, more than 500 physicians on staff, approximately 2,500 employees and 600 volunteers who provide services in five buildings on the hospital's 20-acre campus in Mountain View.

El Camino Hospital is a busy place. Its high-volume emergency department sees 30,000 patients annually. And, at 4,000 babies a year, El Camino has one of the largest labor and delivery birthrates in Santa Clara county.

"Women who deliver at El Camino Hospital can be confident that if their baby has a problem our level of care available is the finest," states the hospital's medical director. The neonatologists and nurses care for a complete range of mothers and infants—from those who experience a normal delivery to patients who need high-risk medical services. The unit includes a Level III intensive care nursery for treatment of premature and ill newborns.

El Camino reaches out to the community in many ways. Concern, its unique Employee Assistance Program(EAP)—one of the first hospital-sponsored EAPs in the country—helps thousands of Silicon Valley employees each year. Lifecheck, the hospital's health promotion and risk-reduction program, helps participants quit smoking, achieve a healthful weight, and reduce stress. RotaCare, a collaborative community medical clinic and health program, helps people who are uninsured and underinsured. Its Older Adult Resource Center focuses on the special needs of seniors and their families. In addition, there are healthcare classes, flu and immunization clinics, wellness checks, patient transportation, gift and snack shops, and other services.

One indication of El Camino's close community ties is its extraordinarily active auxiliary, which dates back to 1958, even before the hospital opened. The 1,000-member auxiliary has donated more than three million hours of volunteer service to the hospital and contributes $100,000 for equipment purchases every year.

"I don't have to wonder why I volunteer 180 hours here each month. It's because I've always seen the caring, the understanding, the outreach, and the support that El Camino gives people—regardless of who you are, how much you make, or what you do," affirms the auxiliary president. "This doesn't feel like a hospital to me—it feels like family." ✦

El Camino has one of the largest labor and delivery birthrates in Santa Clara county.

Acknowledgements

San Jose & Silicon Valley: Primed For The 21st Century only came together because of all of the wonderful area experts who gave up their valued time to help me with the direction of this publication. First of all, I would like to thank Carol Beddo, assistant to Frank Taylor of the Redevelopment Agency, for helping me think through the project and connecting me with important people such as Dennis Korabiak, Mary Stokes, and John Weis from the agency. Mary was available for every and any question that I had, Dennis took the time to take me on a walking tour of downtown San Jose, and John was a great source of information.

Former Santa Clara County Supervisor Rod Diridon, currently executive director of the International Institute for Surface Transportation Policy Studies, who was instrumental in the restructuring of San Jose and Silicon Valley's transportation system, also gave time for an interview and directed me to appropriate sources.

Cathy Gaskell, marketing and promotion officer, San Jose International Airport, supplied me with much information regarding the airport and also took the time to be interviewed.

Jan Carey, former director communications services, Santa Clara Office of Education, assisted with important data regarding education statistics in the area; and Sylvia Hutchinson, public affairs officer, San Jose State University, provided me with current information about San Jose State University.

I truly appreciate the time of Thuan Nguyen, founder/president, Vietnamese Chamber of Commerce, who shared with me the nuances of the Vietnamese community of the area.

Who better to know what is available as far as museums, parks, and entertainment but Julie Mark, deputy director, City of San Jose, Visitor Services & Facilities Division. Julie was a tremendous source and provided me with ample brochures and information about the area.

I am sure there are many more knowledgeable people that assisted me with the information for this book. To those I haven't mentioned, a big "Thank you!"

Below are many books and articles I utilized as a source for this publication.

Chris Di Salvo
Author

Bibliography

Books:

Arbuckle, Clyde. *History of San Jose*. Smith McKay Printing Co., 1985.

Beilharz, Edwin A. & Donald O.De Mers. *San Jose, California's First City*. Continental Heritage Press, Inc., 1980.

Laffey, Gloria Anne & Robert G Detlefs. "County Leadership," *Santa Clara County Government History*. World Dancer Press, Fresno, CA 1995.

McCaleb, Charles S. "Rails, Roads & Runways," *The 20-Year Saga of Santa Clara County's Transportation Agency*. World Dancer Press, Fresno, CA 1994.

McEnery, Tom. *The New City-State*. Roberts Rinehart Publishers, 1994.

Muller, Kathleen. *San Jose City With a Past*, 1988.

Reports and Publications:

"Choices 1996-1997, San Jose Unified School District."

City of San Jose Project Diversity, Steering Committee Report, August 1991.

Hispanic Magazine, May 1996.

McCormack's Guides For Newcomers and Families, Santa Clara County, 1996.

Vital Signs, A Sourcebook for School Planners in Santa Clara County. Santa Clara County Office of Education, Colleen B. Wilcox, Ph.D., Superintendent, Winter 1995.

Enterprises Index

Index

This book was set in Berthold Baskerville and Formata at Community Communications, Inc. in Montgomery, Alabama.